Liability for Environm

Liability for Environmental Harm

John Bates

His Honour Judge William Birtles

Charles Pugh

LexisNexis™ UK

Members of the LexisNexis Group worldwide

United Kingdom	LexisNexis UK, a Division of Reed Elsevier (UK) Ltd, Halsbury House, 35 Chancery Lane, LONDON, WC2A 1EL, and 4 Hill Street, EDINBURGH EH2 3JZ
United Kingdom	LexisNexis UK, a Division of Reed Elsevier (UK) Ltd, 2 Addiscombe Road, CROYDON CR9 5AF
United Kingdom	LexisNexis IRS, member of the Eclipse Group Ltd, 18–20 Highbury Place, LONDON N5 1QP
United Kingdom	LexisNexis UK, a Division of Reed Elsevier (UK) Ltd, 4 Hill Street, EDINBURGH EH2 3JZ and Halsbury House, 35 Chancery Lane, LONDON WC2A 1EL
Argentina	LexisNexis Argentina, BUENOS AIRES
Australia	LexisNexis Butterworths, CHATSWOOD, New South Wales
Austria	LexisNexis Verlag ARD Orac GmbH & Co KG, VIENNA
Canada	LexisNexis Butterworths, MARKHAM, Ontario
Chile	LexisNexis Chile Ltda, SANTIAGO DE CHILE
Czech Republic	Nakladatelství Orac sro, PRAGUE
France	Editions du Juris-Classeur SA, PARIS
Germany	LexisNexis Deutschland GmbH, FRANKFURT and MUNSTER
Hong Kong	LexisNexis Butterworths, HONG KONG
Hungary	HVG-Orac, BUDAPEST
India	LexisNexis Butterworths, NEW DELHI
Ireland	LexisNexis, DUBLIN
Italy	Giuffrè Editore, MILAN
Malaysia	Malayan Law Journal Sdn Bhd, KUALA LUMPUR
New Zealand	LexisNexis Butterworths, WELLINGTON
Poland	Wydawnictwo Prawnicze LexisNexis, WARSAW
Singapore	LexisNexis Butterworths, SINGAPORE
South Africa	LexisNexis Butterworths, DURBAN
Switzerland	Stämpfli Verlag AG, BERNE
USA	LexisNexis, DAYTON, Ohio

A CIP Catalogue record for this book is available from the British Library.

ISBN 0 406 97007 6

Typeset by Columns Design Ltd, Reading, Berkshire
Printed and bound in Great Britain by Hobbs the Printers Ltd, Totton, Hampshire

Visit LexisNexis UK at www.lexisnexis.co.uk

Foreword

By Lord Justice Carnwath, CVO

One of the strengths of the common law is its adaptability. 'Environmental Law' is a relative newcomer to the English legal scene. A Department of the Environment was created as long ago as 1970, but it was not until 1990 that we had a fully-fledged environmental statute (the Environmental Protection Act 1990). Of course, much of the content of the 1990 Act was familiar. There was a large body of legislation for the protection of public health, and the control of all kinds of pollution. However, the drawing together of the many different strands of statute and case law into a coherent body of environmental law has inevitably taken some time.

At the same time we have found strength in the principles of the common law developed over centuries. For example, the recent *Transco* case (discussed in the text at para 2.96) shows how the *Rylands v Fletcher* principle (first articulated in the 1860s, as a response to public concerns following the loss of 250 lives in the Bradfield reservoir disaster in 1864) remains a powerful tool today to deal with dangerous uses of land. As Lord Bingham said:

> 'Common law rules do not exist in a vacuum, least of all rules which have stood for over a century during which there has been detailed statutory regulation of matters to which they might potentially relate.'

Thus, the common law has had to adapt itself to the complex legislative framework governing every aspect of activity in the environment, much of it strongly influenced by European requirements.

The present work provides a clear and readable guide through the different categories of legal liability for environmental harm. There is a common sense and practical division of the Parts: between causes of action, practice and procedure, and substantive practice. I strongly welcome the treatment of the individual forms of claim as parts of the more general issue of environmental liability. By approaching it in this way, the authors help to dispel the mystery and complexity of different sources of law confronting judges, practitioners and students. This comprehensive treatment is particularly timely given the vigorous debate currently under way in the European Union on the proposed Directive on Environmental Liability (see para 5.14).

RC
Royal Courts of Justice
February 2004

Preface

In an age in which scientific knowledge is rapidly increasing, fuelling the production of new substances or showing that older substances are more harmful than was first thought, the law too needs to advance. New laws are needed for new and potentially harmful products such as genetically modified organisms. Traditional bases for causation are not capable of dealing with 'toxic torts'. An increased demand for better environmental regulation goes hand in hand with a sense that the polluter should pay for the harm he has done.

This book aims to give an overview of the practical and legal aspects of liability for environmental harm. The practical guidance has been derived from the 10 years' litigation experience of the Environmental Team at Old Square Chambers. The book is targeted at the non-specialist wanting a guide through the maze of different bases on which liability can be founded. Thus there is a certain amount of overlap in some chapters, particularly concerning statutory nuisance, but we feel that this is necessary to give a clearer guide to the law.

It is a pleasure to be able to record the help we have received from a number of people, in particular other members of the Old Square team including Philip Mead (noise) and Daniel Bennett (personal injury) and Stuart Brittenden, Betsan Criddle and Ben Cooper all of Old Square Chambers, who were kind enough to look at the chapters and suggest some amendments for which we are duly grateful.

We should also acknowledge the help of Penny Jewkes whose seminal article on light pollution in the Journal of Planning Law a few years ago made us realise the importance of this developing area; and to James Rickards for research (noise), and last but certainly not least to Sue Jones, our patient typist.

The law in this book is stated as at 20 February 2004.

Contents

Chapter 3   Statutory nuisance 41
William Birtles

Table of statutes

References in the right-hand column are to paragraph number. Paragraph references printed in **bold** type indicate where the Act is set out in part or in full.

Table of statutory instruments

References in the right-hand column are to paragraph number. Paragraph references printed in **bold** type indicate where the SI is set out in part or in full.

Table of European legislation

References in the right-hand column are to paragraph. Paragraph references printed in **bold** type indicate where the provision is set out in part or in full.

Table of Conventions

References in the right-hand column are to paragraph. Paragraph references printed in **bold** type indicate where the article is set out in part or in full.

Table of cases

A

B

C

D

I

J

K

M

O

P

T

X

Y

Z

Decisions of the European Court of Justice are listed below numerically. These decisions are also included in the preceding alphabetical table.

PART I

Causes of action

CHAPTER 1

Negligence

INTRODUCTION

1.01 Environmental liability claims in the tort of negligence have the advantage that compensation for personal injuries is certainly available,[1] and that the claimant need have no interest in the land to mount a claim.[2] On the other hand, negligence actions have significant disadvantages: injunctions are not available; pure economic loss is not recoverable; and exemplary damages are not recoverable. Most importantly, the claimant must always establish fault in the negligence action, and this can be difficult and expensive.

1   It is now clear that damages for personal injury cannot be obtained in nuisance or *Rylands v Fletcher* (1868) LR 3 HL 330: see *Transco plc v Stockport Metropolitan Borough Council* [2003] UKHL 61, [2004] 1 All ER 539.
2   *Hunter v Canary Wharf Ltd* [1997] AC 655, HL.

1.02 It has been conventional in an environmental liability case to plead causes of action in: nuisance, negligence and under the rule in *Rylands v Fletcher*. This applies now only where compensation is sought in respect of actual physical damage. Where the action is in respect of personal injury, the cause of action will be confined to negligence. Where it is for interference with enjoyment of land, the cause of action will be nuisance. Furthermore, in a physical damage claim, modern case management may dictate, in given circumstances, that the negligence action will be stayed pending trial of the nuisance action, since the latter will be less expensive as it does not involve an allegation of breach of duty.

DUTY OF CARE

1.03 An owner/occupier of land has a duty of care to his or her neighbour: if the owner/occupier creates, negligently, a dangerous state of affairs on his or her own land which will foreseeably harm his or her neighbour's land and it does so, the owner/occupier will be liable in negligence for his or her action.

1.04   However, the common law does not generally impose liability for omissions to act. So, for example, where the claimant's land was flooded by seawater and the defendant Board, although under no duty to repair the breach in the sea-wall, undertook the repairs negligently, it was held that the Board was not liable because its neglect did not inflict any more damage than would a total omission.[1]

1   *East Suffolk Rivers Catchment Board v Kent* [1941] AC 74, HL.

1.05   However, an owner/occupier is under a common law duty to take positive action to remove or to reduce hazards to his or her neighbours, even though the hazard is not one that the owner/occupier brought about. The owner/occupier must take reasonable steps to this end, for the benefit of his or her neighbours.[1] If an occupier's tree is struck by lightning and catches fire, the occupier must take reasonable steps to prevent the fire spreading. This duty to take 'reasonable steps' applies in cases of natural causes such as lightning[1] or soil subsidence collapsing onto neighbouring houses,[2] or loss of support due to a landslip[3] or incursion of tree roots.[4] The owner/occupier of land has a similar duty where the source of nuisance is man-made, e g by a trespasser.[5]

1   *Goldman v Hargrave* [1967] 1 AC 645, PC.
2   *Leakey v National Trust for Places of Historic Interest or Natural Beauty* [1980] QB 485, CA.
3   *Holbeck Hall Hotel Ltd v Scarborough Borough Council* [2000] QB 836, CA.
4   *Delaware Mansions Ltd v Westminster City Council* [2001] UKHL 55, [2002] 1 AC 321.
5   *Sedleigh-Denfield v O'Callaghan* [1940] AC 880, HL.

1.06   Though the duty to take 'reasonable steps' is resonant of negligence, the duty is limited and qualified and therefore different from the duty of care in negligence. The standard of care is limited to that which is reasonable to expect of the owner/occupier in his or her individual circumstances. The owner of a small property, where a hazard arises which threatens a neighbour with substantial interests, will not be required to do as much as one with larger interests and greater resources to protect them. It has been emphasised that this approach entails a 'broad and not a detailed assessment' of the defendant's means.[1]

1   *Leakey v National Trust for Places of Historic Interest or Natural Beauty* [1980] QB 485, CA.

BREACH OF DUTY

1.07

'Negligence is the omission to do something which a reasonable man, guided upon those considerations which ordinarily regulate the conduct of human affairs, would do, or do something which a prudent and reasonable man would not do'.[1]

1   *Blyth v Birmingham Waterworks Co* (1856) 11 Exch 781.

1.08   The test refers to the standard of the 'reasonable man'; the standard of the defendant himself or herself is irrelevant. In the environmental context, this means the reasonable waste disposal operator, the reasonable factory owner and so on. The reasonable operator will be judged objectively, but by the standards of knowledge prevailing in the relevant industry at the material time, and not at the time the case goes to trial.

1.09   There is considerable overlap here with foreseeability and the court will take a number of factors into account, including the following:
(a)   the object to be attained by the defendant's conduct;
(b)   the practicability of precautions. The court will look at any approved or general practice prevailing at the time of and prior to the alleged breach of duty. The fact that the defendant complied with the prevailing custom or practice will be a persuasive argument in the defendant's favour, although it is not conclusive;
(c)   the court will balance the practicability of any suggested precautions that the defendant could have taken against the risk of harm.

1.10   A conviction for a criminal offence, where material to the matters complained of, can be pleaded and used in evidence in the civil compensation proceedings.[1] This would apply, for example, to a public nuisance conviction. Such a conviction, notwithstanding that the standard of proof is higher in a criminal court than in a civil court, is not conclusive of the issue in the civil court. However, unless the defendant can persuade the civil court that the criminal conviction is in some material sense irrelevant or was the product of a technical irregularity (in which case the civil court would want to know why it had not been successfully appealed), the presence of a criminal conviction is likely to be conclusive on the issue of fault.

1   Civil Evidence Act 1968, s 11.

1.11   The finding of fault in the design of the operation of a plant which gives rise to toxic emissions may be a matter of the most complex expert evidence and an extremely laborious discovery process. In such a case, the doctrine of *res ipsa loquitur* can assist the claimant.[1]

> 'There must be some reasonable evidence of negligence. But where the thing is shown to be under the management of the defendant or his servants, and the accident is such as in the ordinary course of things does not happen if those who have the management use proper care, it affords reasonable evidence, in the absence of explanation by the defendants, that the accident arose from want of care.'

1   *Scott v London and St Katherine Docks Co* (1865) 3 H & C 596, Ex Ch.

1.12   So, for example, if a single incident explosion produced a poisonous gas cloud causing environmental damage, the doctrine of *res ipsa loquitur* could be invoked. It could similarly be invoked if there was an incident involving a leak from a waste disposal site and the emission of dangerous substances into a river. However, the position is likely to be different with long-term, steady seepage cases where the causes tend to be multi-factorial.

1.13   Compliance with a statutory standard can be a conclusive answer to an allegation of breach of duty; or, at the least, make fault much harder to prove. In *Budden v BP Oil Ltd*[1] actions were brought by infant claimants against oil companies claiming in negligence damages for personal injury caused by the lead content of the defendants' petrol. The alleged negligence was that the company should have ceased before July 1978 to add any lead to the petrol which they refined and sold or at least should have reduced the proportion of lead in their petrol. The defendants averred that they had complied with regulations which set maximum limits for the lead content in petrol made under the Control of Pollution Act 1974, s 75(1).

1   [1980] JPL 586, CA.

1.14   The Court of Appeal struck out the claim on the basis that the claimants could not show fault. The court held that the prescribed maximum lead limits in the regulations were arrived at by an independent person which Parliament, by its tacit assent to the regulations, approved and enforced. In the circumstances the court was unable to see how a judge could hold that the oil companies had breached any duty owed to the children once it was clear that they had complied with the requirements prescribed by the Secretary of State. The Court of Appeal made the point that were it to do otherwise, the courts would, in effect, be laying down a permissible limit which would be determined as being of universal application and inconsistent with the permissible limit prescribed by Parliament, which would result in an unacceptable constitutional anomaly.

1.15   On the other hand, in water quality and air quality cases compliance with a statutory standard may only be persuasive rather than conclusive. The grant of a licence to discharge polluting matter into water courses (known as a 'consent') does not affect the common law rights of a riparian owner to sue a discharger even where the discharges complained of are within the limits of the consent. The fact of compliance with the consent is relevant and persuasive on the side of the defendant in determining whether there was nuisance and/or negligence, but it is not conclusive of the issue.

1.16   There is nothing in the Control of Pollution Act 1974, s 75 which expressly states that Parliament intended to give a statutory defence to air polluters in regard to their normal common law liabilities by laying down maximum concentrations, any more than in providing the imposition of 30-mph speed limits. Parliament intended statutory defence to negligence actions in respect of drivers travelling at 30 mph.

CAUSATION

1.17   In order to succeed in a negligence action, the claimant must prove a causal connection between the defendant's careless conduct and the damage.

This can be particularly difficult in environmental liability claims, particularly where the damage complained of is personal injury. The subject is addressed in Chapter 12.

FORESEEABILITY

1.18 In order to succeed in a negligence action the claimant must surmount the 'foreseeability' hurdle, ie must show that the particular kind of damage to the particular claimant is not so unforeseeable as to be too remote.

1.19 The 'foreseeability' test will be applied in negligence just as in nuisance cases.[1] In this respect nuisance and negligence and the rule in *Rylands v Fletcher* are indistinguishable.[2]

1   *The Wagon Mound (No 2)* [1967] 1 AC 617, PC.
2   *Cambridge Water Co Ltd v Eastern Counties Leather plc* [1994] 1 All ER 53, HL.

1.20 In *Cambridge Water* the claimant had to spend a million pounds because of the spillage of chlorinated solvent over many years up to 1976 resulting from the defendant company's practice of lifting by fork-lift truck, and on occasion puncturing, large drums of solvent which led to the borehole from which the company derived a water supply being contaminated to the extent that it was unsaleable by reason of being in breach of Water Quality Regulations.[1] The claimant sought to recover damages in negligence, nuisance and *Rylands v Fletcher*.

1   Now to be found in the Water Supply (Water Quality) Regulations 1989, SI 1989/1147, Sch 2, Tables, item 10.

1.21 The House of Lords applied *The Wagon Mound (No 2)* and held that the recovery of damages, whether in private nuisance, negligence or *Rylands v Fletcher*, depends on 'foreseeability by the defendants of the relevant type of damage'. The House of Lords ruled that, on the particular facts of the *Cambridge Water* case, the relevant type of damage was not reasonably foreseeable in 1976 when the spillage occurred.

1.22 It would, for example, have been reasonably foreseeable at the time that regular small spills of this solvent may lead to toxic fumes, perhaps giving rise to respiratory illness, but not that the solvent would descend 30 metres into the ground and then start spreading laterally so as to affect a borehole 1.3 miles away.

1.23 In approaching foreseeability in this way the House of Lords implicitly found that foreseeability of general 'pollution of some kind' was not sufficiently specific for the imposition of liability. Future cases will give guidance as to degree of specificity required.

1.24   For example, up to the 1950s tar works were common in industrial areas. The tar would be made in large vats. When the time came to empty or clean the vats it was typical to open the valves and let the surplus tar drain into the ground. Thus large quantities of excess tar washings were deliberately and repeatedly spread across the same area of land and, forty years later, before such land could be used for, say, residential development, it would need considerable treatment (to avoid health hazards to children playing and so forth). To take another example, 'drum graves' were a typical method of 'waste disposal' thirty years ago, but now, when corroded, the toxic contents contaminate the land, and if redeveloped for residential use major expenditure would be required to make the land safe. Another example would be a landfill site becoming methane active thirty years or more after being tipped by a local authority.

1.25   In these instances it was foreseeable to anybody who asked themselves the question that these actions would pollute the land in a general sense. The point is that, according to the standards and practices of those times, nobody ever thought to question what type of damage would arise. It remains to be seen how the 'relevant type of damage' test will be applied in such cases.

1.26   Foreseeability can raise difficult questions. In the *Abbeystead* disaster case,[1] the Court of Appeal (with a powerful dissenting judgment by Bingham LJ) upheld the finding of liability in negligence against the defendant engineers for failing to take sufficient account of the risk of leakage of reservoir methane gas in designing a deep tunnel construction project. In consequence, inadequate precautions were taken and a methane explosion occurred killing 16 people and injuring many more. Russell LJ, giving the majority judgment, approached the question of foreseeability in this way:

'We were referred to a number of authorities dealing with the spectrum of the likelihood of events, ranging from probabilities to remote possibilities. For my part I derive most assistance from the words of Lord Reid, in *Wagon Mound (No. 2)* [1967] 1 AC 617. Dealing with the remote risks, he said (at 642):

"But it does not follow that, no matter what the circumstances may be, it is justifiable to neglect a risk of such a small magnitude. A reasonable man would only neglect such a risk if he had some valid reason for doing so, e.g. that it would involve considerable expense to eliminate the risk. He would weigh the risk against the difficulty of eliminating it. If the activity which caused the injury to Miss Stone had been an unlawful activity, there can be little doubt that *Bolton v Stone* [1951] AC 850 would have been decided differently. In their Lordships' judgment *Bolton v Stone* did not alter the general principle that a person may be regarded as negligent if he does not take steps to eliminate a risk which he knows or ought to know is a real risk and not mere possibility which would never influence the mind of a reasonable man. What that decision did was to recognise and give effect to the qualification that it is justifiable not to take steps to eliminate the risk if it is small and if the circumstances are such that a reasonable man, careful of the safety of his neighbour, would think it right to neglect it."

The test, formulated in this way, then has to be applied to the facts of the instant case. Was it foreseeable that methane would be encountered? If it was encountered, were the defendants entitled to assume that such methane was merely stress relief methane, and would not adversely affect the permanent works? Did the defendants ever consider the distinction between stress relief methane and reservoir methane? These are the questions with which the Judge has to deal.'

1   *Eckersley v Binnie* (1988) 18 Con LR 1.

1.27 In the *Abbeystead* case there was a vigorous dispute between experts as to whether, at the date of the tunnel design, a reasonable engineer would have foreseen reservoir methane gas leakage as something to be taken into account. The Court of Appeal held that the trial judge was entitled to resolve this in favour of the claimants against the defendant engineers.

1.28 The comparison between *Cambridge Water* and *Abbeystead* illustrates the wide margin of discretion enjoyed by the court and the scope for judicial control by the exercise of this discretion.

DAMAGE

1.29 Negligence and nuisance are actions on the case: in neither cause of action is the tort complete, so that damages are recoverable, unless and until damage has been caused to the claimant. Pollution cases, particularly long-term low-level pollution cases, involve difficult questions as to when and if damage has in fact occurred. These are questions of fact and degree for the courts to determine and the answer to these questions not only governs whether or not a tort has been committed but also whether or not the limitation period has expired before proceedings were commenced.

1.30 Just because something is 'contaminated' or even 'harmful' in statute law, that does not mean that the contamination amounts to 'damage' for the purposes of actions in negligence.

1.31 In *Cambridge Water* the imposition of a statutory standard which meant that Cambridge Water had to withdraw the borehole from use was held to constitute the actionable damage. It should be noted, of course, that the actual level of water contamination by the solvent was identical prior to the imposition of the standard but yet, at that point in time, no actionable damage would have arisen.

1.32 In *The Orjula*[1] a ship's deck and hatch covers had been contaminated by hydrochloric acid leaking from containers which had been negligently loaded. The ship had to be decontaminated by using soda to neutralise the acid and then washed down with fresh water. The trial judge found that this was physical damage sufficient to found a case in negligence even though there was no physical alteration to the fabric of the ship,[2] but he attached importance to the fact that specialists were engaged to undertake the decontamination work, and the vessel was required by the authorities to be decontaminated before she could sail.

1   [1995] 2 Lloyd's Rep 395.
2   At 398.

1.33 In *Hunter v London Docklands Development Corpn*[1] an action in negligence was brought because of the deposit of dust arising from major construction works. The defendants claimed that dust deposits were not capable of constituting damage. The Court of Appeal held that excessive dust, for example, trodden into the fabric of the carpet in such a way as to lessen the value of the fabric, would be actionable. The damage was 'in the physical change which rendered the article less useful or less valuable'.[2]

1   [1996] 2 WLR 348, CA.
2   Pill LJ at 366 F.

1.34 In *Blue Circle Industries plc v Ministry of Defence*[1] contamination of land by radioactive material was held to constitute physical damage to the land even though the consequence was economic, in that the property was worth less and expenditure was incurred in removing the contaminated top soil. The extensive cleansing operations and restrictions on use of the land were sufficient to demonstrate physical damage.[2]

1   [1999] Env LR 22, CA. For a case going the other way, see *Merlin v British Nuclear Fuels plc* [1990] 3 All ER 711.
2   For the purposes of the Nuclear Installations Act 1965, s 7(1). However, the court stated that it was seeking to apply common law principles.

1.35 In deciding whether actual damage has occurred, can the court take into account future and continuing damage? At first instance, in the *Cambridge Water* case, Kennedy J answered this question (which is important in the context of chronic pollution cases) in the negative:

'The damage must be substantial, and it must be, in my view, actual; that is to say the court has, in dealing with questions of this kind, no right to take into account contingent, prospective, or remote damage ... so if it were made out that every minute a millionth of a grain of poison were absorbed by a tree, a millionth of a grain of dust deposited upon a tree, that would not afford a ground for interfering, although after the lapse of a million minutes the grains of poison or the grains of dust could be easily detected.'

1.36   There is an arguable parallel here with the special situation of withdrawal of support. The mere withdrawal of support is not actionable in itself as a nuisance; it only becomes wrongful if and when a subsidence occurs.[1]

1   *Midland Bank plc v Bardgrove Property Services Ltd* [1992] 2 EGLR 168, CA.

1.37   The claimant is caught in something of a trap here. There is interplay between actual damage as a pre-condition to the tort being complete on the one hand, and the limitation period beginning to run on the other. If the claimant issues proceedings and the court holds that no actual damage has yet occurred, then no tort has been committed and the action fails. If the claimant stays his or her hand in issuing proceedings until it is beyond any doubt that actual damage has occurred, then, if the court finds on a true analysis that the actual damage had in fact occurred years earlier, the claimant's action could be statute-barred (notwithstanding, perhaps, the provisions of the Latent Damage Act 1986).

LIMITATION

1.38   The Limitation Act 1980, ss 14A and 14B (as amended by the Latent Damage Act 1986) deal with actions in respect of latent damage. By s 14A(4), the limitation period is either:
(a)   six years from the date on which the cause of action accrued; or
(b)   three years from the 'starting date' if that period expires later than the six-year period mentioned at (a).

1.39   The 'starting date' is the earliest date on which the claimant, or any person in whom the cause of action was vested before the claimant, had both the knowledge required for bringing an action and the right to bring it. 'Knowledge' in this sense means knowledge of material facts about the damage and other facts such as causation and the identity of the defendant. It includes knowledge which the claimant might reasonably have been expected to acquire from facts observable or ascertainable by him or her, or from facts ascertainable with the help of appropriate expert advice which it is reasonable for the claimant to seek.

1.40   By the Limitation Act 1980, s 14B, an overriding time-limit is applied to actions for negligence not involving personal injuries: this is a period of 15 years from the date (or, if more than one, the last of the dates) on which there occurred any act or omission:
(a)   which is alleged to constitute negligence; and
(b)   to which the damage in respect on which damage is claimed is alleged to be attributable.

1.41   Accordingly there is a 'long-stop' of 15 years from the date of the negligent act or omission after which no action can be brought in the tort of negligence. This will apply even where the cause of action in negligence has not yet accrued because no actual damage has occurred.

1.42 Suppose, for example, that in *Cambridge Water* the statutory standards relating to maximum permissible levels of the solvent in question were not brought into effect until 1992 (rather than the actual date which was 1982), ie 16 years after the last spillage that could be relied on in 1976. Since there was no actionable damage for 16 years, no action in negligence could have been brought, and by the time it could properly have been brought, the action would be statute-barred. This long-stop does not, however, apply to actions in nuisance, so that the statute of limitations would not begin to run until 1992 and the action in nuisance would be within time providing it was brought before 1998.

NEGLIGENCE ACTIONS AGAINST PUBLIC AUTHORITIES

1.43 In general terms, a negligence action against a public authority is attended by special difficulties. No action will lie against a statutory undertaker for doing that which the legislator has authorised, or where the legislator has directed that the power is to be exercised in the manner complained of.[1] If a public authority exercises a statutory power negligently, there is no liability if the damage results from the bona fide exercise of its discretionary powers.[2] For decisions of policy, no duty of care can arise unless the claimant has first proved that the public body was acting ultra vires. Where the activity of the body does not involve the exercise of discretion but the body has carried out a purely operational task negligently and in excess of its statutory power, it may be liable in negligence.[3]

1   *Metropolitan Asylum District Managers v Hill* (1881) 6 App Cas 193 at 213, HL.
2   *East Suffolk Rivers Catchment Board v Kent* [1941] AC 74, HL.
3   *Geddis v Proprietors of Bann Reservoir* (1878) 3 App Cas 430 at 455, 456, HL.

1.44 In any proposed action against a statutory undertaker the practitioner will have to consider a fresh set of principles in determining whether a private claim can be mounted. One factor is whether the damage alleged is personal injury, physical damage, or merely pecuniary loss. Another factor is whether the terms of this instrument, properly construed, are intended primarily to benefit the individual or the public at large. Another factor is whether the complaint concerns an act, or an omission, or advice. The following examples illustrate the range of factors involved.

1.45 In *Stovin v Wise*[1] the claimant sustained injury in a road traffic accident caused in part by a restricted view for which the highway authority was responsible. It was held that the highway authority was not liable. The question of whether the existence of a statutory power gave rise to a common law duty of care required an examination of the policy of the statute. The absence of a statutory duty would normally exclude the existence of a common law duty of care. The minimum preconditions for basing a duty of care on a statutory power were, first, that it would have been irrational not to have exercised the power so that there was in effect a public law duty to act; and second, that there were exceptional grounds for holding that the policy of the statute required compensation to be paid to persons who suffered loss because the power was not exercised. In *Kane v New Forest District Council*[2] the decision was in favour of liability. *Stovin* was distinguished on the basis that *Stovin* was an omission whereas in *Kane* it was an act.

1   [1996] AC 923, HL.
2   [2002] 1 WLR 312.

1.46   In *Marcic v Thames Water Utilities Ltd*[1] the harm complained of was physical damage of a particularly unpleasant kind. For years the claimant's house, which was at a low point of the drainage system, had endured serious and repeated sewage flooding from overloaded sewers for which the defendants were responsible pursuant to a statutory scheme under the Water Industry Act 1991. Notwithstanding arguments which had persuaded the Court of Appeal, including human rights arguments under the Human Rights Act 1998, the House of Lords held that on a true and proper construction of the Water Industry Act 1991, and particularly s 18(1) thereof, common law remedies were excluded.

1   [2003] UKHL 66, [2004] 1 All ER 135.

1.47   An example involving economic loss may be found in the planning field: *Ryeford Homes Ltd v Sevenoaks District Council*.[1] The claimants were property developers who sued the local planning authority for damages for the negligent grant of a planning permission for the development of a neighbouring site. The judge concluded that no special relationship or proximity arose between the parties and that no duty of care was owed in respect of the grant of planning permission. Alternatively, he would have come to the same conclusion on the basis of public policy on the footing that the authority's duty is primarily one of good government owed to the public as a whole. Finally, as the third basis for his decision, the judge held that even if there was liability in negligence, a breach of duty would normally only give rise to irrecoverable economic loss which was a further bar to a remedy.[2]

1   [1989] 2 EGLR 281.
2   See also *Strable v Dartford Borough Council* [1984] JPL 329; *Lam v Brennan and Borough of Torbay* [1997] PIQR P488, CA.

1.48   To find a statutory authority liable for negligent advice, the court will look at the purpose for which the advice was given. The nature of the purpose will be defined in relation to the power the authority is exercising in giving the advice. In addition, the court will consider whether the claimant falls within the class of those who will foreseeably rely on the advice.[1] In general, the courts will be slow to impose a duty of care on statutory authorities for the advice they give[2] but such a duty has been imposed in certain circumstances.[3]

1   *Reeman v Department of Transport* (1997) 2 Lloyd's Rep 674.
2   *Tidman v Reading Borough Council* [1994] PLR 72.
3   *Lambert v West Devon Borough Council* (1997) 96 LGR 45.

1.49 In May 2003 the Court of Appeal in *Health and Safety Executive v Thames Trains Ltd*[1] – dealing with an application to strike out under the Civil Procedure Rules 1998, r 3.4(2) – briefly reviewed the authorities on liability of statutory bodies. It considered that a duty of care could be imposed for actions they perform as part of their executive functions, such as granting planning permissions etc, or accept responsibility for – *Kane v New Forest District Council*[2] – or for failure to exercise a power – *Larner v Solihull Metropolitan Borough Council*.[3] Thus the law is still developing in this area but it is only in the exceptional case that a claim in respect of the granting of permissions or licences or failure to exercise a power is likely to succeed.

1   [2003] EWCA Civ 720.
2   [2002] 1 WLR 312.
3   [2001] RTR 469.

1.50 In *Perrett v Collins*[1] a passenger recovered damages for personal injury sustained in an aircraft which crashed, and it was held that his action could lie against the authority which certified the aircraft as fit to fly. By contrast, where a surveyor allegedly reported that water in Bangladesh was safe to drink, the Court of Appeal struck out environmental liability claims by people who suffered arsenicosis from drinking it, on the basis that the surveyor was not a statutory authority and had no power or control over the water or its availability to those who might drink it.[2]

1   [1998] 2 Lloyd's Rep 255, [1999] PNLR 77.
2   *Binod Sutrahdur v Natural Environment Research Council* [2004] LTL 20/2/04.

CHAPTER 2

Nuisance

WHAT IS PRIVATE NUISANCE?

2.01   The essence of the tort is unlawful interference with a person's use or enjoyment of land. As befits a legal remedy whose essence concerns *land*, this is a cause of action of great antiquity. The nineteenth-century innovation of *statutory* nuisance has led many to predict the demise of this private law remedy. The prophets have been confounded; private nuisance has enjoyed a new lease of life, consistent with the growth of concern about environmental protection generally.

2.02   In recent times the higher courts have repeatedly been called upon to refine and sharpen principle in the law of nuisance. The process began with *Cambridge Water Co Ltd v Eastern Counties Leather plc*[1] (foreseeability). This was followed by *Hunter v Canary Wharf Ltd*[2] (standing to sue). The House of Lords comprehensively reviewed the law relating to liability for damage caused by encroaching tree roots in *Delaware Mansions Ltd v Westminster City Council*.[3] The House of Lords has recently reviewed liability in nuisance of sewerage undertakers for damage caused by flooding in *Marcic v Thames Water Utilities Ltd*.[4] *Rylands v Fletcher*[5] has been reconsidered by the House of Lords in *Transco plc v Stockport Metropolitan Borough Council*.[6]

1   [1994] 2 AC 264, HL.
2   [1997] AC 655, HL.
3   [2001] UKHL 55, [2001] 4 All ER 737.
4   [2003] UKHL 66, [2004] 1 All ER 135.
5   (1868) LR 3 HL 330.
6   [2003] UKHL 61, [2003] 3 WLR 1467, [2004] 1 All ER 539.

CATEGORIES OF PRIVATE NUISANCE

2.03   There are three categories of nuisance: (1) encroachment on the claimant's land, where the nuisance closely resembles trespass; (2) physical damage to the claimant's land; and (3) interference with the claimant's use and enjoyment of the land (which is usually referred to as a 'sensibility' claim).

Encroachment on land

2.04   This category of nuisance is a specialist subject which is reviewed in Chapter 4.

Physical damage

2.05   The term 'physical damage' covers damage to premises, trees, shrubs and chattel damage such as livestock on the plaintiff's land (eg *St Helen's Smelting Co v Tipping*[1]). The term also covers damage to curtains or car bodywork (*Halsey v Esso Petroleum Co Ltd*[2]). The physical damage must be material or substantial and damage is one of the essentials of nuisance. Its existence must be proved, except in those cases in which it is presumed by law to exist: see *R v Battsby*;[3] *A-G v Kingston-on-Thames Corpn*;[4] *Salvin v North Brancepeth Coal Co.*[5]

1   (1865) 11 HL Cas 642.
2   [1961] 1 WLR 683.
3   (1850) 16 QB 1022.
4   (1865) 34 LJ Ch 481.
5   (1874) 9 Ch App 705.

2.06   The definition of physical damage is not always straightforward. In negligence damage has been defined as a 'change of state', see *Hunter v Canary Wharf Ltd.*[1] We think that the same definition applies in nuisance.

1   [1997] AC 655, CA.

2.07   In *Hunter v Canary Wharf Ltd*[1] it was held that dust could constitute physical damage for example where it was trodden into carpets such as to amount to a change of state. This is consistent with old cases involving coal dust soiling shop produce. In *The Orjula*[2] acidic contamination of a ship's surface structure required by regulation to be steam-cleaned was held to constitute physical damage. In *Blue Circle Industries plc v Ministry of Defence*[3] radioactive contamination requiring expensive remediation under statute was held to constitute physical damage. These were all cases in the tort of negligence. They demonstrate where a statutory scheme requires clean-up at great expense the court will be quick to find that physical damage has occurred. In *Merlin v British Nuclear Fuels plc*[4] where the trial judge held that there was no 'physical damage' for the purposes of the Nuclear Installations Act 1965, the concentrations of radionucleides identified did not exceed any statutory levels, and therefore the claim for compensation under the Act failed.

1   [1997] AC 655, CA.
2   [1995] 2 Lloyd's Rep 395.

3   [1999] Ch 289, CA.
4   [1990] 2 QB 557.

2.08 Subject to proof of physical damage, a nuisance action in this second category ought to be straightforward. We emphasise that the Latent Damage Act 1986 which clearly applies to negligence actions apparently has no application in a nuisance action.

2.09 The airborne pollution 'actual damage' cases have involved a number of industrial processes. The St Helen's case involved copper smelting. *Walter v Selfe*[1] involved brick burning. *Salvin v North Brancepeth Coal Co*[2] involved emissions from a coking plant and *Wood v Conway Corpn*[3] involved a gas works. *Halsey v Esso Petroleum Co Ltd*[4] involved smuts from an oil distribution dept. *Pwllbach Colliery Co Ltd v Woodman*[5] involved coal dust from a coal stocking depot that soiled shop produce.

1   (1851) 4 De G & Sm 315.
2   (1874) 9 Ch App 705.
3   [1914] 2 Ch 47, CA.
4   [1961] 2 All ER 145.
5   [1915] AC 634, HL.

2.10 In all these cases relief was granted to the persons affected by the industrial processes, notwithstanding arguments put forward by the industrial operators to the general effect that they were using best practicable means to reduce or eliminate the pollution and that they were fulfilling an important function by supplying goods and services and employing people.

Sensibility claims

2.11 The third category is where no physical damage has occurred but there is injury to enjoyment caused by such things as noise, vibration, smell and dust. These are usually called sensibility claims, but in *Hunter v Canary Wharf Ltd*[1] Lord Hoffmann described this as 'injury to amenity'.

1   [1997] AC 655, HL.

2.12 The standard of 'injury' needed to found an action in a sensibility claim is well settled. It is

'inconvenience materially interfering with the ordinary physical comfort of human existence, not merely according to elegant or dainty modes and habits of living, but according to plain and sober and simple notions and habits obtaining among the English people': *Sturges v Bridgman*.[1]

1   (1879) 11 Ch D 852, CA.

2.13 Accordingly, the court will not allow the hypersensitive plaintiff to impose excessive restraints on his or her neighbour: *Robinson v Kilvert*.[1] It is interesting to compare the position in negligence where, of course, the defendant must take his or her victim as the defendant finds the victim, however susceptible that victim may be.

1   (1889) 41 Ch D 88, CA.

2.14   In *Devon Lumber Co Ltd v MacNeill*,[1] the plaintiff, at first instance, recovered personal injury damages in private nuisance against a cedar mill which created fine dust which exacerbated the plaintiff's allergy. On appeal, the award to the plaintiff was reduced, it being held that in a nuisance action her allergy must be ignored, so damages were only recoverable using the yardstick of a normal person of ordinary habits and sensibilities. This is a rare instance of damages being awarded for personal injury in nuisance and would not be followed.[2]

1   (1987) 45 DLR (4th) 300, NB CA.
2   See paras **2.50** and **2.51**.

2.15   Although the standard of *material* interference with *ordinary* habits is easy to state in principle, it is more difficult to define in practice. It is a matter of degree, and always a question of fact. The following are the main matters that will be taken into account:
*   time (particularly day or night);
*   duration (transitory or permanent);
*   locality;[1]
*   manner;
*   deliberate or within rights;
*   social value.

1   See paras **2.26–2.31** below.

PRE-CONDITIONS TO A NUISANCE ACTION

2.16   Before considering the court's approach to sensibility claims in more detail, it is important to underline pre-conditions which must be satisfied for any nuisance claim.

Foreseeability

2.17   The claimant must establish that the relevant damage was a reasonably foreseeable consequence of the user at the time when the user occurred. In the *Cambridge Water*[1] case, the defendants escaped liability for pollution of the underground water supply caused by seepage into it of chemicals accidentally spilt during their leather-tanning process, on the ground the damage had not been foreseeable.

1   [1994] 2 AC 264, HL.

Unreasonable user

2.18 'The very essence of a private nuisance ... is the unreasonable user by a man or his land to the detriment of his neighbour': per Lord Denning MR in *Miller v Jackson*.[1] In *Cambridge Water* Lord Goff emphasised that this is still an important pre-condition (at 301):

'It is still the law that the fact that the defendant has taken all reasonable care will not of itself exonerate him from liability, the relevant control mechanism being found within the principle of reasonable user'.

1   [1977] QB 966 at 980, CA.

2.19 The scale of the defendant's operation and the potential effect on others will be relevant in determining whether user is reasonable. Lord Goff identified this as a parallel concept with 'non-natural user' in *Rylands v Fletcher*. A large-scale industrial operation will generally be an 'unreasonable user', e g a hazardous waste incinerator: see *Graham v Rechem International*.[1] A small-scale operation, such as central-heating fuel storage tanks for a public house might at first sight appear to be a 'reasonable user', particularly if the scale is not much larger than a domestic dwelling. But if the leakage will foreseeably contaminate an adjacent property, and the contamination is substantial, the user would probably be held to be unreasonable.

1   [1996] Env ER 158.

Continuous state of affairs

2.20 The general rule is that, in order to constitute nuisance, the interference must arise from a 'continuous state of affairs' on land not belonging to the plaintiff: *Bolton v Stone*.[1] As has recently been clarified by the House of Lords in *Cambridge Water*, the rule in *Rylands v Fletcher* was a development of the law of nuisance which enabled a remedy, exceptionally, to be provided for an isolated escape as opposed to a continuous state of affairs.

1   [1951] AC 850, HL.

Interest in property

2.21 In *Hunter v Canary Wharf*[1] the House of Lords, by a majority, reaffirmed the proposition that a private nuisance is primarily a wrong to the owner or the occupier of the land affected. Accordingly, standing to sue in private nuisance was based on demonstrating an interest in the property affected. In his dissenting speech Lord Cooke relied on, amongst other things, Article 8 of the European Convention on Human Rights and it is certainly possible that the restrictive requirement of a legally protected interest in land, as a pre-requisite for a successful nuisance claim, may now need to be reconsidered. In *McKenna* *v British Aluminium Ltd*,[2] it was held that it was arguable that this aspect of the common law might require modification in the light of the Human Rights Act 1998.

1   [1997] AC 655.
2   [2002] Env LR 721.

Coming onto the land of the claimant

2.22 Following *Hunter v Canary Wharf* where interference with television reception was held not to constitute a nuisance on the ground, amongst others, that the presence of a large building blocking television reception did not fulfil an essential requirement of something coming on to the land of the claimant, it is probably important to check that this is a pre-condition that the claimant can satisfy. In *Anglian Water Services Ltd v Crawshaw Robbins & Co Ltd*[1] it was held that the negligent interruption of a supply of gas by a third party is not actionable as a private nuisance. The claim failed to meet the pre-condition that nuisance requires something coming on to the land of the claimant.

1   [2001] BLR 173.

THE COURT'S APPROACH

2.23 The essence of the exercise is that of balancing the defendant's right to conduct his or her operations as he or she pleases, with the claimant's right to have the use and enjoyment of his or her neighbouring property without undue interference. In addressing this balancing exercise, the courts take a number of matters into account in approaching the central question to be determined on the facts of each case, namely, whether the defendant is using his or her property reasonably or not.

2.24 In *Colls v Home and Colonial Stores Ltd*[1] Lord Halsbury said:

'What may be called the uncertainty of the test (i.e. the unreasonable user test) may also be described as its elasticity. A dweller in towns cannot expect to have as pure air, as free from smoke, smell, and noise as if he lived in the country and distant from other dwellings, yet an excess of smoke, smell and noise may give a cause of action. In each of such cases it becomes a question of degree, and whether in each case it amounts to a nuisance which will give a right of action.'

1   [1904] AC 179, HL.

2.25 While numerous circumstances are taken into account in the balancing exercise, the cases show that the three factors most commonly given weight are (1) locality; (2) whether the defendant has used best practical means to minimise interference; and (3) the social value of the defendant's operation.

Locality

2.26 Locality is clearly a factor. Lord Halsbury's famous allusion to Bermondsey and Belgravia has been given recent emphasis in the decision by Buckley J in *Gillingham Borough Council v Medway (Chatham) Dock Co Ltd.*[1]

1   [1993] QB 343, [1992] 3 All ER 923.

2.27 In that case a former naval dockyard was given planning permission to operate as a commercial port. Access to the port was limited to two residential roads. Very quickly heavy traffic was using the road for 24 hours a day, causing great disturbance to the local community.

2.28 When the planning application had been made, the local authority had been aware that an increase in heavy traffic was likely to take place. The defendant had in fact estimated that some three to four hundred lorry movements would occur per day, thus increasing noise levels, particularly at night. Planning permission had been granted because the economic benefit of having a commercial port was considered to outweigh the environmental disadvantages.

2.29 In 1990, no doubt faced with many complaints by residents, the local authority commenced an action under the Local Government Act 1972, s 222 seeking an injunction to prevent traffic movement between 7pm and 7am on the grounds of public nuisance (on this point public and private nuisance are indistinguishable). The trial judge ruled that the effect of the grant of planning permission was to change the character of the neighbourhood to the extent that a nuisance action was to be considered in the light of the existing environment, not the one that existed in the past. The local authority's action was dismissed.

2.30 In *Wheeler v J J Saunders Ltd,*[1] planning permission had been granted for two pig-rearing houses. The neighbouring plaintiffs subsequently brought a successful nuisance action in respect of the smells from the units. The question on appeal was whether the planning permission provided a good defence to such an action. The Court of Appeal distinguished the *Chatham Dock* case on the basis that it concerned a major redevelopment and rejected any interpretation giving rise to a wider proposition that a planning decision automatically authorised any nuisance which would inevitably result from it, and dismissed the appeal in *Wheeler's* case upholding the trial judge's award of damages and injunction.

1   [1996] Ch 19, CA.

2.31 In *Hunter v Canary Wharf* the defendants sought to rely on *Chatham Dock* but the Court of Appeal was not prepared to hold that the planning permission conferred an immunity, and this point was not appealed to the House of Lords.[1]

1   See para **2.39** below.

Best practicable means

2.32   A factor which will be taken into consideration is whether the defendant is using best practicable means to eliminate or reduce the inconvenience caused to the plaintiff. The finding that the defendant is not using best practicable means, though not conclusive, may well render the defendant liable in nuisance. On the other hand, the fact that the defendant has used best practicable means is by no means conclusive in the defendant's favour, save in building and construction cases.[1]

1   See paras **2.60–2.66** below.

Social value

2.33   The 'social value' of the defendant's activity is only a factor, but not a conclusive one, in the balancing exercise. For example in *Shelfer v City of London Electric Lighting Co*[1] Lindley LJ said

> 'neither has the circumstance that the wrongdoer is in some sense a public benefactor (e.g. a gas or water company or a sewer authority) ever been considered as sufficient reason for refusing to protect by injunction an individual whose rights are being persistently infringed'.

This dictum was applied by the Court of Appeal in *Kennaway v Thompson*[2] where the claim succeeded for an injunction restraining noisy speedboat racing.

1   [1895] 1 Ch 287, CA.
2   [1981] QB 88, CA.

DEFENCES IN A NUISANCE ACTION

2.34   In the standard works, the defences of (i) prescription, (ii) grant of rights, (iii) act of God and (iv) act of trespasser are dealt with. In toxic tort claims, however, the defence of most importance and that which has seen the most recent development in the case law is the defence of statutory authority.

Statutory authority

2.35   This defence has been the subject of consideration by the House of Lords in three cases in the 1980s: *Allen v Gulf Oil Refining Ltd*,[1] *Tate & Lyle Industries Ltd v Greater London Council*[2] and *Department of Transport v North West Water Authority*.[3]

1   [1981] AC 1001, HL.
2   [1983] 2 AC 509, HL.
3   [1984] AC 336, HL.

2.36   In the *Gulf Oil* case the residents of a previously quiet village sought to bring nuisance proceedings in respect of the Milford Haven Oil Refinery development. The action was struck out. The House of Lords construed the special Act authorising the construction of the refinery as conferring immunity on the Company provided they could prove it was inevitable that despite their using all reasonable care the local residents would still sustain the harm about which they were complaining. The court was unable to award any damages to the plaintiff as no compensation for that harm was directly given by the Act. The plaintiff's only remedy was to the extent that the actual nuisance exceeded that for which such immunity was conferred, ie, to the extent that the Company did not use reasonable care.

2.37   Thus, once nuisance has been established, the burden is effectively transferred to the company to show that it has exercised all reasonable care to minimise the nuisance. To the extent that it is able to do so, immunity has been conferred by the courts.

2.38   This was well illustrated the in *Tate & Lyle* case. This action, as in the case of *Gulf Oil*, was based on public nuisance, although on this point there is no distinction between public and private nuisance. The Greater London Council, acting with statutory authority, constructed ferry terminals at Woolwich. Because of the faulty design and construction of the ferry terminals the river bed became heavily silted which meant that the plaintiffs had insufficient depth of water to gain access to their jetties. The plaintiffs had to spend more than £500,000 dredging the river to regain access. It was held that the defendants should bear three-quarters of this cost and the plaintiffs one-quarter on the footing that due diligence by the defendants would still have left the plaintiffs with some dredging to do (hence conferring an immunity to that extent).

2.39   Whilst a special Act authorising a development confers statutory authority and invokes the above principles, it is by no means clear whether lesser or more general instruments are capable of having the same effect. In *Hunter v Canary Wharf Ltd*,[1] the docklands action for interference with television reception, the Canary Wharf development was undertaken pursuant to Enterprise Zone consents which were in turn expressly authorised by Parliament pursuant to the Local Government Planning and Land Act 1980. The defendants argued that this statutory scheme operated to confer the defence of statutory authority on the development. The Court of Appeal rejected this.

1   [1997] AC 655, CA.

2.40   Another attempt to obtain what Americans call 'statutory pre-emption' (ie an immunity providing a compliance with a statutory scheme can be demonstrated) occurred in the context of a local authority certificate for noisy construction works pursuant to the Control of Pollution Act 1974, s 60. In *Lloyds Bank plc v Guardian Assurance plc and Trollope & Colls Ltd*[1] the Court of Appeal held that the fact that a local authority, exercising its powers under s 60, had granted a certificate allowing certain working hours for a construction site did not confer an immunity on the developer from injunction proceedings in private nuisance at the instance of a private party seeking further and greater restrictions on the hours that could be worked than those laid down in the s 60 Certificate. Where, by contrast, a cause of action in nuisance is held not to be consistent with a statutory scheme, then the claim in nuisance will be dismissed: see *Marcic v Thames Water Utilities Ltd*[2] where the House of Lords, reversing the decision of the Court of Appeal, held that the statutory right to complain to the Director General of Water Services was the exclusive remedy for sewage flooding.

1   (1986) 35 BLR 34.
2   [2003] UKHL 66, [2004] 1 All ER 135.

2.41   Under the Environmental Protection Act 1990 and in its successors there is an extensive system for the licensing of scheduled industries involving a far more exacting scrutiny of the applicant's activity than has ever previously been the case. It may well be that the defendant will try to use the existence of an operating licence or permit granted by a statutory authority as a defence against a nuisance action. This point remains to be tested in English courts, although it was touched upon in *Blackburn v ARC Ltd*[1] in relation to a waste disposal licence.

1   [1998] Env LR 469 at 525.

Reasonable precautions taken

2.42   Where the defendant is the *creator* of the nuisance the fact that the defendant has taken reasonable precautions to reduce or prevent the nuisance will not constitute a defence, see *Cambridge Water* reaffirming established law, for example Lord Symonds in *Read v J Lyons & Co Ltd*:[1]

> 'If a man commits a legal nuisance, it is no answer to his injured neighbour that he took the utmost care not to commit it. There the liability is strict.'

1   [1947] AC 156, HL.

2.43   If, on the other hand, the defendant is not the creator of the nuisance, but is a 'continuer' in the sense that he comes into ownership or occupation of the land and subsequently has knowledge actual or constructive that a nuisance is being caused, then the fact that he has used all reasonable means to reduce or prevent the nuisance continuing does constitute a defence to a nuisance action: see *Goldman v Hargrave*;[1] *Leakey v National Trust*;[2] and *Cambridge Water*.[3]

1   [1967] 1 AC 645, PC.
2   [1980] QB 485, CA.
3   [1994] 2 AC 264.

2.44   In this context, however, the practitioner should beware if the proposed defendant is a statutory undertaker exercising powers. Public authorities have special responsibilities and their liabilities have to be considered in the light of statutory functions. Where the statutory scheme provides a remedy, the court may hold that this is an exclusive remedy, thus depriving an individual of his right to claim damages in nuisance. Providing decisions of the proper authority under the statutory scheme are susceptible to judicial review, it is unlikely that there will be any breach of duty under the Human Rights Act 1998, s 6: see *Marcic v Thames Water Utilities Ltd.*[1]

1   [2003] UKHL 66, [2004] 1 All ER 135.

Coming to a nuisance

2.45   It is commonly thought that it is a defence that the plaintiff 'comes to the nuisance'. It is not. The Court of Appeal so held in *Miller v Jackson*[1] where the plaintiffs lived on a new residential estate which bordered a long-standing cricket pitch from which balls were intermittently hit into the plaintiffs' garden. In so doing the Court of Appeal affirmed the old authority of *Bliss v Hall*.[2] The exception to this rule is where a right has been acquired to any easement by prescription, ie for more than a 20-year term. We know of no reported modern case in which a prescriptive right has been upheld as a defence to a nuisance action.

1   [1977] QB 966.
2   (1838) 4 Bing NC 183.

One of many

2.46   It is also sometimes assumed that a company defending a nuisance action will succeed by saying that the company was 'one of many'. Again this is wrong. 'One of many' does not constitute a defence. It was so held in the water pollution case of *Blair v Deakin*[1] where several manufacturers, having their works upstream, caused nuisance to a riparian owner below. It was held no answer in a nuisance action brought by the riparian owner against one of the manufacturers for such manufacturer to say that the share he contributed to the nuisances was infinitesimal and inappreciable. It should be emphasised, however, that this was an application for injunction. It is by no means clear the same approach would be taken in a damages action.

1   (1887) 57 LT 522.

REMEDIES

2.47   Chapters 10 and 11 deal with remedies in general terms. There are some particular matters in respect of remedies for private nuisance that call for additional comment.

Injunctions

2.48   An injunction is one of the most significant of the available remedies in private nuisance actions. For example in *Crump v Lambert*[1] an injunction was granted which would have had the effect of closing a factory in Walsall in a 'sensibility' case. This was notwithstanding the point that Walsall was an industrial locality, and an acceptance that the factory served the public interest in conferring economic benefit on the community. In *Allison v Merton Sutton and Wandsworth Area Health Authority*[2] an injunction was granted where the noise from a hospital boiler kept the plaintiff awake at night resulting in feelings of depression. In *Halsey v Esso Petroleum Co Ltd*[3] an injunction in private nuisance was granted in respect of noise from the boilers, the Esso plant generally, and from Esso's vehicles. In *A-G v Gastonia Coaches Ltd*[4] the judge granted a suspended injunction where a firm's coaches emitted diesel fumes and 'revved' their engines in a residential street. The general principles of injunctive relief are dealt with in Chapter 10.

1   (1867) LR 3 Eq 409.
2   [1975] CLY 2450.
3   [1961] 1 WLR 683.
4   [1977] RTR 219.

Compensation for property damage

2.49   It is settled law that damages are recoverable in respect of property damage (*St Helen's Smelting Co v Tipping*[1]) and chattel damage (*St Helen's Smelting* and *Halsey*[2]); see also, generally, *Hunter v Canary Wharf Ltd*.[3] The property and chattel must, of course, be connected with the plaintiff's land, for example the livestock in *St Helen's Smelting* and the washing hanging on the line in *Halsey*. By contrast, in the *Halsey* case where the car was parked, not on the plaintiff's property, but in the road between the plaintiff's house and the factory, the bodywork damage from oil smuts was not recoverable in private nuisance. It was, however, held to be recoverable in public nuisance. Had Mr Halsey had a driveway to his house in which he habitually parked his car, then the damage to his car would have been recoverable as a private nuisance.

1   (1865) 11 HL Cas 642.
2   [1961] 1 WLR 683.
3   [1997] AC 655, HL.

Compensation for personal injury

2.50 Damages for personal injury do not appear to be recoverable in private nuisance. Although such damages have not infrequently been recovered in public nuisance, Lord Goff, in *Hunter v Canary Wharf Ltd*[1] expressed the view that 'personal injury claims should be altogether excluded from the law of nuisance'.[2] This stance is consistent with his speech in *Cambridge Water*,[3] and also the speech of Lord Macmillan in the House of Lords in *Read v J Lyons & Co Ltd*[4] where he said:

> 'Whatever may have been the law of England in early times I am of the opinion that as the law now stands an allegation of negligence is in general essential to the relevancy of an action of reparation for personal injuries.'[5]

1   [1997] AC 655, HL.
2   At 692.
3   [1997] 2 AC 264.
4   [1947] AC 156, HL.
5   See also *Transco plc v Stockport Metropolitan Borough Council* [2004] 1 All ER 539.

2.51 Evidence of illness is of course admissible in a nuisance action to demonstrate the seriousness of the nuisance, for example respiratory illness in an airborne dust nuisance claim, or depressive illness in a noise nuisance claim. The relevance is strictly confined to demonstrating the injury to the amenity of the property.

Quantum in 'sensibility' claims

2.52 In personal injury claims quantum will be determined on principles and precedents which are fully set out in such works as *Kemp and Kemp: The Quantum of Damages*.[1] However, the principles and precedents in respect of quantum in sensibility cases are a good deal more difficult to locate.

1   D Kemp and M S Kemp (looseleaf, Sweet & Maxwell).

2.53 Formerly the only guidance from the Court of Appeal in recent times was in the case of *Bone v Seale*[1] (a pig farm smells case). There the court stated that damages in personal injury cases may provide a loose analogy for appropriate awards in nuisance cases.

1   [1975] 1 WLR 797.

2.54 However, such an approach was disapproved by the House of Lords in *Hunter v Canary Wharf Ltd*,[1] but in the three speeches touching on the subject the approach that was to be substituted is not easy to understand. It was said that in cases involving interference with amenity and enjoyment of property the court must place a value on an intangible loss which cannot be assessed mathematically (per Lord Lloyd at 696). *Ruxley Electronics and Construction v*

Forsyth[2] was relied upon as demonstrating the court's wide and flexible approach to the valuation of intangibles. Lord Hoffmann in an important passage (at 706) says that estate agents evaluate these 'intangibles' all the time, impliedly saying that expert evidence will usually be called for.

1   [1997] AC 655.
2   [1996] AC 344, HL.

2.55   We would submit, at least where the expert's expenses are proportionate to the sums claimed, that expert valuations should be obtained. In a case where the injury to amenity is permanent, the valuer will be addressing the injury to the freehold or reversion. In the more usual case where the injury to amenity is transitory the expert's starting point may well be the rental value in the open market (unaffected) compared with the rental value (with the nuisance). The duration of the nuisance can then be brought into the computation. A reported case after *Hunter v Canary Wharf Ltd*[1] where valuers were used is *Blackburn v ARC Ltd*.[2]

1   [1997] AC 655.
2   [1998] Env LR 469.

Loss of profits

2.56   Where an actionable nuisance interferes with the claimant's property and in addition damages the claimant's chattels which the claimant uses in his or her business, the claimant can recover consequential damages including loss of profit: see *Hunter v Canary Wharf Ltd*,[1] particularly the speech of Lord Hoffmann at 706.

1   [1997] AC 655, HL.

The award must not exceed extent of the nuisance

2.57   Where in a nuisance claim the defendant incurs liability because his or her otherwise lawful activity causes excessive interference with the claimant's use or enjoyment of land, the court will ensure that the defendant is only required to pay compensation for the extent to which the defendant's interference is unreasonable and hence actionable.

2.58   In many cases there will be a discount because of the effect on the claimant of those activities which the defendant could lawfully have carried on.

2.59   This limiting principle is likely to be of particular relevance in construction works cases. Indeed in the leading case, *Andreae v Selfridge & Co Ltd*,[1] where the plaintiff succeeded in proving that a nuisance had been caused by the defendants as a result of noise and dust produced during their building operations, it was emphasised that a lesser degree of interference would not have been actionable, and, in reducing damages which had been awarded at first instance, Sir Wilfred Greene MR said:

'... one must be careful not to penalise the defendant company by throwing into the scales against it the loss ... caused by operations which it was legitimately entitled to carry out. It can be made liable only in respect of matters, in which it has crossed the permissible line.'

1   [1938] Ch 1, CA.

Building and construction operations

2.60 Building and construction operations, including demolition, almost invariably cause some disturbance through noise, dust and vibration to the local residents. By their very nature such works are 'temporary', although in the case of a huge project, such as the London Docklands development, temporary can mean many years. Faced with the need to respect the public interest in regeneration, redevelopment and restoration the courts have evolved special principles for dealing with this category of cases.

2.61 The law is well settled and was restated by the Court of Appeal in *Andreae v Selfridge & Co Ltd*[1] by Sir Wilfred Greene MR dealing with a case of demolition in the West End of London as follows:

'The Judge found that by reason of all three operations, there was a substantial interference with the comfort of the plaintiff in the reasonable occupation and use of her house, such that, assuming damage to be established, an actionable nuisance would be constituted. But it was said that when one is dealing with temporary operations, such as demolition and re-building, everybody has to put up with a certain amount of discomfort, because operations of that kind cannot be carried on at all without a certain amount of dust. Therefore, the rule with regard to interference must be read subject to this qualification, and there can be no dispute about it, but in respect of operations of this character, such as demolition and building, if they are reasonably carried on and all proper and reasonable steps are taken to ensure that no undue inconvenience is caused to neighbours, whether from noise, dust or other reasons the neighbours must put up with it.'[2]

1   [1938] Ch 1.
2   [1938] Ch 1 at 5–6.

2.62 In construction cases, therefore, nuisance is effectively put on the same footing as negligence, with one significant difference. Whereas in a negligence action it is for the plaintiff to establish fault on the defendant's part, in a construction nuisance case, once the claimant has established the prima facie actionable nuisance arising from the construction works, the burden shifts to the defendant to show non-negligence in relation to prevention and abatement of nuisance. This latter distinction is however more apparent than real. A claimant would still need the reassurance of technical evidence which would probably rebut such a defence before launching proceedings.

2.63   In determining whether the defendant has or has not taken all reasonable precautions it will not avail the defendant, in general terms, to advance the propositions either that a particular precaution would cost him more, or, (as in the case of a restriction of hours of working, eg at night) would delay the termination of works. There is a balancing exercise here. The court is unlikely to bankrupt the project at the instigation of local residents temporarily affected.

2.64   So, for example, in *Hart v Aga Khan Foundation*[1] the plaintiff, who lived in Thurlow Place, brought injunction proceedings in respect of the construction of the Ismaili Cultural Centre opposite the Victoria and Albert Museum in the Cromwell Road. Lawson J granted injunctions relating to the type of equipment to be used, and restricting the hours of work. The Court of Appeal substantially set aside the injunction on the grounds that the restricted hours would give rise to a cost over-run of the order of £1.2 million. However, all major construction projects have built in timescales underpinned by financial penalties and involving third-party obligations, and it remains to be seen how far the courts will permit the contractual structure to limit the claimant's ability to obtain relief in nuisance.

1   (13 February 1981, unreported), CA, Bar Library Transcript 1980 M4893.

2.65   In the *Hart* case Stephenson LJ thought it right to require greater precautions to be taken when the temporary work of demolition and rebuilding is likely to take a matter of months or years rather than only weeks or days. If this principle of proportionality is invoked by the courts huge projects taking five years or more would call for state-of-the-art techniques to minimise dust, vibration and noise. This should mean that the courts will not just consider equipment available on the English market, but what is available worldwide.

2.66   Time restrictions and the introduction of best equipment costs money and the residents' actions will always be met with the 'injury to profits' defence. Nonetheless, in the instance of a long-term construction project the balance ought to favour the resident. Construction projects lasting days or weeks usually enhance the amenity of the neighbourhood because they involve refurbishment and restoration so that, at the price of temporary inconvenience, the claimant will see some long-term benefit. In the case of a long-term project however, the impact is usually a permanent and radical alteration of the neighbourhood, involving the destruction of a community sometimes of very long standing and the relocation of many of its members. In this instance there is little, if any, long-term enhancement for the claimant to balance against the years of injury to amenity whilst construction is undertaken. In every sense, the profit, social and environmental gain will belong to persons other than the long-standing residents.

PUBLIC NUISANCE

2.67 A whole community is up in arms because of the repeated and dreadful stench from an animal waste processing business. A neighbourhood complains en masse when a paper mill which had worked a 12-hour day now works a 24-hour day, giving rise to night-time noise and lorry movements, forklift trucks and bailing machines. A village downwind of an old quarry, long disused, is concerned to find that the quarry is now being filled with tons of fibrous asbestos waste. The population of a given area finds the supply of drinking water has been contaminated making it temporarily unfit for human consumption.

2.68 These are all potential public nuisance claims. There is a lot of common ground between public and private nuisance, and in many instances claims can be made good in both.

Principles

2.69 Public nuisance is a criminal offence, as well as a tort. Public nuisance is one which inflicts damage, injury or inconvenience on all the Queen's subjects or on all members of a class who come within the sphere or neighbourhood of its operation.

2.70 *Stephens Digest of Criminal Law*[1] describes public nuisance in this way:

'Every person is guilty of an offence at common law, known as public nuisance, who does an act not warranted by law, or omits to discharge a legal duty, if the effect of the act or omission is to endanger the life, health, property, morals, or the comfort of the public, or to obstruct the public in the exercise or enjoyment of rights common to all Her Majesty's subjects.'

1   9th edn, p 179.

2.71 By way of recent examples, the South West Water Authority was prosecuted to conviction for public nuisance in the Crown Court at Exeter arising out of the Camelford Water contamination incident in 1988. In the *Sea Empress* oil pollution case, the Port Authority was charged on indictment with public nuisance, although this charge was not proceeded with as a result of a plea bargain.[1]

1   See Chapter 7 at paras **7.52–7.56**.

2.72 The essential ingredients are:
(a) an actionable wrong (falling within the *Stephens Digest* definition above);
(b) material effect on a large number of people, sufficient to constitute a class.

2.73 As to the second point, the wrong may affect some members of the public to a greater extent than others. The question whether the number of persons affected is sufficient to constitute a class is one of fact. Not every member needs to be affected in the neighbourhood. The leading case on the point is *A-G v PYA Quarries Ltd*[1] in which Romer LJ said (at 184):

> 'It is, however, clear in my opinion that any (public) nuisance which materially affects the reasonable comfort and convenience of life of a class of Her Majesty's subjects. The sphere of the nuisance may be described generally as "the neighbourhood"; but the question whether the local community within that sphere comprises a sufficient number of persons to constitute a class of the public is a question of fact in every case. It is not necessary, in my judgment, to prove that every member of the class has been injuriously affected; it is sufficient to show that a representative cross-section of the class has been so affected for an injunction to issue.'

1   [1957] 2 QB 169, CA.

Who may bring proceedings in public nuisances?

2.74 Public nuisance actions, in modern times, are usually brought by local authorities. Importantly, where certain specific matters can be established, individual citizens can bring public nuisance actions and this is also considered below. Finally, the Attorney General still has a jurisdiction, now rarely exercised, and we make reference to this.

Local authorities: public nuisance

2.75 The Local Government Act 1972, s 222 allows local authorities to institute civil proceedings 'in their own names'. This is separate from their statutory nuisance powers.

2.76 A good example of the local authority instituting civil proceedings is *Shoreham-by-Sea UDC v Dolphin Canadian Proteins Ltd.*[1] The defendants owned a long-established factory in an industrial area. The factory produced feeding stuffs, fertiliser and tallow from boiling down chicken feathers, chicken offal, fats, bones and other forms of offal. Emission of unpleasant smells arising from this processing was a nuisance to local inhabitants.

1   (1972) 71 LGR 261.

2.77 The evidence of nuisance was compelling, consisting of, for example, the fact that a school situated about 100 yards away from the factory occasionally had to keep the windows closed in summer such that the children were so hot they were unable to pay attention to what they were doing. Another nearby factory found that on occasion its workers could not eat their lunch because the smell from the defendants' premises affected their stomachs. There were numerous complaints from local householders who had to keep their windows closed and could not sit out in their gardens in the summer. Donaldson J reminded himself that this was a 'sensibility' case and that this was an industrial area. The local inhabitants were not entitled to expect to sit in a sweet-smelling orchard. He was not, however, satisfied that the best practicable means to abate had in fact been employed ('there is no profit in anti-pollution measures'), and he would have granted an injunction but for the fact that the defendant company gave undertakings to abate the nuisance within nine months. The company then breached the undertakings. The local authority moved for leave to issue a writ of sequestration against the defendant company for contempt of court. The court stayed its hand and substituted a heavy fine for contempt.

2.78 Nowadays the local authority would bring such proceedings by way of statutory nuisance under the Environmental Protection Act 1990, s 79, and particularly s 79(1)(d): 'any dust, steam, smell or other effluvia arising on industrial, trade or business premises and being prejudicial to health of a nuisance'. It is, however, a complete defence under s 80(7) of the Act to show that best practicable means were used to prevent or counteract the effects of the nuisance; see Chapter 3 generally.

2.79 However, a private action based on common law nuisance (see below) has a better prospect of success, because, whilst the use of best practicable means will be a factor to be taken into account by the court in looking at the reasonableness of the defendant's conduct, it is not conclusive. Parliament has conferred a statutory defence on an alleged polluter facing local authority proceedings in statutory nuisance which the polluter will not enjoy if a private person brings a common law nuisance action.

2.80 When a neighbourhood action group, suffering substantial inconvenience from an industrial operation, having exhausted negotiations with the industrial operator, then goes to the local environmental health officer, the two legal remedies which the local authority will have at the forefront of its mind will be statutory nuisance proceedings under the Environmental Protection Act 1990, Pt III and common law public nuisance.

2.81 However, the local authority will not always act and even when it does there are very clear limits to what such an action can achieve for the aggrieved individual. In the first place a local authority common law public nuisance action may only achieve an injunction to stop the nuisance. It cannot achieve compensation and damages for the aggrieved citizens. Whilst for most citizens the abatement of the nuisance will be more significant than the money, in circumstances where abatement is impossible money compensation is at least a mitigating factor, and where the nuisance has gone on for a long period and has affected a lot of people, the compensation claim could be substantial.

2.82   The local authority may decide that an injunction is unlikely to be awarded. In an interlocutory case the local authority will be unwilling to give a cross-undertaking in damages (although it should be noted that public authorities seeking to enforce the law have been held to be exceptions to the usual rule on undertakings as to damages: *Kirklees Metropolitan Borough Council v Wickes Building Supplies Ltd*[1]). Every local authority has a finite budget and it is bound to prioritise in terms of the number of industrial processes it is prepared to take on in the courts in any given period. For all these reasons, some meritorious cases may not be taken up by a local authority.

1   [1993] AC 227, HL.

Public nuisance actions by individuals

2.83   A private individual may bring an action in his or her own name in respect of a public nuisance when, and only when, the individual can satisfy the 'particular damage' test, namely, that the individual has suffered some particular, foreseeable and substantial damage over and above that sustained by the public at large, or when the interference with the public right involves a violation of some private right of his or her own.

2.84   In some cases the 'particular damage' test is straightforward. So, for example, in *Tate & Lyle Industries Ltd v Greater London Council*[1] it was held that the interference with the public right of navigation of the river was a public nuisance and the fact that the plaintiffs could not use their jetties was a particular damage enabling the plaintiffs to bring their own action successfully in public nuisance.

1   [1983] 2 AC 509, HL.

2.85   In *Halsey v Esso Petroleum*,[1] the smuts descending on vehicles in the public street were held to be a public nuisance but the damage to the plaintiff's car was particular damage entitling the plaintiff to claim damages in public nuisance. In the same case, the defendants were held liable in public nuisance for the noise of their lorries entering the plant at night in respect of which the plaintiff had suffered particular damage in that his sleep was disrupted.

1   [1961] 1 WLR 683.

2.86   Other cases will need more careful analysis. It should be noted that the 'particular damage' not only has to be 'over and above' that sustained by the public at large, but also arguably 'different in kind': see *Ricket v Directors etc of the Metropolitan Rly Co.*[1] In relation to obstruction of a highway, Lord Chelmsford LC said (p 190):

'It is doubtful whether the owner of the house sustained any injury different in kind, though it might be greater in degree, from that of the rest of the public; and therefore it is questionable whether he could have maintained an action ...'.

1   (1867) LR 2 HL 175.

2.87   Whilst in certain instances establishing 'particular damage' may involve difficulty, once the pre-condition has been satisfied, the individual is in as good a position as the local authority to sue in public nuisance for damages and injunction.

The Attorney General

2.88   The unique constitutional position of the Attorney General has long been recognised. In *Gouriet v Union of Post Office Workers*[1] it was regarded as settled that he alone stands as *parens patriae* and therefore normally only he can bring a public action in respect of 'public wrongs'. Unfortunately the Attorney is not seen very often, partly because the local authorities now do his work, partly because he is not often asked and partly because, when asked, he wants to know where the money is coming from to underwrite the legal costs of his intervention. Nonetheless, if it was not possible to satisfy the 'particular damage' test and if the local authority refused to bring statutory nuisance proceedings, private individuals could nonetheless apply to the Attorney General who would have jurisdiction to bring the proceedings.

1   [1978] AC 435, HL.

Establishing public nuisance

2.89   In establishing the nuisance the court will take into account similar factors as in private nuisance, ie locality, 'best practicable means' and social value. Defences to a claim in public nuisance are also similar, notably the defence of statutory authority, the defence which was used with partial success in *Tate & Lyle Industries Ltd v Greater London Council*.[1]

1   [1983] 2 AC 509, HL.

2.90   As Sir Thomas Bingham MR has stated, 'public nuisance is private nuisance writ large': *AB v South West Water Services Ltd*.[1] In the context of that case he did point to two significant distinctions, namely that public nuisance is a criminal offence, and that public nuisance is likely to lead to many complaints and therefore many plaintiffs.

1   [1993] 1 All ER 609 at 627G, CA.

2.91   From the standpoint of the practitioner who is considering possible proceedings, the two most important distinctions between public nuisance and private nuisance are probably these:

(a)   an interest in property is not required to bring an action in public nuisance;

(b)   there is ample authority that personal injury damages are recoverable in public nuisance, but such authority must now be doubtful in the light of Lord Goff's obiter dictum that personal injury claims should be altogether excluded from the law of nuisance.[1]

1   See para **2.50**.

Rylands v Fletcher

2.92   In the mid-nineteenth century, a mine owned by the plaintiff was flooded when independent contractors employed by the defendant failed to block off underground shafts leading to the mine before filling the reservoir with water. The flooding had occurred without any fault on the part of the defendant but he was held liable on the ground that anyone who brought onto his land or collected there something likely to cause damage if it escaped, was under a strict duty to prevent an escape.

2.93   Blackburn J said:[1]

'We think that the true rule of law is, that the person who for his own purposes brings on his lands and collects and keeps there anything likely to do mischief if it escapes, must keep it in at his peril, and if he does not do so, is prima facie answerable for all the damage which is the natural consequence of this escape. He can excuse himself by showing the escape was owing to the plaintiff's default; or perhaps that the escape was the consequence of vis major, or the act of God; but as nothing of this sort exists here, it is unnecessary to enquire what excuse would be sufficient. The general rule, as above stated, seems on principle just. The person whose grass or corn is eaten by the escaping cattle of his neighbour, or whose mine is flooded by the water from his neighbour's reservoir, or whose cellar is invaded by the filth of his neighbour's privy, or whose habitation is made unhealthy by the fumes and noise and vapours of his neighbour's alkali works, is damnified without any fault of his own; and it seems both reasonable and just that the neighbour, who has brought something on his property which was not naturally there, harmless to others so long as it is confined to his own property, but which he knows to be mischievous if it gets on his neighbour's, should be obliged to make good the damage which ensues if he does not succeed in confining it to his own property. But for his act in bringing it there no mischief could have accrued, and it seems but just that he should at his peril keep it there so that no mischief may accrue, or answer for the natural and anticipated consequences. Upon authority, this we think is established to be the law whether the things so brought be beasts, or water or filth or stenches.'

1   (1866) LR 1 Exch 265 (at 279–280).

Rylands v Fletcher[1] in the House of Lords

2.94 Lord Cairns adopted this passage of the judgment of Blackburn J, but he also introduced an element of discretion, and certainly opened the door to judicial policy-making, by restricting the rule to circumstances where the defendant had made 'a non-natural use' of the land: *Rylands v Fletcher*.

1   (1868) LR 3 HL 330, [1861–73] All ER Rep 1.

2.95 In *Cambridge Water* the House of Lords reviewed in depth *Rylands v Fletcher*, and restated the principles, holding in effect, that *Rylands v Fletcher* had not introduced any radical new departure from the well-settled principles of nuisance, but was an extension of the law of nuisance to deal with 'one-off escapes'.

Transco v Stockport

2.96 Nearly ten years later in *Transco plc v Stockport Metropolitan Borough Council*,[1] the House of Lords re-visited *Rylands v Fletcher*. In this case a local authority piped a water supply to a block of flats. This water main led to tanks in the basement of the blocks for onward distribution of water to 66 flats and therefore the capacity of the main pipe was much greater than the capacity of a pipe supplying any single dwelling. Without negligence on the part of the Council the main pipe failed and a great deal of water escaped over a prolonged period. The water escape caused the subsidence of an embankment which supported Transco's 16-foot high-pressure gas main. The embankment collapsed leaving the gas main exposed and unsupported. Since there was an immediate serious risk that the gas main may crack with potentially devastating consequences, Transco took prompt and effective remedial measures and sought to recover the cost from the Council.

1   [2003] UKHL 61, [2003] 3 WLR 1467, [2004] 1 All ER 539.

2.97 The House of Lords upheld the dismissal of Transco's claim for compensation, finding that, since Transco had failed to establish 'non-natural user', *Rylands v Fletcher* did not apply. However, Lord Bingham set out to restate the rule in *Rylands v Fletcher* 'so as to achieve as much certainty and clarity as was attainable'. The salient points, of general application, may be summarised as follows:

(a)   The rule in *Rylands v Fletcher* was a sub-species of nuisance, which was itself a tort based on the interference by one occupier of land with the right in or enjoyment of land by another occupier of land.

(b)   It was a pre-condition that there should be an escape from one tenement to another.

(c)   A claim in *Rylands v Fletcher* could not include a claim for death or personal injury.

(d)   A claimant had to satisfy the 'mischief or danger test'; ie the precondition of liability that the thing which the defendant had brought onto his or her land had to be 'something which will naturally do mischief if it escaped out of his land' (see the citation from *Rylands* above).

(e)   The mischief or danger test should not be at all easily satisfied. It had to be shown that the defendant had done something which the defendant recognised, or ought to have recognised, as giving rise to an exceptionally high risk or danger or mischief if there should be an escape however unlikely an escape might have been thought to be.

(f)   As to 'non-natural user', the rule in *Rylands v Fletcher* was engaged only where the defendant's use was shown to be 'extraordinary and unusual'. An occupier of land who could show that another occupier of land had brought or kept on his or her land an exceptionally dangerous or mischievous thing in extraordinary or unusual circumstances was entitled to recover compensation from that occupier for any damage caused to his or her property interest by the escape of that thing, without the need to prove negligence. The defendant, where the rule in *Rylands v Fletcher* applied, would only have the defences of act of God or of a stranger.

Escape

2.98   The rule in *Rylands v Fletcher* only applies where the thing which does the damage has escaped: see *Transco.*[1] For the purposes of the rule, escape means escape from a place where the defendant has occupational control over land to a place which is outside his occupational control: *Read v J Lyons & Co Ltd.*[2] It seems that the rule does not apply to an escape from a ship: *The Wagon Mound (No 2)*,[3] a case in which the appeal was allowed on different grounds.

1   [2003] UKHL 61, [2003] 3 WLR 1467.
2   [1947] AC 156, HL.
3   [1963] 1 Lloyd's Rep 402 (NSW).

Remoteness of damage

2.99   Foreseeability of damage of the relevant type as well as an escape from the land of things likely to do mischief is a pre-requisite of liability. Accordingly, strict liability for the escape from their land of things likely to do mischief only arises if the defendant knew or ought reasonably to have foreseen, applying standards and knowledge of the date of the acts or omissions complained of, that those things might if they escaped cause damage: *Cambridge Water.*[1]

1   See para **2.17** above.

2.100 Difficulties may be caused however in assessing the degree of specificity of the 'type of damage' which needs to be foreseeable for liability to attach. The fact that pollution of some kind is foreseeable is not sufficiently specific for liability to be imposed, but there has not been any authority since *Cambridge Water* on this point.

2.101 The rule in *Rylands v Fletcher* does not apply where the escape is caused by an act of God. Nor does it apply if the escape was due to the act of a stranger of whose acts the defendant has no control and which was not an act which the defendant ought reasonably to have anticipated and guarded against: *Perry v Kendricks Transport Ltd.*[1] Once the defendant has proved that the escape is caused by the act of a stranger, the defendant avoids liability unless the claimant can go on to show that the act which caused the escape was an act of the kind which the defendant could reasonably have anticipated and guarded against.

1   [1956] 1 All ER 154, [1956] 1 WLR 85, CA.

2.102 The rule does not apply where the escape was due to some act or default of the claimant.

2.103 The rule does not apply where the claimant has consented to the presence of the thing which escapes: *A Prosser & Son Ltd v Levy.*[1] This exception is chiefly exemplified in cases concerning water, but there is no reason in principle why it should be confined to such cases. Consent has sometimes been implied where common benefit can be shown.

1   [1955] 3 All ER 57, CA.

2.104 It would be wrong to take the view that a finding of general benefit to the community always excludes the application of the rule. The rule has been applied to gas companies: see *Northwestern Utilities Ltd v London Guarantee and Accident Co Ltd*;[1] water companies: see *Charing Cross Electricity Supply Co v Hydraulic Power Co*;[2] tram companies: see *West v British Tramways Co*;[3] railway companies: see *Jones v Festiniog Rly Co*;[4] and colliery companies: see *Rylands v Fletcher* itself.

1   [1936] AC 108, PC.
2   [1914] 3 KB 772, CA.
3   [1908] 2 KB 14, CA.
4   (1868) LR 3 QB 733.

2.105 When a dangerous thing is used under statutory authority, it is generally necessary to prove negligence in order to establish liability: see *Geddis v Proprietors of Bann Reservoir.*[1] Where a thing is brought onto the land under the authority of a statute which provides that there is no liability for a nuisance caused by the exercise of the statutory power, there is no liability for an escape: see *Marcic v Thames Water Utilities Ltd.*[2] Where the prospective defendant is a statutory undertaker the practitioner must take special precautions to ensure that the claim can be properly founded, because statutory undertakers acting with statutory powers are generally in a special position and their obligations and liabilities can only be understood in the context of the statutory scheme within which they operate.

1   (1878) 3 App Cas 430, HL.
2   [2003] UKHL 66, [2004] 1 All ER 135.

Remedies

2.106   On the footing that *Rylands v Fletcher* is an extension of the law of nuisance, then the 'nuisance' remedies of compensatory damage and/or injunction are available.

Damages for personal injuries

2.107   There are numerous examples of personal injury awards in *Rylands v Fletcher* cases.[1] The House of Lords has now ruled that a claim for damages for death or personal injury cannot be brought under the rule in *Rylands v Fletcher*[2] because such a claim does not relate to any right in or enjoyment of land.

1   *Miles v Forest Rock Granite Co (Leicestershire) Ltd* (1918) 34 TLR 500, CA; *Shiffman v Venerable Order of the Hospital of St John of Jerusalem* [1936] 1 All ER 557; *Hale v Jennings Bros* [1938] 1 All ER 579, CA; *Perry v Kenricks Transport Ltd* [1956] 1 All ER 154, [1956] 1 WLR 85, CA.
2   *Transco plc v Stockport Metropolitan Borough Council* [2003] UKHL 61, [2003] 3 WLR 1467, [2004] 1 All ER 539.

CHAPTER 3

Statutory nuisance

WHAT IS STATUTORY NUISANCE?

Background

3.01 Part III of the Environmental Protection Act 1990 ('EPA 1990') is titled 'Statutory Nuisance and Clean Air' and deals with statutory nuisances, clean air and controls over offensive trades.

3.02 Sections 79–82 of the EPA 1990 replace the previous provisions of the Public Health Act 1936 ('PHA 1936') and the Public Health (Recurring Nuisances) Act 1969 ('PH(RN)A 1969') with a more streamlined system of procedures which are similar to those contained in the Control of Pollution Act 1974 relating to noise. Noise nuisance which was formerly covered by those provisions has now been incorporated into Pt III of the EPA 1990.

3.03 How the new provisions should be interpreted and whether light can be shed on their meaning by reference to previous case law and practice is of importance. The long title of the EPA 1990 describes itself as an Act 'to restate the law defining statutory nuisances and improve the summary procedures for dealing with them'.

3.04 This supports the presumption that for those definitions which remain unchanged from the PHA 1936 the old case law may be followed. Where the definition has changed, then careful consideration should be given to whether application of the case law under the previous Act is appropriate.

Duty to investigate and follow up complaints

3.05 Under the EPA 1990, s 79(1) every local authority is placed under a duty to ensure their area is inspected from time to time to detect any statutory nuisance. They are also required to take such steps that are reasonably practicable to investigate a complaint of statutory nuisance made by a person living in its area. Total inaction would not satisfy the requirement and a once-only inspection is unlikely to either. Where a local authority fails to satisfy the requirements the Secretary of State has power to take action.[1]

1   In *R (on application of Anne) v Test Valley Borough Council* [2001] EWHC Admin 1019, [2002] Env LR 22 the court considered the adequacy of an investigation into an alleged statutory nuisance and found the steps the Council took were those which were reasonably practicable in the circumstances of the case.

How does the common law fit in?

3.06   Because the EPA 1990 does not include a definition of 'nuisance', it is necessary to re-examine the essential common law principles and cases which will help in assessing whether an activity or operation complained of is an actionable nuisance under the EPA 1990. In *R v Carrick District Council, ex p Shelley*[1] Carnwath J (as he then was) said:

'The word "nuisance" has given rise to more controversy, in the context of the Public Health Act 1936 and its predecessor. In principle "nuisance" has its common law meaning, either public or a private nuisance.'[2]

1   [1996] Env LR 273. For a full detailed analysis of the common law see Chapter 2, which must be read together with this chapter.
2   At 278.

PUBLIC NUISANCE

3.07   'Public nuisance' is defined as:

'an act, not warranted by law, materially affecting the reasonable comfort of a class of Her Majesty's subjects who come within the sphere or neighbourhood of its operation'.

The question of whether a local community can amount to a 'class' is a question of fact in every case.

3.08   There is no need to have an interest in land for a claim in public nuisance so that if a whole family including children wants to claim damages, the action must be made in public nuisance. If the only remedy sought is an injunction, then the householder can claim in private nuisance alone.

3.09   The usual examples of public nuisance given relate to such things as carrying on an offensive trade, keeping a brothel and obstructing the highway. Many of the areas that used to be classed as public nuisances are now specifically covered by statute. Examples that are more relevant today might be contaminating water making it unfit to drink, stench from a nearby factory or noise from building works.

How public nuisance relates to statutory nuisance

'Best practicable means'

3.10 Nowadays local authorities are more likely to use the EPA 1990, s 79, but under s 80(7) the use of best practicable means ('BPM') provides a defence to a prosecution in certain circumstances. As a result, an individual citizen's case for public nuisance may stand a better prospect of success because although BPM is a factor that the court will take into account, it will not automatically provide a defence (except in cases where the activity is being conducted under statutory authority or construction works).

Apart from BPM, what other differences are there?

3.11 A local authority cannot get compensation on behalf of its residents, only an injunction to stop the nuisance. Sometimes a nuisance may not be abatable, for example, when the court thinks BPM have been used and the works must continue, in which case compensation will be an important remedy to mitigate the problem. Or, if the nuisance is serious and has gone on for some time, the damages might be substantial. Finally, local authorities have finite resources and may have problems with undertakings as to damages when they get an injunction against the perpetrator of the nuisance.

TYPES OF STATUTORY NUISANCE

3.12 A 'statutory nuisance' is defined by the EPA 1990, s 79(1) as meaning:

'(a)   any premises in such a state as to be prejudicial to health or a nuisance;

(b)   smoke emitted from premises so as to be prejudicial to health or a nuisance;

(c)   fumes or gases emitted from premises so as to be prejudicial to health or a nuisance;

(d)   any dust, steam, smell or other effluvia arising on industrial, trade or business premises and being prejudicial to health or a nuisance;

(e)   any accumulation or deposit which is prejudicial to health or a nuisance;

(f)   any animal kept in such a place or manner as to be prejudicial to health or a nuisance;

(g)   noise emitted from premises so as to be prejudicial to health or a nuisance;

(ga)   noise that is prejudicial to health or a nuisance and is emitted from or caused by a vehicle, machinery or equipment in a street or in Scotland, road;

(h)   any other matter declared by any enactment to be a statutory nuisance'.

New areas of statutory nuisance

3.13 The definition in the EPA 1990, s 79, broadly speaking, is in similar terms to that set out in the PHA 1936, s 92. It should be noted, however, that paras (b), (c), (ga) and (h) are new categories of statutory nuisance.

- para (b) specifically includes smoke;
- para (c) specifically includes fumes or gases;
- para (ga) specifically includes noise emitted from or caused by a vehicle, machinery or equipment in a street;
- para (h) refers to any other matters declared by any enactment to be a statutory nuisance.

See below for examples.

Further information on the categories of statutory nuisance

EPA 1990, s 79(1)(a) re-enacts the PHA 1936, s 91(1)(a): 'any premises in such a state as to be prejudicial to health or a nuisance'

3.14 'Premises' is defined as land, building, vessels and there is no requirement relating to whether the premises are occupied or as to ownership. Such considerations are only relevant when considering on whom to serve proceedings. The only fact to take into account is that the premises exist and their state. It is necessary to look at the premises as a whole and not individual defects and their effects. For example, in the case of water penetration it is the effect of the water coming into the premises that needs to be looked at rather than the source when assessing whether a nuisance exists. In *Haringey London Borough Council v Jowett*,[1] the Divisional Court held that traffic noise from vehicles, machinery or equipment in the street rendering premises to be in such a state as to be prejudicial to health or a nuisance did not constitute a statutory nuisance for the purposes of the EPA 1990, s 79(1)(a) as amended by the Noise and Statutory Nuisance Act 1993, s 2.

1   (1999) 32 HLR 308.

3.15 The leading authority is now *Birmingham City Council v Oakley*[1] where the House of Lords ruled that for the premises to be in 'such a state as to be prejudicial to health' there must be some factor that is so prejudicial. As Lord Hoffmann put it:[2]

> 'The section contemplates a case in which the premises as they stand present a threat to the health of the occupiers or neighbours which requires summary removal.'

1   [2001] Env LR 648.
2   At para 45.

EPA 1990, s 79(1)(b) 'smoke emitted from premises'

3.16 'Smoke' is defined by the EPA 1990, s 79(7) as including soot, ash, grit and gritty particles emitted in smoke. It is likely that the words 'emitted from premises' mean that the smoke must affect other premises and that it is not enough for the smoke to cause a nuisance to occupiers of that same premises. Section 79(2) exempts premises occupied on behalf of the Crown for naval, military, air force or defence purposes and those occupied by a visiting force. Other circumstances are exempted by s 79(3) including smoke emitted from steam railways, industrial or trade premises and chimneys of a private dwelling within a smoke-controlled zone.

EPA 1990, s 79(1)(c) 'fumes or gases emitted from premises'

3.17 This is a new category of statutory nuisance. The EPA 1990, s 79(7) defines fumes and gas as meaning 'any airborne solid matter smaller than dust and vapour and moisture precipitated from vapour'. The words 'emitted from premises' are likely to have the same meaning as above. Section 79(4) restricts this section to private dwelling emissions although commercial or industrial premises might well be caught under s 79(1)(d) below and may be subjected to local authority air pollution control under Pt I of the EPA 1990.

EPA 1990, s 79(1)(d) broadly re-enacts the PHA 1936, s 92(1)(d): 'any dust, steam, smell or other effluvia arising on industrial trade or business premises ...'

3.18 'Dust' does not include chimney smoke which is dealt with under para (b).[1] This is the only category of statutory nuisance specifically confined to 'industrial, trade or business premises', which are defined in the EPA 1990, s 79(7). The definition of 'trade' in past case law is wide enough to include manufacturing and processing and the term 'business' has been construed as being almost anything which is occupational as distinguished from pleasure. It is clear from the case law that most activities other than those that are purely domestic or recreational and one off transactions would be included.

1   See para **3.16** above.

EPA 1990, s 79(1)(e) re-enacts the PHA 1936, s 93(1)(c): 'any accumulation or deposit ...'

3.19 It must be shown that the accumulation is a 'threat to health in the sense of a threat to disease, vermin or the like': see *Coventry City Council v Cartwright*.[1] It was held not to extend to 'an accumulation of inert matter, building materials, scrap iron, broken glass or tin cans merely because that matter may cause physical injury to a person coming on to the land'. It must, however, be arguable that such an accumulation could encourage vermin to collect.

1   [1975] 1 WLR 845, DC.

EPA 1990, s 79(1)(f) re-enacts the PHA 1936, s 92(1)(b) 'animals'

3.20   There is contradictory case law on whether this provision is able to regulate noise as well as smell and other matters prejudicial to health or a nuisance caused by keeping animals. Since the wording of the statute is not restricted, any matter that comes within the definition of a statutory nuisance should be covered by it.

EPA 1990, s 79(1)(g) 'noise emitted from premises …'

3.21   Section 79(7) defines 'noise' as including vibrations. The noise must be emitted from premises as stated above. 'Premises' is now expressly defined as to include land. Previous case law indicates that premises would not cover noise made in streets or public places. Practically speaking this type of action may still be difficult to bring. An exemption to statutory noise nuisance is included in the EPA 1990, s 79(6) which states that the provisions do not apply to noise from aircraft except model aircraft.

EPA 1990, s 79(1)(ga) 'noise that is prejudicial to health or a nuisance and is emitted from or caused by a vehicle, machinery or equipment in a street (or in Scotland, road)'

3.22   This was introduced by the Noise and Statutory Nuisance Act 1993 and covers noise or vibration from equipment, machinery or vehicles in a street. It overcomes some of the difficulties which arose under para (g) ('noise from premises') in cases of street noise. The special procedures introduced in respect of nuisances, contained in the EPA 1990, ss 80A and 81(1A) and (1B) should be noted, and so should the fact that this category of statutory nuisance is disapplied in various circumstances (traffic noise, noise from certain military sources and noise from demonstrations), by s 6A.

EPA 1990, s 79(1)(h) 'any other matter declared by any enactment to be a statutory nuisance'

3.23   Matters now covered include:
- PHA 1936, s 141 relating to unsanitary cisterns, etc;
- PHA 1936, s 259 in connection with watercourses, etc;
- PHA 1936, s 268 relating to tents, vans, etc;
- Mines and Quarries Act 1954, s 151 relating to fencing abandoned and disused mines and quarries.

ANTICIPATED NUISANCES

3.24   The EPA 1990, s 80(1) allows the local authority to take action in anticipation of a statutory nuisance occurring, which should assist an authority when dealing with transient sources/causes of nuisance.

SUPPLEMENTARY PROVISIONS

3.25 The EPA 1990, s 81(1) provides that where more than one person is responsible for a nuisance, s 80 will apply to each of those persons whether or not they would be responsible individually. Section 81(2) allows an authority to take action in respect of a statutory nuisance, totally or partly outside their area but which affects their area. If the recipient of the Notice[1] appeals, then the case must be heard in a court in the area where the alleged nuisance occurred.

1   See paras **3.34–3.36** below.

'PREJUDICIAL TO HEALTH OR A NUISANCE'

3.26 The EPA 1990, s 79(1) states, in respect of each class of statutory nuisance, that it must be 'prejudicial to health or a nuisance'.

Nuisance

3.27 'Nuisance' is a separate test and it is not necessary to show that the activity is prejudicial to health in order for it to be a statutory nuisance. In the case of *Betts v Penge UDC*[1] where the premises were in a state of disrepair, the front door and some of the windows having been removed by the landlord, this was sufficient to constitute a statutory nuisance. It was held that it is sufficient to show the premises or activity in question are such as 'to interfere with personal comfort and thus constitute a nuisance'.

1   [1942] 2 KB 154, DC.

3.28 More recently it has been argued that a nuisance under the Public Health Acts must be qualified by reference to the general spirit and intention of the Acts as dealing with matters relating to health, disease and vermin. This interpretation might limit those cases where the activity complained about relates purely to whether it is a nuisance and where there is no risk to health (see *Salford City Council v McNally*[1]).

1   [1976] AC 379, HL.

3.29 It has also been held that a nuisance in terms of what could be defined as a statutory nuisance has to be given a common law interpretation, ie either private nuisance or a public nuisance (see *National Coal Board v Neath Borough Council*[1]). On that basis, interference with neighbouring property is a prerequisite for private nuisance and something which affects the comfort of the public at large is necessary for public nuisance. In that case the court said:

'a nuisance could not arise if what has taken place affects only the person or persons occupying the premises where the nuisance is said to have taken place'.

1   [1976] 2 All ER 478, DC.

3.30   *Wivenhoe Port Ltd v Colchester Borough Council*[1] was a case in relation to statutory nuisance caused by dust from the handling of soya meal. It was held in the Crown Court that a nuisance within the definition of statutory nuisance must interfere materially with the personal comfort of residents in the sense that it materially affected their well-being although it might not be prejudicial to their health. Dust falling on vehicles might be an inconvenience to their owners and might even diminish the value of the car but this would not be a statutory nuisance. In the same way dust falling on a garden, or inside a shop would not be a statutory nuisance but dust in the eyes or hair even if not shown to be prejudicial to health would be an interference with personal comfort.

1   [1985] JPL 175.

3.31   The above cases were decided before the EPA 1990 came into force. It is arguable that they should not be followed because the spirit and intention of the EPA 1990 is to improve procedures that enable local authorities to exercise control over certain activities that detract from the environment as opposed to being solely concerned with matters that threaten public health. Activities that cause a nuisance only should be actionable and the legislation provides that this is the case. Any interpretation that restricts a claim of statutory nuisance to a situation where there is a risk to health or interference with personal comfort incorrectly interprets the spirit and express purposes of the EPA 1990. If the *Wivenhoe* case is followed it will severely limit the application of the EPA 1990 to improve environmental quality where there is an absence of interference with human comfort.

Prejudicial to health

3.32   The EPA 1990, s 79(7) defines 'prejudicial to health' as meaning 'injurious or likely to cause injury to health'. This is the same definition as used by the PHA 1936, and it makes it clear that likelihood of injury to health is included as well as actual injury. The definition of 'prejudicial to health' could also be widely interpreted by the courts, particularly if it is seen in the light of the World Health Organization's definition of health. This states that health is 'a state of complete physical, mental and social well-being and not merely the absence of disease or infirmity'. So far the English courts' interpretation of 'health' has been narrow, although with increased health and environmental awareness there is scope for broadening this.

3.33   Examples of cases where the issue of health has been addressed are:
* *Coventry City Council v Cartwright*[1] which dealt with whether an accumulation of inert matter was prejudicial to health. The court stated the underlying concept which it struck at is an accumulation of something which produces a threat to health in the sense of a threat of disease, vermin or the like.

- *Greater London Council v Tower Hamlets London Borough Council*[2] where the court held that condensation and its associated mould growth could make premises prejudicial to health.
- *Southwark London Borough Council v Ince*[3] where premises were regarded as prejudicial to health by reason of noise from road and rail traffic penetrating the dwelling because of inadequate sound insulation.
- In *Cunningham v Birmingham City Council*[4] a two-judge Divisional Court held that the test of 'prejudicial to nuisance' was an objective one and held that a Stipendiary Magistrate was wrong in determining the case by relating the Respondent's duties to the particular health requirements of the Appellant's son who suffered from autistic-spectrum syndrome, which caused behavioural problems and made him a hazard in limited space. The kitchen to the property was very small and argued to be dangerous, having regard to the son's condition.
- In *R v Bristol City Council, ex p Everett*[5] the Court of Appeal upheld Richards J who held that the statutory nuisance regime was not intended to apply in cases where the sole concern was that, by reason of the state of the premises, there was a likelihood of an accident causing personal injury. Although the language in the statutory provisions were capable of embracing accidental physical injury, it was reasonably clear from the legislative history that the expressions were not intended to be so wide in their scope: that kind of problem fell outside the legislative purpose. Thus if premises could not amount to a statutory nuisance by reason of the fact that they were in such a state as to create a likelihood of accident causing personal injury, it followed that a steep staircase could not give rise even if it created such a likelihood. The Court of Appeal went on to hold that there was an implied power on the part of a local authority to withdraw an Abatement Notice which it had served. The exercise of such a discretion could only be challenged on Wednesbury grounds.

1   [1975] 1 WLR 845.
2   (1983) 15 HLR 54.
3   (1989) 21 HLR 504.
4   [1998] Env LR 1.
5   [1999] Env LR 587.

THE ABATEMENT NOTICE

3.34   The EPA 1990, s 80 provides that where a local authority is satisfied a statutory nuisance exists or is likely to occur or recur, it must serve an Abatement Notice which will require abatement or prohibit or restrict its occurrence or recurrence and may require the execution of work or taking of steps for such purposes, specifying the time within which compliance is required. In the *Carrick* case,[1] Carnwath J held that 'must' means *must*.

1   See para **3.06** above.

3.35   The Abatement Notice may be dismissed or varied on appeal, but if the Abatement Notice stands, or stands in a modified form, there is a discretion to prosecute for breach, with stiff financial sanctions in the event of conviction. Recent case law has focused on the form of Abatement Notices since defendants to criminal proceedings have sought, sometimes successfully, to have the proceedings struck down as a nullity by reason of defective Abatement Notices. There is now a significant body of case law to give guidance both to those drafting an Abatement Notice, and to those seeking to challenge the Notice.

3.36 So far as material EPA 1990, s 80 provides as follows:

'80(1) Where a local authority is satisfied that a statutory nuisance exists, or is likely to occur or recur, in the area of the authority, the local authority shall serve a notice ("an Abatement Notice") imposing all or any of the following requirements—

(a) requiring the abatement of the nuisance or prohibiting or restricting its occurrence or recurrence;

(b) requiring the execution of such works, and the taking of such other steps, as may be necessary for any of those purposes,

and the notice shall specify the time or times within which the requirements of the notice are to be complied with'.

So far as the term 'statutory nuisance' is concerned, this term is defined in the EPA 1990, s 79 and its eight subparagraphs (each dealing with a separate head eg smoke, fumes, dust, animals etc) and each subparagraph ending with the words: 'so as to be prejudicial to health or a nuisance'.

Challenging an Abatement Notice

3.37 Challenges to Abatement Notices in the reported cases range from the hopeless to the hopeful, as follows.

3.38 Examples of *hopeless* challenges are the following:
- A failure to specify whether the nuisance alleged comes under the limb of prejudicial to health on the one hand or nuisance on the other. What was important was that the acts constituting the nuisance were sufficiently alleged so that the person served with the Notice knew what was required to abate it: see *Lowe and Watson v South Somerset District Council.*[1]
- A failure to insert the time for compliance: see *R v Tunbridge Wells Justices, ex p Tunbridge Wells Borough Council.*[2]

1   [1998] Env LR 143.
2   [1996] Env LR 88.

3.39 An example of a *fairly hopeless* challenge is a failure within the Notice to specify the nature of the nuisance (see the EPA 1990, s 80 (1)(a)). The nature of the nuisance will generally be treated as *obvious* to the recipient of the Notice. This was so even in respect of a Notice so sloppily drafted as to make no reference whatsoever to noise, barking or dogs, in a dog barking case: *Myatt v Teignbridge District Council.*[1] Accordingly, whilst the nature of the nuisance ought always to be specified, we are not aware of any decided case in which a Notice has been struck down for a failure so to do. The same approach applies to a complaint by an individual: *East Staffordshire Borough Council v Fairless.*[2]

1   [1994] Env LR 78.
2   [1999] Env LR 525.

3.40   An example of a *hopeful* challenge is a failure to specify works required under the EPA 1990, s 80(1)(b). This has proved to be very fertile terrain for challenges and it is only very recently that a settled approach to this difficult problem is emerging.

3.41   In summary form, the challenges to Notices on grounds of failure to specify work required to be carried out to abate the nuisance *have failed*, and *will fail*, in noise nuisance cases involving:
● crowing cockerels;
● barking dogs (*Budd v Colchester Borough Council*[1]);
● raves and discos (*East Northamptonshire District Council v Fossett*[2]);
● live entertainment at a jazz bar (*Surrey Free Inns plc v Gosport District Council*[3]);

Challenges to Notices for failure to specify works required to be carried out to abate the nuisance have *succeeded* in respect of:
● structural insulation work to be carried out in a residential building to prevent noise/vibration from an adjacent stamping press (*Sterling Homes (Midlands) Ltd v Birmingham City Council*[4]);
● soundproofing of a void between two residential flats (*Network Housing Association v Westminster City Council*[5]);
● ensuring the safety of a rock face in danger of collapsing onto houses (*Kirklees Metropolitan Borough Council v Field*[6]).

1   [1997] Env LR 128.
2   [1994] Env LR 388.
3   [1999] Env LR 750, CA.
4   [1996] Env LR 121.
5   [1995] Env LR 176.
6   [1998] Env LR 337.

3.42   Although it is easy to recite a list of successes and failures it has proved more difficult to elicit the statement of principle.

3.43   In particular, following *Sterling Homes*, it appeared that the draftsman had a *choice* as to whether to specify works required to be carried out to abate the nuisance. If he chose to do so, however, then the words used had to be sufficiently clear and specific to tell the recipient exactly he would have to do to avoid criminal prosecution. Needless to say, given a free choice, draftsmen avoided making any such requirement since it would readily be challenged for failure to be sufficiently specific, and merely relied upon a straightforward 'abate the nuisance'.

3.44   However, the Divisional Court in *Kirklees*, whilst approving the judgment in *Sterling Homes*, refined it by holding that where it is implicit that works of some kind must be carried out in order to abate the nuisance, those works must be specified. Accordingly, in those circumstances, it was not a matter of choice on the part of the draftsman.

3.45   *Surrey Free Inns* has further refined the principle. The issue arose as to whether the draftsman of the Notice must specify works in a case where the nuisance could be abated by carrying out works (eg sound insulation works), or could alternatively be carried out by other means (eg turning the music off; selling one's dogs or cockerels). In this situation, it was held by the Court of Appeal, the draftsman had a choice as to whether to specify works. Accordingly a failure to specify works in this situation did not give rise to a nullity.

3.46   The Divisional Court in *Kirklees* remarked that it regarded the position as now fully clear and did not expect to see any further cases on the point. However, as a result of this decision more Abatement Notices will be required to specify works, and this is a minefield. So, for example, in *Network Housing Association* case the relevant part of the Notice required the recipient to:

> 'Provide suitable and effective sound insulation in the void between flats D and C so as to provide a level of airborne sound insulation (measured as Dn Tw in accordance with BS 2750 part 4 1980 and BS 5821 part 1 1984) of not less than 42dB or carry out such other works as will achieve the above required degree of airborne sound insulation between flats D and C. In improving the airborne sound insulation take all reasonable steps to ensure that no degradation occurs in the existing level of structure borne sound insulation'.

3.47   This was struck down by the Divisional Court for want of particularity. Whilst it was adequate to inform the recipient of the *result required*, it was held defective because it *left the way in which that result was to be achieved to the recipient of the Notice*.

3.48   In *R v Falmouth and Truro Port Health Authority, ex p South West Water Ltd*[1] the Court of Appeal analysed the cases and concluded that McCullough J's reasoning in *Sterling* was correct and that an authority does not have to specify works.

> 'In *all* cases the local authority can if it wishes leave the choice of means of abatement to the perpetrator of the nuisance. If, however, the means of abatement *are* required by the local authority, then they must be specified.'

Kirklees overruled.

1   [2001] QB 445, [2000] Env LR 658.

3.49   The principle is now reasonably clear:

(i)   the Notice need not specify any works, and will normally not do so;

(ii)   where a Notice does do more than merely say 'abate the nuisance and do works or take steps to that end' – in that it specifies a means to abate the nuisance – those means must be fully particularised.

Withdrawal of Notices

3.50   There is an implied power for an authority to withdraw a Notice that it has served: *R v Bristol City Council, ex p Everett.*[1]

1   [1998] 3 All ER 603, [1999] Env LR 256.

Appeals against Abatement Notices

3.51   A person who is served with an Abatement Notice may appeal against it to a magistrates' court within a period of 21 days beginning with the date on which he or she was served with the Notice.[1]

1   EPA 1990, s 80(3).

Making the appeal

3.52   An appeal is made by way of complaint to the magistrates' court and the Magistrates' Courts Act 1980 ('MCA1980') applies to the proceedings.[1]

1   EPA 1990, Sch 3, para 1(2).

3.53   The main provisions of the MCA 1980 concerned are ss 51 to 64, which set out a rudimentary procedure. They are more designed to deal with complaints in relation to non-payment of maintenance etc than with civil trials. It is fair to say that there is very little substantive law on the way in which this type of appeal should be dealt with.

3.54   One useful provision may be the MCA 1980, s 123, which provides that no objection shall be allowed to any complaint in respect of a defect in its substance or form or in any variance between it and the evidence adduced by the complainant. If the defendant considers himself or herself misled, then the defendant should ask the court for an adjournment.

Grounds of appeal

3.55   The permissible grounds of appeal are set out in reg 2(2) of the Statutory Nuisance (Appeals) Regulations 1995.[1]

1   SI 1995/2644.

3.56   *Ground (a)* is that the Abatement Notice is not justified by the EPA 1990, s 80. This in effect means that there is no nuisance or prejudice to health from the complainant's premises.

3.57   The use of the present tense in the regulation has led the courts to say that one looks to see if there is a nuisance at the date of the magistrate's hearing: see *Johnsons News of London v Ealing London Borough Council*.[1] However, in *Surrey Free Inns plc v Gosport Borough Council*[2] the Court of Appeal held that *Johnsons News* was wrongly decided and the correct date for determining whether or not there was a nuisance was at the time of the service of the Abatement Notice. That decision has been applied by the Divisional Court in *R v Crown Court at Knightsbridge, ex p Cataldi*.[3] The Divisional Court held that at the date of the service of the Abatement Notice the local authority was entitled to have regard to three possible situations: (i) if there was an existing statutory nuisance; (ii) that a statutory nuisance was likely to occur; or (iii) that there was no statutory nuisance on that date but there had been such a nuisance in the past and it was likely to recur. Any of these situations entitled the local authority to serve an Abatement Notice.

1   (1989) 154 JP 33.
2   [1999] Env LR 750.
3   [1999] Env LR 1, 62, CA.

3.58   The onus in this situation is on the local authority to justify its Notice: see *Budd v Colchester Borough Council*.[1] It must therefore show, on the balance of probabilities, that there is a nuisance from the complainant's premises or operations or that they are prejudicial to health. A nuisance here is one that would constitute a public or private nuisance in common law: *National Coal Board v Thorne*.[2] However, the nuisance may have to be one that affects health as opposed to comfort and enjoyment of property: see *National Coal Board* (above) and *Wivenhoe Port Ltd v Colchester Borough Council*.[3]

1   [1997] Env LR 128.
2   [1976] 1 WLR 543, DC.
3   [1985] JPL 175.

3.59   One aspect of any nuisance case is whether the defence of reasonable user applies. The question here is whether the activity concerned is one that is necessary for the ordinary use and occupation of land or houses and so comes within the principle of give and take as between neighbouring occupiers of land: see, eg, *Graham and Graham v Rechem International*.[1] Thus if the nuisance is caused by bonfires it may be considered that having occasional bonfires is part of the ordinary use and occupation of land with which neighbours must put up.

1   [1996] Env LR 158.

3.60   *Ground (b)* is that there has been some informality, error or defect in the Notice. If, on hearing the appeal, the court is satisfied that the defect etc was not material it must dismiss the appeal.[1] 'No informality, defect or error is a material one unless it is such as to produce injustice': per Lord Denning in *Miller-Mead v Minister of Housing and Local Government.*[2]

1   SI 1995/2644, reg 2(3).
2   [1963] 1 All ER 459 at 467G, CA.

3.61   *Ground (c)* is concerned with the reasonableness of the local authority's requirements. If it is for the local authority to justify its Notice then logically the local authority must also justify any requirements it makes. However, given the trend of authorities not to specify detailed requirements, the onus may be on the complainant to show that his or her scheme of works is the best solution to the problem.

3.62   *Ground (d)* is that more time is needed in order to be able to comply with the Notice. Given the time between the service of the Notice and the appeal hearing a court might expect the complainant to have complied with the Notice by the time the appeal is heard. In such a case, if this is the only ground of appeal, the sensible approach would be to withdraw the appeal on suitable terms as to costs.

3.63   *Ground (e)* concerns the use of best practicable means. This is dealt with later in this chapter.[1]

1   See paras **3.95–3.99** below.

3.64   *Grounds (f) and (g)* deal with noise cases where other legislation or Notices cover the noise in question.

3.65   *Grounds (h), (i) and (j)* are concerned with service on some other person than the complainant. If the appeal is brought under either of grounds (i) or (j) then the Notice of appeal must also be served on any other such person referred to.[1]

1   SI 1995/2644, reg 2(4).

Suspension of Notice

3.66   A Notice may be suspended pending the outcome of an appeal in accordance with reg 3 of the Statutory Nuisance (Appeals) Regulations 1995.[1] For a suspension to be permissible, compliance with the Notice must involve expenditure on works before the hearing of the appeal or, in relation to noise, that the noise is necessarily caused in the course of the Appellant carrying out a duty imposed on the Appellant by law.

1   SI 1995/2644.

3.67   The local authority can prevent this suspension if the nuisance to which the Notice relates is prejudicial to health or is likely to be of such limited duration that to suspend the Notice would make it useless. In addition they can state that they consider that any expenditure on works before the hearing would not be out of proportion to the public benefit to be gained from compliance with the Notice. If they set out any of these reasons in the Notice then that Notice will not be suspended pending the appeal.

3.68   Where such objections are stated in the Notice the only way to get over them will be to apply for a judicial review of the authority's decision and for a stay of that decision – not to suspend the Notice – pending the hearing of the judicial review application.

Evidence

3.69   The hearing of an appeal against an Abatement Notice is a hearing *de novo* into the matter. The court is entitled to hear any evidence about the case, even if this involves hearsay: *Kavanagh v Chief Constable of Devon and Cornwall.*[1] The magistrates' court acts under the MCA 1980, s 53(2), providing that 'the court, after hearing the evidence and the parties, shall make the order for which the complaint is made or dismiss the complaint'. This does not mean that hearsay must be excluded but if it is to be adduced the court must carefully consider the weight to be given to it: *Westminster City Council v Zestfair Ltd.*[2]

1   [1974] 2 All ER 697, CA.
2   (1989) 153 JP 613.

3.70   It is advisable to ask for a pre-trial review hearing at which the court can be asked to issue directions as to the exchange of witness statements, expert evidence, meetings of experts etc. The degree of detail involved will depend on the complexity of the case and whether the parties are co-operating or at loggerheads.

3.71   Where experts are to be called they should be carefully briefed as to the nature of the court (particularly if there is to be a bench of lay justices) and the hearing. Their evidence should be easy to follow and a glossary of terms should always be included. In *Southwark London Borough Council v Simpson*[1] the tenant alleged that her house was damp and in such a state that it was prejudicial to health and thereby constituted a statutory nuisance. The magistrates heard evidence from a chartered surveyor who said he had no medical knowledge of whether the damp problems were prejudicial to health but he had read articles in which similar damp problems had been considered prejudicial. He did not produce any of those articles nor was he able to give any details of them. The magistrates concluded that the property was suffering from severe damp problems and therefore a statutory nuisance. The Divisional Court allowed the council's appeal and held that although an expert witness did not have to be medically qualified in order to provide evidence about whether a nuisance was prejudicial to health, that expert was required to have some experience in the relevant field. In this case the expert witness had said that he had no relevant experience and accordingly he was in no better position than a layperson. Magistrates were not entitled to consider the evidence provided by him.

1   [1999] Env LR 553, DC.

Withdrawal of appeal

3.72 Often, either before the case or during it, the parties will reach an agreement. They may then wish to withdraw the appeal on agreed terms. There are no rules as to this. Some courts will allow a withdrawal on undertakings, others hold that the court has no power to determine an appeal without hearing the evidence.[1]

1   See MCA 1980, s 53.

3.73 One solution, if the court agrees, is for one party simply to give evidence of the proposed agreement and then the advocates should both ask the court if it is willing to make an order in the terms sought. If it does not agree then full evidence will have to be called. If it agrees then it has heard evidence and can make the proposed order.

Procedure

3.74 There are five stages:
(1) complainant opens his or her case and calls evidence;
(2) defendant opens his or her case and calls evidence;
(3) complainant can call rebutting evidence;
(4) defendant can address court if he or she has not already done so;
(5) either party may ask for leave to address the court a second time; if one party is allowed to do this the other side must also have a second turn. The defendant goes first and the complainant has the last word.

The decision of the court

3.75 After hearing the evidence the court may:
(a)   quash the Abatement Notice to which the appeal relates;
(b)   vary the Abatement Notice in favour of the Appellant in such manner as it thinks fit; or
(c)   dismiss the appeal.

A Notice that is varied will be final and have effect as if it had been made by the local authority.[1]

1   SI 1995/2644, reg 2(5).

3.76   Where there is a dispute as to who should do the works and the people who should pay for them, the court may say who is to execute the work and make contribution orders.[1] It may also make orders for the payment of the authority's expenses in carrying out any necessary works.[2]

1   SI 1995/2644, reg 2(6)(a) and (7).
2   SI 1995/2644, reg 2(6)(b) and (7).

Costs

3.77   Provision for costs is made by the MCA 1980, s 64. This gives the court a wide discretion to make an order for costs that it considers 'just and reasonable'. The amount must be specified and that amount must also be 'just and reasonable'.

3.78   Ideally where there is a large amount to be sought each side should give the other a breakdown of their costs before the end of the hearing. If necessary there may need to be an adjournment to enable a more detailed examination of the amount claimed. However the High Court will rarely interfere with a costs order and then only because the order was 'perverse': *R v Southend Stipendiary Magistrate, ex p Rochford District Council*.[1]

1   [1994] Env LR D15.

Appeals

3.79   An appeal on the facts can be made to the Crown Court.[1] Either party may institute such an appeal. The appeal must be made within 21 days of the magistrates' decision.[2] The Statutory Nuisance (Appeals) Regulations 1995[3] do not apply to such an appeal so that any application for suspension of the Notice pending the Crown Court's decision must be made to that Court: *Surrey Free Inns plc v Gosport Borough Council*.[4]

1   EPA 1990, Sch 3, para 1(3).
2   Crown Court Rules 1982, r 7.
3   SI 1995/2644.
4   [1999] Env LR 750, CA.

3.80   Alternatively the court can be asked to state a case for the opinion of the High Court. If such an application is made the Appellant's right of appeal to the Crown Court ceases. The magistrates' court should be asked to state a case within 21 days of the decision concerned.[1] The application should set out the questions on which the High Court's opinion is sought.[2]

1   MCA 1980, s 111.
2   Magistrates' Courts Rules 1981, r 76.

PROSECUTION FOR FAILURE TO COMPLY

3.81   A prosecution is brought under the EPA 1990, s 80(3):

'If a person on whom an abatement notice is served, without reasonable excuse, contravenes or fails to comply with any requirement or prohibition imposed by the notice, he shall be guilty of an offence.'

3.82 An offence is punishable on summary conviction by a fine not exceeding level 4 on the standard scale.[1] An offence on industrial, business or trade premises attracts a fine of up to £20,000.[2]

1   EPA 1990, s 80(5).
2   EPA 1990, s 80(6).

3.83 A court can also impose a further fine of an amount equal to one-tenth of that level for each day on which the offence continues after conviction.[1]

1   EPA 1990, s 80(6).

The nature and standard of proof

3.84 *Cunningham v Birmingham City Council*[1] deals with the test by which one measures what is 'prejudicial to human health'. The case concerned the special needs requirements of a child suffering from autistic-spectrum syndrome, living in (restricted) local authority property. The court held that the test was objective.

1   [1998] Env LR 1.

3.85 It follows that looking at what is prejudicial to health in some cases may not require evidence of actual damage/injury/prejudice but expert evidence as to whether something would be prejudicial to average people. That expert evidence may be necessary for many cases which are not 'obvious' was indicated in *R v Carrick District Council, ex p Shelley*.[1]

1   [1996] Env LR 273 at 278.

3.86 Where a defendant who has been prosecuted for failing to comply with an Abatement Notice pleads by way of defence that he or she had a reasonable excuse for not complying with the Notice, it is for the prosecution to demonstrate, to the criminal standard of proof, that the excuse was not reasonable: *Polychronakis v Richards & Jerrom Ltd*.[1]

1   [1998] Env LR 346.

Who or what is responsible for the nuisance?

3.87 The following cases assist in identifying what is the nuisance complained of and equally important who is responsible. The wording in the EPA 1990, s 79(7)(a) refers to the person to whose act, default or sufferance the nuisance is attributable. In *Network Housing Association v Westminster City Council*,[1] the court held that where there was no noise insulation between adjoining flats, the nuisance was attributable to the local authority, and not to the person occupying an adjacent flat who was the original author of the noise.

1   [1995] Env LR 176.

3.88   In *Carr v Hackney London Borough Council*[1] the magistrate, applying *Coventry City Council v Doyle*,[2] concluded that at the time of the hearing, although there had been a nuisance, there was not likely to be a reoccurrence because of efforts on the part of the Respondent. The local authority had attempted to fit convector heaters which the complainant refused. Held that the likelihood of reoccurrence of a nuisance, for lack of heating, was due to the complainant's refusal and not the fault of the local authority.

1   [1995] Env LR 372.
2   [1981] 2 All ER 184.

3.89   The question of who is responsible for a nuisance was discussed in the *Carrick* case[1] where, in relation to sewage discharged into the sea, Carnwath J held that the proper test was whether on the balance of probabilities the material came from the water authority's outfalls; the fact that any nuisance might depend on the vagaries of the tide did not preclude the authority's responsibility.

1   [1996] Env LR 273.

3.90   It is necessary for any Abatement Notice to name and be served on the person responsible to fulfil the requirements of the EPA 1990, s 160 and the Local Government Act 1972, s 233. Therefore, a wrongly addressed Notice indicating an associated company, although received by the offending company at the same address, was not properly served: *AMEC Building Ltd v Camden London Borough Council*.[1]

1   [1997] Env LR 330.

3.91   *AMEC* may be contrasted with *Wiltshier Construction (London) Ltd v Westminster City Council*.[1] In this case the Notice incorrectly identified the relevant premises as 21–23 Victoria Street rather than 21–29 Victoria Street. The Divisional Court upheld the finding of the magistrate that the Appellant had been undertaking works to which the Notice related and that although there might have been a serious disadvantage to the Appellant, in this case on the evidence there had been no misunderstanding.

1   [1997] Env LR 321.

DUTY OF THE LOCAL AUTHORITY

3.92   The *Carrick* case[1] is also helpful in indicating that whether there is or is not a nuisance under the EPA 1990, s 80 is a question of fact, not discretion.

Once the authority is satisfied that there is, on the balance of probabilities, a statutory nuisance, then the authority has a duty to serve an Abatement Notice, and – possibly – to prosecute for failure to comply.

1   [1996] Env LR 273.

THE NEED TO CHALLENGE ABATEMENT NOTICES

3.93   In *AMEC* it was argued that it was necessary for the prosecution to establish that there had been a pre-existing nuisance prior to the issue of the Notice. This argument was rejected, applying *A Lambert Flat Management Ltd v Lomas*,[1] an authority under the Control of Pollution Act 1974 ('CPA 1974'), s 58. Any question of the validity of the Notice could be challenged by appeal. The offence concerned breach of the Notice, and not whether there was originally a nuisance.

1   [1981] 1 WLR 898.

3.94   *Butuyuyu v Hammersmith and Fulham London Borough Council*[1] concerned failure to appeal a Notice due to illness. It was held that it was not possible to define what was a reasonable excuse under the EPA 1990, s 80(4), which could vary from case to case. It should not be construed narrowly so as to exclude the personal circumstances of the Appellant.

1   (1996) 29 HLR 584, [1997] Env LR D13.

DEFENCE OF 'BEST PRACTICABLE MEANS'

3.95   The defence of 'best practical means' ('BPM') is set out in the EPA 1990, s 80(7) and (8). Section 80(7) provides that it is a defence to a charge under s 80(4) to prove that the BPM were used to prevent, control or counteract the effects of the nuisance.

3.96   The EPA 1990, s 79(9) provides that 'best practicable means' is to be interpreted by reference to the following provisions:
(a)   'practicable' means reasonably practicable having regard among other things to local conditions and circumstances, to the current state of technical knowledge and to the financial implications;
(b)   the means to be employed include the design, installation, maintenance and manner and periods of operation of plant and machinery, and the design, construction and maintenance of buildings and structures;
(c)   the test is to apply only so far as compatible with any duty imposed by law;
(d)   the test is to apply only so far as compatible with safety and safe working conditions, and with the exigencies of any emergency or unforeseeable circumstances;

and, in circumstances where a code of practice under the Control of Pollution Act 1974, s 71 (noise minimisation) is applicable, regard shall also be had to guidance given in it.

3.97   The EPA 1990, s 80(8) limits this defence mainly to offences arising on industrial, trade or business premises, for smoke[1] only if emitted from a chimney and disapplies it totally in cases of fumes and gases[2] and in the miscellaneous provisions.[3]

1   EPA 1990, s 79(1)(b).
2   EPA 1990, s 79(1)(c).
3   EPA 1990, s 79(1)(h).

3.98   In *Manley v New Forest District Council*[1] Newman J set out the general concept of the defence:

> '... it may assist if I say a little more about the concept of "best practicable means". Prior to it being defined in statute, but which is now exemplified in section 79(9) of the 1990 Act, the phrase had not been statutorily defined. It was regularly used in relation to different processes and its meaning was exemplified in the past by notes published by Her Majesty's Inspectorate of Pollution and the predecessors. An important feature of the doctrine or concept has always been that it allowed for flexibility to cater for local and individual circumstances. The concept itself was developed as a basis for environmental pollution control. Traditionally such control has been discretionary and technical in a scientific sense. "Best practicable means", so far as my research goes, first applied in 1842 in an attempt to control smoke emissions in Leeds. It then subsequently played a large part in control enacted in the Alkali Act 1874. Its introduction reflected a conciliatory and co-operational approach, so that the method of enforcement would not place an undue burden on manufacturing industry and on businesses.'

In that case the judge held that the concept cannot include the carrying on of the business from other premises nor can the statutory duty on an authority to serve an Abatement Notice overrule the defence by way of the EPA 1990, s 79(9)(c) – the defence is only to apply so far as is compatible with any duty imposed by law.

1   [1999] PLR 36.

3.99   In *East Devon District Council v Farr*[1] the court held that magistrates have an obligation to conclude that the defendant has explored all possible options. However, the court upheld, in that case, a determination that the defendant had used BPM on the basis that he had explored various options such as extraction and air-conditioning, but the noise level of air-conditioning could be greater. The efficiency of the air-conditioning was said to be question-able and the cost of either equipment could be prohibitive.

1   [2002] EWHC 115, [2002] Env LR 735.

COMPENSATION

3.100   A court can order a person convicted of an offence to pay compensation for any personal injury, loss or damage resulting from that offence 'on application or otherwise'.[1] Magistrates may only award a maximum of £5,000 in respect of any offence.[2]

1   Powers of Criminal Courts (Sentencing) Act 2000, s 130.
2   Powers of Criminal Courts (Sentencing) Act 2000, s 131(1).

3.101   The limitations on claiming compensation in cases in the magistrates' court are clear from the following cases. In *R v Horseferry Road Magistrates, ex p Prophet*,[1] the Divisional Court cited earlier obiter dicta of Woolf LJ in *Herbert v Lambeth London Borough Council*[2] that compensation should only be awarded in cases which are simple and straightforward, and where no great amount is at stake. It was unsuitable for personal injury.

1   [1995] Env LR 104.
2   (1991) 24 HLR 299.

3.102   *Davenport v Walsall Metropolitan Borough Council*[1] indicates that as long as the court has some information put before it, it may be sufficient for information to be given by advocates in order to determine a compensation order. The fact that there is no civil remedy is one matter to be considered in exercising a discretion whether to award compensation, but not determinative. The dicta of Woolf LJ were also approved.

1   [1997] Env LR 24.

3.103   In *R v Crown Court at Liverpool, ex p Cooke*,[1] the Divisional Court held that compensation in relation to statutory nuisance should only be awarded for injury, loss or damage caused by the continuation of the nuisance from the date when the period stated in the Notice expired to the date of hearing. If the complainant delayed in bringing proceedings for over six months after the expiry of the Notice, then compensation would be limited to the six-month period prior to the making of the complaint.

1   [1996] 4 All ER 589.

Fines

3.104   There is a detailed discussion about fines for environmental offences in Chapter 7 at paras **7.49–7.63**.

3.105   Whilst the EPA 1990, s 80(5) provides for fines at one-tenth of level 5 for a continuing failure to comply, there is a discretion to impose a lesser penalty: see *Canterbury City Council v Ferris*.[1]

1   [1997] Env LR 14.

Costs[1]

3.106   There is clear authority that in cases like these a court can award the prosecuting authority a reasonable sum for the time and trouble it has expended in connection with the offence: *R v Tottenham Justices, ex p Joshi*.[2] This was confirmed by the Court of Appeal in *R v Associated Octel Co Ltd*[3] as being part of the court's jurisdiction under the Prosecution of Offences Act 1985, s 18 to award the prosecution such costs 'as it considered just and reasonable'. In the circumstances it may be just and reasonable for the sentencer to order the defendant to pay all the costs of the investigation.

1   See also Chapter 7 at para **7.64**.
2   [1982] 2 All ER 507.
3   [1997] 1 Cr App Rep (S) 435, CA.

3.107   However, this has to be balanced with the proposition that a costs order should not be disproportionate to the fine. In *R v Northallerton Magistrates' Court, ex p Dove*,[1] the court held that:

> 'While there was no requirement that any sum so ordered should stand in any arithmetical relationship to any fine imposed, the costs ordered to be paid should not in the ordinary way be grossly disproportionate to the fine.'

1   (1999) 163 JP 657, DC.

3.108   Justices should ordinarily begin by deciding on the appropriate fine to reflect the criminality of the defendant's offence, always bearing in mind the defendant's means and ability to pay; and then consider what, if any, costs the defendant should be ordered to pay to the prosecutor.

3.109   If, when the costs sought by the prosecutor were added to the proposed fine, the total exceeded the sum which the defendant could be reasonably ordered to pay, it was preferable to achieve an acceptable total by reducing the sum of costs ordered rather than by reducing the fine.

3.110   If the court had it in mind to make any unusual or unconventional order potentially adverse to a defendant, it should alert the defendant and his or her advisers to that possibility.

3.111   As far as the making of the costs order is concerned the Court in *R v Associated Octel Co Ltd*[1] considered that:

> 'the prosecution should serve on the defence, at the earliest time, full details of its costs, so as to give the defendant a proper opportunity to consider them and make representations on them, if appropriate.
>
> If the defendant, once served with the prosecution's costs, wished to dispute the whole or any part of the schedule, he should give proper notice to the prosecution of the objections which it was proposed to

make; at least it should be clear to the court what the objections were. It might be that in some exceptional cases that a full hearing would need to be held for the objections to be resolved, as there was no provision for the taxation of the prosecution's costs in a criminal case.'

1   [1997] 1 Cr App Rep (S) 435, CA.

POWERS AND RESPONSIBILITIES OF LOCAL AUTHORITIES

3.112   The *Vale of White Horse District Council v Allen & Partners*[1] case is authority for the proposition that s 222(1) of the Local Government Act 1972 is not a free-standing right. A local authority, if it wishes to bring proceedings, must do so in accordance with the EPA 1990, s 80.

1   [1997] Env LR 212.

3.113   There is no private cause of action for breach of statutory duty for failure by a local authority to enforce preventative or remedial action resulting from a nuisance by a neighbouring landowner: *R v Lam and Brennan (t/a Namesakes of Torbay)*.[1]

1   [1997] 3 PLR 22, CA.

CIVIL PROCEEDINGS

3.114   An individual adversely affected by a statutory nuisance cannot bring civil proceedings against the person responsible for damages for breach of statutory duty. It cannot be implied into the Act that Parliament intended to create a civil remedy at the time of the enactment: *Issa v Hackney London Borough Council*.[1]

1   [1997] 1 All ER 999, [1997] Env LR 157, CA.

NOISE ACT 1996

3.115   The Noise Act 1996 is discussed in Chapter 13 at paras **13.49–13.51**.

INDIVIDUAL ACTION UNDER THE EPA 1990, S 82

3.116   The EPA 1990, s 82 enables an individual to bring proceedings in a magistrates' court for the abatement of a nuisance. To limit frivolous complaints, certain safeguards are built in.

The nature of the proceedings

3.117   The EPA 1990, s 82(1) provides that: 'A magistrates' court may act under this section on a complaint ...'. A complaint is the usual way of starting civil proceedings.

3.118   The question whether proceedings under the EPA 1990, s 82(1) are civil or criminal arose in *Botross v London Borough of Hammersmith and Fulham*,[1] when a magistrates' court in a case stated asked whether s 35(1) of the Power of Criminal Courts Act 1973 had any application. The Divisional Court held that reference to a fine not exceeding level 5 in the EPA 1990, s 82(2) meant that the proceedings were criminal in nature. Further following *Pepper v Hart*[2] the intention of Parliament had been to follow the status quo of previous Acts.

1   [1995] Env LR 217.
2   [1993] AC 593, HL.

3.119   Thus earlier cases such as *Northern Ireland Trailers Ltd v Preston Corpn*[1] are still relevant here.

1   [1972] 1 WLR 203.

3.120   Proceedings under the EPA 1990, s 82 should therefore be commenced by the laying of an information and the issuing of a summons under the criminal jurisdiction of the magistrates' court.

Person aggrieved

3.121   Under the EPA 1990, s 82(1) a complaint can only be made 'by any person on the grounds that he is aggrieved by the existence of a statutory nuisance'.

3.122   In *A-G of the Gambia v N'Jie*[1] Lord Denning said:

'The words "person aggrieved" are of wide import and should not be subjected to a restricted interpretation. They do not include, of course, a mere busybody who is interfering in things that do not concern him; but they do include a person who has a genuine grievance because an order has been made which prejudicially affects his interests.'

1   [1961] 2 All ER 504 at 511, PC.

3.123   In *Birmingham District Council v McMahon*[1] it was held that a council tenant in a block of flats who complained of a statutory nuisance affecting the block in general but not his flat was not a 'person aggrieved' for these purposes. This decision may depend on the facts of the individual case. Thus an occupier of the block affected by a smell as he or she leaves the block may be a 'person aggrieved' by it.

1   (1987) 151 JP 709.

INTIMATION NOTICE

3.124   The EPA 1990, s 82(6) requires that before instituting proceedings the person aggrieved must give to the proposed defendant a notice in writing of his or her intention to bring the proceedings and must specify the matter complained of. This is commonly known as an *intimation notice*.

3.125 In most cases the notice must allow the proposed defendant at least 21 days to respond before proceedings can be issued, however for noise nuisances under the EPA 1990, s 79(1)(g) or (ga) the period is only three days.[1]

1   EPA 1990, s 82(7).

3.126 In *Pearshouse v Birmingham City Council*[1] a strong Divisional Court (Lord Bingham CJ; Collins J) held that the purpose of giving notice under the EPA 1990, s 82(6) was to enable the recipient of the notice to make any necessary inspection and, if so advised, take practical and effective steps to cure or eliminate the subject matter of the complaint. The aggrieved person did, however, have to give the recipient of the notice such detail as was reasonable in all the circumstances. The procedure was intended to be a simple one and should not be bogged down in unnecessary technicality or undue literalism. See also *East Staffordshire Borough Council v Fairless*.[2]

1   [1999] Env LR 536.
2   [1999] Env LR 525.

3.127 These are the only requirements a person aggrieved has to follow before laying an information before the court.

'He is under no obligation to heed requests for a longer period within which to undertake work or to wait until after the expiry of 21 days to see whether any promises are honoured.'[1]

1   *R v Dudley Magistrates' Court, ex p Hollis* [1998] Env LR 354 at 361 per Moses J.

EPA 1990, s 82 proceedings

3.128 The criminal nature of the proceedings means that the prosecution will have to satisfy the court, so that it can be sure, that the nuisance exists and the defendant is responsible for the nuisance in question.

3.129 If the court is satisfied that either the nuisance exists, or that though abated it may recur, it can make an order under the EPA 1990, s 82(2) requiring abatement or prohibiting recurrence and may order the execution of works necessary for that purpose. Given the principles set out above in relation to Abatement Notices the court may be wiser simply to require abatement or prohibit recurrence.

3.130 The court may also impose a fine not exceeding level 5 on the standard scale.

3.131   If the nuisance relates to a dwelling which the court finds is unfit for human habitation as a result of the nuisance the court may order that it should not be occupied until made fit.[1]

1   EPA 1990, s 82(3).

3.132   The proceedings are brought against either the person responsible for the nuisance[1] or in relation to a structural defect, the owner of the premises[2] or where the person responsible for the nuisance cannot be found, the owner or occupier of the premises.[3] The premises here will have to be the premises from which the nuisance originates. Specific provision is made in respect of noise in streets.[4]

1   EPA 1990, s 82(4)(a).
2   EPA 1990, s 82(4)(b).
3   EPA 1990, s 82(4)(c).
4   EPA 1990, ss 82(4)(d), (5) and (5A).

3.133   If no person responsible can be found the court may, after hearing from the local authority, direct them to deal with the problem.[1]

1   EPA 1990, s 82(13).

Offences

3.134   Similar provisions as to offences against Abatement Notices are made in the EPA 1990, s 82(8) and the defence of best practicable means is applied by s 82(9) and (10).

3.135   Given the nature of the EPA 1990, s 82 proceedings, s 82(11) gives the court convicting a person of an offence under s 82(8) a power, after hearing the relevant local authority, to order that authority to do anything required by the defendant under the court's order.

Costs

3.136   Under the EPA 1990, s 82(12) where in these proceedings it is proved that the alleged nuisance existed at the date of the making of the complaint (this actually means the laying of the criminal information) then, whether or not the nuisance still exists at the time of the hearing the court shall order the defendant to pay to the complainant such amount as the court considers reasonably sufficient to compensate the complainant for any expenses properly incurred by him or her in the proceedings.

3.137   A magistrates' court is not entitled to refuse costs under the EPA 1990, s 82(12). It is bound to order costs provided that it was satisfied that the statutory nuisance existed at the time of the complaint. Its consideration of costs is limited to questions as to whether particular items of expenditure were necessary and the amounts claimed are warranted by the particular proceedings. The costs which could be recovered include expenses incurred in proving the existence of a statutory nuisance and in the steps required by the statute prior to the making of the complaint: *R v Dudley Magistrates' Court, ex p Hollis.*[1]

1   [1998] Env LR 354.

3.138   Contingency fee arrangements were considered in *Hughes v Kingston upon Hull City Council.*[1] H (a tenant of K) claimed that K was responsible for a statutory nuisance (relating to damp) at his premises and brought proceedings under the EPA 1990, Pt III. The works required to abate were carried out by K and the proceedings were withdrawn. However, the Appellant sought an order for costs under s 82(12). The magistrate accepted that the Appellant had not been made fully aware of the potential liability for costs by his solicitors and the rate at which costs were accruing and found that the retainer had been specifically worded by the solicitors to avoid the difficulties evident in *British Waterways Board v Norman*[2] which set out how such agreements may be unenforceable. He further found that the solicitors did not intend to pursue costs against H if his case failed, would have realised from the outset that this would not have been possible and that the retainer amounted to a contingency arrangement which was contrary to public policy (particularly with a criminal trial) and unenforceable in such cases. He rejected the contention that there was a binding contract between the solicitors and their clients. On a case stated the Divisional Court held that the Solicitors' Practice Rules provided that solicitors should not enter into contingency fee arrangements in respect of contentious proceedings. The magistrate had found that there was a contingency fee and that the arrangement was unenforceable. The agreement was contrary to the Solicitors' Practice Code and the decision in *Thai Trading Co v Taylor*[3] did not render the magistrate's decision incorrect.

1   [1999] Env LR 579.
2   (1993) 26 HLR 232.
3   [1998] QB 781, CA.

3.139   In *Taylor v Walsall and District Property and Investment Co Ltd*[1] the Divisional Court held that when a substantial sum was claimed by way of costs, a court must take proper steps to investigate just how the claim was arrived at and the detailed grounds upon which any challenge to those costs was made. It was essential to determine the basis upon which any item or head of costs was said not have been properly incurred, whether wholly or in part. A complainant should also, as a matter of course, provide the Respondent with notice of any costs they intended to claim prior to the hearing and the Respondent should, in return, either state that they accepted the claim or set out the reasons why they disputed it. It would be appropriate to use Calderbank letters, setting out the parties' without prejudice positions, so that Respondents who admitted some responsibility might be afforded protection and the issue of costs should be resolved as cheaply as possible.

1   [1998] Env LR 600.

3.140   If the nuisance has continued because the complainant has refused access to inspect or repair, then costs are unlikely to be awarded to the complainant: *Jones v Walsall Metropolitan Borough Council.*[1]

1   [2003] Env LR 140.

CHAPTER 4

Trespass to land

DEFINITION

4.01 Trespass to land consists in any unjustifiable intrusion by one person. The slightest crossing of the boundary is sufficient. Examples of trespass are the removal of any part of the land in the possession of another or any part of a building or other erection which is attached to the soil so as to form part of the realty. Placing rubbish against a wall, or dumping rubbish on another's land is trespass. However, it is probable that causing land to become fouled by a discharge of oil in a navigable river is not a trespass.[1]

---

1   *Overseas Tankship (UK) Ltd v Morts Dock and Engineering Co Ltd, The Wagon Mound* [1961] AC 388, PC where such a cause of action was treated as sounding in negligence. See also Chapter 15 at paras **15.05–15.13**.

4.02 Every continuance of a trespass is a fresh trespass, in respect of which a new cause of action arises from day to day as long as the trespass continues.

4.03 It may also be a trespass to invade the airspace above land. Intrusion into airspace at any height, however high, is not automatically wrongful, but it is clear that it is a wrong where such airspace is necessary for the full use of land below.

THE DEFENDANT'S INTENTION OR NEGLIGENCE

4.04 It is no defence to a claim for trespass that the trespass was due to a state of law or fact, provided the physical act of entry onto the claimant's land was *voluntary*. If the entry is quite *involuntary*, no liability is incurred. If the entry is voluntary, then an intention to enter (without actual or implied licence) makes the entrant a trespasser. This is so whether the entrant intends to act rightfully or wrongfully. Even negligent entry, where there is no intention to enter at all, also amounts to trespass.[1] Where there is unintentional non-negligent entry (eg straying over a boundary in the dark) there would be no trespass.

1   *League Against Cruel Sports v Scott* [1986] QB 240.

TRESPASS VERSUS NUISANCE

4.05   Trespass is a *direct*, as opposed to a *consequential*, injury, and is actionable without proof of damage, whereas damage must be proved in nuisance. If a defendant deposits rubbish of any kind on the land of another, or if a defendant sends polluted water from his or her land onto his or her neighbour's land, these are acts of trespass for which the defendant will be responsible without any proof of damage. However, if the defendant allows the root of his or her trees to grow into his or her neighbour's land or permits sewage to flow onto the neighbour's land, these are acts of nuisance, not trespass. The claimant must therefore establish the existence of appreciable damage.[1]

1   The distinction is not always obvious: compare *Esso Petroleum Co Ltd v Southport Corpn* [1956] AC 218, HL, with *Jones v Llanrwst UDC* [1911] 1 Ch 393.

4.06   Because a claim for trespass can be brought without proof of actual damage, the trifling nature of the trespass is no defence. It follows that where entry is merely threatened *a quia timet* injunction can be sought. The continuing trespasser may be restrained by injunction.

WHO MAY SUE?

4.07   A claim for trespass can be brought by the person in possession of land, who can claim damages or an injunction or both. A tenant in occupation can sue, but not a landlord, except in cases of injury to the reversion of the lease. Similarly, a person in possession can sue although he or she neither is the owner nor derives title from the owner, and indeed may be in adverse possession. All that 'possession' means is the occupation or physical control of the land. Proof of ownership is prima facie proof of possession, unless there is evidence that another person is in possession. Even then the presumption is that the person having a title to the land is in possession. Possession of the surface of the land includes possession of any minerals under the surface and thus possession prima facie operates to exclude others from access to the minerals. A lodger in a private house cannot bring a claim for trespass because possession remains in the landlord. However, a sub-tenant – ie a person to whom rooms in the house are demised so that he or she becomes the actual tenant of those rooms – has possession and can bring a claim in trespass. The test is one of exclusive possession.[1] Similar principles apply to business premises.[2]

1   *Street v Mountford* [1985] AC 809, HL.
2   *Ashburn Anstalt v Arnold* [1989] Ch 1, CA. See also *Monsanto plc v Tilly* [2000] Env LR 313 where the Court of Appeal held that Monsanto's agreement with a farmer whereby it did not actually own or occupy the site gave it sufficient interest to bring a trespass claim.

CRIMINAL OFFENCES OF ENTERING PROPERTY

4.08 The Criminal Law Act 1977 ('CLA 1977'), Pt II, as amended by the Criminal Justice and Public Order Act 1994 ('CJPOA 1994'), Pt V, enacts the following new offences:
  (i)   using or threatening violence to secure entry;[1]
  (ii) remaining on residential premises, having entered as a trespasser and after being required to leave by a 'displaced residential occupier' or a 'protected intending occupier' of residential premises;[2]
  (iii) having, as a trespasser, a weapon of offence without lawful authority or excuse;[3]
  (iv) trespassing on premises of a diplomatic mission;[4]
  (v)   obstructing a Court Officer executing process for possession against unauthorised occupiers.[5]

1   CLA 1977, s 6.
2   CLA 1977, s 7.
3   CLA 1977, s 8.
4   CLA 1977, s 9.
5   CLA 1977, s 10.

4.09 A further offence of criminal trespass is provided by the CJPOA 1994, s 61. A 'senior Police Officer' may direct persons to leave land if he reasonably believes that two or more persons are trespassers and 'are present there with the common purpose of residing there for any period'.[1] The Police have to be satisfied that the occupier has asked the trespassers to leave and that they are causing damage or using threatening behaviour or have six or more vehicles on the land. If the trespassers do not comply they become criminally liable.[2] The CJPOA 1994 has also created a new offence of 'aggravated trespass' whereby persons who trespass on land in order to disrupt a lawful activity taking place on that land become criminally liable.[3] Thus hunt saboteurs and similar groups would be caught by this provision.

1   CJPOA 1994, s 61(1).
2   CJPOA 1994, s 61(4).
3   CJPOA 1994, s 68.

THE SUBJECT MATTER OF TRESPASS

4.10 Any land, subsoil and superstructure can be the subject matter of trespass. The owner of what is called a profit á prendre can bring a claim for trespass in respect of the interference. So the owner of an exclusive right of fishing can maintain a claim for trespass against anyone who pollutes or interferes with that fishing right.[1] However, an owner of an easement cannot maintain a claim for trespass but can maintain a claim for private nuisance.[2]

1   *Rawson v Peters* (1972) 225 Estates Gazette 89, CA.
2   *Nicholls v Ely Beet Sugar Factory Ltd* [1936] Ch 343, CA.

JUSTIFICATION

4.11   It is not trespass if the entry is *justifiable*.[1] Entry may be made under a right of easement, under a profit á prendre or under a licence. In certain conditions it is permissible to enter to abate a nuisance on an adjacent property, but that right does not extend to entry concerned with repair or improvement of one's own building which cannot be reached externally except by such access. Even pressing necessity, for example a state of danger, does not of itself justify entry in the absence of actual licence. However, the Access to Neighbouring Land Act 1992 does enable the court to order access for preservation work on neighbouring land.

1   Destruction of genetically modified ('GM') crops to protect third parties or the general public from harm is not justifiable: *Monsanto plc v Tilly* [2000] Env LR 313, CA.

4.12   The licence at common law may be given to go upon the adjoining land to abate a nuisance or to prevent the spread of fire. Also if a claimant wrongfully deposits goods or property (e g building materials or rubbish) on the defendant's land the defendant may lawfully go upon the claimant's land for the purpose of removing and depositing them there.[1] Statute law has added to the common law. Section 60 of the National Parks and Access to the Countryside Act 1949 provides as follows:

'Where an access agreement or order is in force as respects any land a person who enters upon land comprised in the agreement or order for the purposes of open-air recreation without breaking or damaging any wall, fence, hedge or gate, or who is on such for that purpose after having so entered thereon, shall not be treated as a trespasser on that land or incur any other liability by reason only of entering or being on the land.'

1   *Rea v Sheward* (1837) 2 M & W 424.

4.13   Section 1(2) of the Access to Neighbouring Land Act 1972 provides that:

'On an application under this section, the Court shall make an access order if, and only if, it is satisfied—

(a)   the works are reasonably necessary for the preservation of the whole or any part of the dominant land; and
(b)   that they cannot be carried out, or be substantially more difficult to carry out without entry upon the servient land.'

4.14   Finally, the Party Wall etc Act 1996, s 8, confers rights of entry in relation to the carrying out of work authorised under that Act.

ENVIRONMENT AGENCY POWERS OF ENTRY

4.15   The Environment Act 1995 ('EA 1995'), s 108 provides that an Officer appointed by the Environment Agency can, when there is no emergency:

(i)   enter premises at any reasonable time;[1]
(ii) be accompanied onto premises by a Police Constable should the Officer apprehend that they will be obstructed in their duty;[2]
(iii) make any investigation as necessary including: measurements, taking samples, photographs and questioning individuals.[3] Answers given to such questions will not be admissible in any prosecution brought against that person although they can, and in practice are, used against another person, for example an employer;
(iv) carry out experimental borings and install and maintain monitoring equipment (with at least seven days' notice).[4]

Where occupants are likely to refuse entry, the Environment Agency Officer can seek a warrant prior to entry onto the premises. Documents which are subject to legal professional privilege are exempt from the above requirements.[5]

1   EA 1995, s 108(4)(a).
2   EA 1995, s 108(4)(b).
3   EA 1995, s 108(4).
4   EA 1995, s 108(8).
5   EA 1995, s 108(13).

4.16   In cases of emergency entry can be gained at any time with force if necessary.[1] In such circumstances no prior notification is required when setting up monitoring equipment or carrying out experimental borings. It is an offence to obstruct intentionally an authorised Environment Agency Officer in the exercise of his or her duties.[2]

1   EA 1995, s 108(4)(a).
2   EA 1995, s 110.

POLICE POWERS OF ENTRY

4.17   The Police have specific powers of entry contained in the Police and Criminal Evidence Act 1984 ('PACE'), supplemented by a Code of Practice. PACE abolishes all common law powers of Police entry without warrant save those concerned with breach of the peace. Section 17 of PACE specifies the lawful occasions on which a Constable may enter to search premises: the Constable may not enter to arrest for a non-arrestable offence. Section 18 allows entry and search after an arrest where there is reasonable cause to suspect the presence of material evidence. Section 32 also allows entry and searching the place where a person was when arrested or where the person was immediately before arrest. PACE also provides certain new powers where the premises are searched under the authority of a warrant and lays down the conditions under which search warrants may be issued.

TRESPASS AB INITIO

4.18   Mention should be made of the old but still extant doctrine of trespass ab initio. In simple language, a person who has entered on another's land under an authority given by law but subsequently abuses that authority, becomes a trespasser ab initio: the person's misconduct relates back so as to make the original entry tortious. This of course is of particular importance in relation to public officials and the Police and also would affect someone exercising a right of way who abuses that right.

4.19   Mention should also be made of justification under a right of way and the fact that any user of a right of way in excess of that right will render the person using it a trespasser. It is therefore a question of degree in each case. The extent of a private right of way depends upon the actual terms of the grant or the Act of Parliament granting it. As far as a public right of way is concerned, the right of the public in respect of a highway is limited to the use of it for the purposes of passing and repassing and for such other reasonable purposes as is usual to use the highway. Any other use would make the member of the public a trespasser. Thus the use of the highway to demonstrate by anti-bloodsports demonstrators could amount to a trespass and interesting arguments under the Human Rights Act 1998 arise here.[1]

1   See also *DPP v Jones* [1999] 2 AC 240 where the House of Lords held that it was not the case that a member of the public who uses the highway for a purpose other than that of passing and repassing, or a purpose ancillary thereto, will necessarily thereby become a trespasser. That case concerned a prosecution under the Public Order Act 1986, ss 70–71, relating to a 'trespassory assembly'. It is still a question of fact and degree in each case.

WATER

4.20   There is no right to pass over the foreshore for the purpose of bathing, or for any other purposes except for fishing or for navigation in the sea and purposes ancillary thereto. There is no right to put down permanent moorings in tidal waters where the bed soil is privately owned. There is no right at common law to tow on the banks of a navigable river and a member of the public cannot acquire, by prescription, the statutory right to navigate upon a river.

4.21   Justification may also occur under customary rights which are local in extent as well as by licence. The law of licences is too complicated to go into in detail here and reference should be made to the appropriate textbooks.[1]

1   A J Gray and S F Gray *Elements of Land Law* (4th edn, LexisNexis UK, 2003).

DAMAGES

4.22   A claimant in trespass is entitled to recover damages even though he or she has suffered no actual loss. The same is true with obtaining an injunction.[1] Where substantial damage has been caused the measure of damages varies. If the trespass consists of a mere user of the soil by passing over it without doing any damage, then the damage recoverable is a price which a 'reasonable man' would be willing to pay for the right of user. Where spoil has been tipped, the measure of damages is not only the loss of open ground but also the value of the site as a tip.[2]

1   *Patel v W H Smith (Eziot) Ltd* [1987] 1 WLR 853, CA.
2   *Whitwham v Westminster Brymbo Coal and Coke Co* [1896] 2 Ch 538, CA.

4.23 Trespass may involve actual physical damage to the land, as where a bank is dug away or a roadway cut up by constant user. The measure of damages here is the amount by which the value of the land has been diminished but not the cost of restoration. Often the diminution in value may be the cost of restoration, but as a rule it will be less. Although diminution in value is the general test, costs of repair and reinstatement exceeding the diminution in value may be awarded where those expenditures are reasonable.[1] Such damages are only awarded where the claimant intends to do the work and make good the damage to his property.[2] The date for assessing such compensation may be the date when repairs could be reasonably undertaken and not the date of the damage itself: *Dodd Properties (Kent) Ltd v Canterbury City Council;*[3] *Ward v Cannock Chase District Council.*[4]

1   *Heath v Keys* (1984) 134 NLJ 888.
2   *Perry v Sidney Phillips & Son* [1982] 1 WLR 1297, CA.
3   [1980] 1 WLR 433, CA.
4   [1985] 3 All ER 537.

4.24 Finally, trespass may involve the severing and carrying away of things attached to the soil. The measure of damages here is the diminution in the value of the land. Thus, for taking fixtures a trespasser could be ordered to pay the value as fixtures.

4.25 Exemplary damages may not be awarded, except where the wrong is an oppressive, arbitrary or unconstitutional act by servants of the Government or where the wrongdoer's conduct has been calculated on a profit exceeding the compensation payable to the plaintiff.[1] However, aggravated damages may be awarded in trespass, eg where the trespass is accompanied by noise and disturbance.

1   *Rookes v Barnard* [1964] AC 1129, HL.

LIMITATION PERIOD

4.26 Subject to the usual exceptions for disabilities, all actions for trespass to land should be brought within six years after the cause of action arose.[1]

1   Limitation Act 1980, s 2.

CHAPTER 5

Breach of statutory duty

STATUTORY POWERS AND DUTIES

5.01 There are two types of authority conferred on statutory bodies such as the Environment Agency or a local authority. The first is a statutory *power*. A power can either be expressed as such, for example in the Water Resources Act 1991, s 166: the Agency, 'shall have power to provide and operate flood warning systems'; or in s 167 of that Act: the Agency 'may dispose of soil in connection with flood defence works'. These are discretionary powers that the authority may choose to exercise or not exercise as long as it reaches its decision in a proper manner.

5.02 Other provisions in a statute may impose a *duty* on an authority. For example, the Environment Protection Act 1990, s 80(1) states that where an authority is satisfied that a statutory nuisance exists, it 'shall' serve an Abatement Notice. This is a mandatory requirement where, if the authority is satisfied on the balance of probabilities that there is a statutory nuisance, it has duty to serve a notice.[1]

1   *R v Carrick District Council, ex p Shelley* [1996] Env LR 273.

5.03 For individuals and companies, statutory duties can be imposed in statutes and regulations for a variety of purposes. These may or may not lead to civil liability. Specific liability may be placed on a person by reason of a statute – for example, in the Occupiers Liability Act 1957 or the Nuclear Installations Act 1965. Some Acts may specifically exclude a right of action, as in s 133 of the Medicines Act 1968. If a right of action is not specifically conferred or excluded by the relevant provision, then the question as to whether liability arises from a breach of the duty depends on judicial interpretation of it.

BREACH OF STATUTORY DUTY ACTION

5.04 In determining whether a particular statutory provision gives rise to liability, the first question is: does it impose a statutory duty on anyone? This can be seen in the words of the statute or regulation. For example, reg 9(1) of the Landfill (England and Wales) Regulations 2002[1] provides that the operator 'shall' not accept certain wastes. It thus imposes a duty on the operator not to accept them.

1   SI 2002/1559.

5.05   In *Todd v Adam*[1] Neuberger J stated:

'It appears to me that the question of whether, by imposing a duty, the legislature intended the breach to give rise to a civil remedy must ultimately depend upon the construction of the particular statutory provision, bearing in mind the language and purpose of the provision, and all other relevant circumstances. Accordingly, as with any question of statutory (or indeed contractual) interpretation, it can be difficult, even dangerous, to attempt to lay down any rules of general application. Of course, cases in which a similar problem has arisen, albeit in relation to a different statutory provision, may provide assistance, particularly so far as the reasoning is concerned. However, in each case the court has to make up its mind by reference to the relevant material available in relation to the particular statutory provision under consideration.'

1   [2002] EWCA Civ 509 at 16, [2002] 2 All ER (Comm) 97 at [16].

5.06   The basic principles are summarised in the speech of Lord Browne-Wilkinson in *X* (*Minors*) *v Bedfordshire County Council*:[1]

'The principles applicable in determining whether [a] statutory cause of action exists are now well established, although the application of those principles in any particular case remains difficult. The basic proposition is that in the ordinary case a breach of statutory duty does not, by itself, give rise to any private law cause of action. However a private law cause of action will arise if it can be shown, as a matter of construction of a statute, that the statutory duty was imposed for the protection of a limited class of the public and that Parliament intended to confer on members of that class a private right of action for breach of a duty'.

1   [1995] 2 AC 633 at 731C–E, HL.

5.07   Lord Browne-Wilkinson went on to say:

'If the statute provides no other remedy for its breach and the Parliamentary intention to protect a limited class is shown, that indicates that there may be a private right of action ... If the statute does provide some other means of enforcing the duty that will normally indicate that the statutory right was intended to be enforceable by those means and not by private right of action ... However, the mere existence of some other statutory remedy is not necessarily decisive. It is still possible to show that on the true construction of the statute the protected class was intended by Parliament to have a private remedy. Thus the specific duties imposed on employers in relation to factory premises are enforceable by an action for damages, notwithstanding the imposition by the statute of criminal penalties for any breach: see *Groves v Wimborne (Lord)* [1898] 2 QB 402.'

5.08 Whilst in *Phillips v Britannia Hygienic Laundry Co*[1] it was said the duty could be owed to the public as a whole, this was discounted in *Todd* on the basis of what was confirmed to be the law in *X (Minors)*. However the final decision in *Todd,* that the relevant legislation did not provide for civil liability, was criticised by another Court of Appeal in *Ziemniak v ETPM Deep Sea Ltd,*[2] a case on the same legislation. These conflicting opinions show how difficult the question of establishing whether a particular provision does impose civil liability is.

1   [1923] 2 KB 832 at 841, CA.
2   [2003] EWCA Civ 636, [2003] 2 All ER (Comm) 283.

LIABILITY OF STATUTORY AUTHORITIES

5.09 Authorities are not usually liable to compensate an individual simply for breaching a duty.[1] Some breaches of duty will trigger a statutory remedy, however. For example, s 93A of the Water Industry Act 1991 ('WIA 1991') imposes a duty on every water undertaker to promote the efficient use of water by its customers. This duty is enforceable by the Secretary of State or OFWAT under s 18 of the Act. The remedy provided by s 18 is exclusive.[2] In addition, in some cases the statute may provide for compensation for a particular act of an authority.

1   *Bourgoin SA v Ministry of Agriculture, Fisheries and Food* [1986] QB 716, CA.
2   WIA 1991, s 18(8).

5.10 Where an authority has breached a duty and caused the claimant loss, the usual route will be to sue in negligence; although in many instances a court may find that the authority owed the claimant no duty of care.[1] Damages may be awarded as part of an action to judicially review the authority's decision. However, a claim for judicial review may only include a claim for damages if they are not the sole relief claimed.[2] The boundary between a private law action and a public law action is flexible, and a claim brought in an ordinary action will not necessarily be struck out because it involves a challenge to a public law act or decision.[3] In addition, damages may be awarded where a court finds that an authority has violated the claimant's human rights.

1   See Chapter 1 at para **1.43**ff.
2   Civil Procedure Rules 1998 ('CPR'), r 54.3(2); and see Supreme Court Act 1981, s 31(4).
3   *Steed v Secretary of State for the Home Department* [2000] 1 WLR 1169, HL.

DIRECT EFFECT OF EC LEGISLATION

5.11 There are three main types of European Community ('EC') legislation: (i) articles of the European Treaty, (ii) EC Regulations and (iii) EC Directives.

Where a Member State, or an emanation of a Member State[1] has caused loss or damage to an individual as a result of a breach of any of these types of legislation, the individual may be able to bring an action against the body concerned. Where the breach is of a Treaty provision or a Regulation, an action may be possible between individuals. The position is usefully summarised in the opinion of the Advocate General in *H J Banks & Co Ltd v British Coal Corpn*:[2]

'The general basis established by the Court in the *Francovich*[3] judgment for State liability also applies where an individual infringes a provision of Community Law to which he is subject, thereby causing loss and damage to another individual. The situation then falls within the terms stated by the Court in paragraph 31 of the *Francovich* judgment (and even earlier in *Van Gend en Loos*[4]) namely breach of a right which an individual derives from an obligation imposed by Community Law on another individual. Once again, the full effect of Community Law would be impaired if the former individual or undertaking did not have the possibility of obtaining reparation from the party who can be held responsible for the breach of Community Law ...'.

1   See *Foster v British Gas plc* [1991] 2 AC 306, HL.
2   Case C-128/92: [1994] ECR I-1209, ECJ.
3   Case C-6, 9/90: *Francovich and Bonifaci v Italy* [1991] ECR I-5357, ECJ.
4   Case 26/62: *Van Gend en Loos v Nederlandse Administratie der Berlastingen* [1963] ECR 1, ECJ.

5.12   To enable an action to be brought, the relevant provision must be 'directly effective'. This means that, first, the provision must be clear, precise and unconditional. Second, its terms must be capable of conferring rights on individuals. Third, in the case of a Directive, the implementation date in respect of it must have expired. An example of how a court reaches its decision on whether a Directive is directly effective can be seen in *R v Secretary of State for Transport, ex p Factortame Ltd (No 2)*.[1]

1   [1991] 1 AC 603, HL.

5.13   In addition to an action in respect of a Directive that has been implemented by a Member State, where an individual suffers damage by the failure of a Member State to implement it, or part of it, the individual may have an action for damages. The law on this aspect was recently clarified by the Advocate General in *Evans v Secretary of State for the Environment, Transport and the Regions*.[1] In particular, he emphasised that the damage complained of must be sufficiently serious for an action to lie and that it is for the national court in any given case to find whether the causal link between non-implementation and damage has been established.

1   Case C-63/01 (24 October 2002, unreported), ECJ.

THE PROPOSED DIRECTIVE ON ENVIRONMENTAL LIABILITY

5.14   This section looks at the principles underlying the Directive. At the time of writing there was a Common Position of the EC Council[1] but this was subject to EC Parliamentary debate. It is the subject of vigorous debate in the European Community and the current text may be changed before it is finally agreed. It is hoped that it will be adopted in April 2004, with implementation in 2007.

1   See Common Position of the EC Council on the Directive – 10933/03, September 2003.

5.15   The full title of the Directive explains its nature: it is on 'Environmental liability with regard to the prevention and remedying of environmental damage'. Thus it is not aimed at giving individuals a right of action in respect of losses they have suffered. No reference is made in the proposal to traditional kinds of damage (personal injury and damage to property), since this is covered by civil liability actions, which are widely used in the Member States. However, the Directive would assist a property owner in having damage caused to his or her lands or waters remediated.

5.16   'Environmental damage' for the purposes of the Directive is defined by reference to biodiversity, waters covered by the Water Framework Directive and land contamination. In accordance with the 'polluter pays' principle, the operator who has caused the environmental damage, or who is faced with an imminent threat of such damage occurring, must bear the costs of repairing the damage. This echoes the clean-up provisions of the Water Resources Act 1991, ss 161A–161D and, to an extent, the contaminated land regime. However, it will be wider in scope as it covers 'biodiversity' – defined in relation to the habitats protected in the Natura 2000 network.

5.17   The key aim of the Directive is set out in its second recital:

'The prevention and remedying of environmental damage should be implemented through the furtherance of the "polluter pays" principle, as indicated in the Treaty and in line with the principle of sustainable development. The fundamental principle of this Directive should therefore be that an operator whose activity has caused the environmental damage or the imminent threat of such damage is to be held financially liable, in order to induce operators to adopt measures and develop practices to minimize the risks of environmental damage so that their exposure to financial liabilities is reduced.'

5.18   The main debate about the Directive has been not so much on the principle, but rather the defences that should be available to an operator. It is not intended to apply retrospectively or to damage caused by the lawful disposal of waste. Thus the UK's contaminated land regime, which does look at historical pollution, should not be affected by it. In addition it is intended that there should be no responsibility for harm caused where the operator was conducting his business in accordance with a relevant permit or authorisation; although this is a matter for Member States. Nor will there be liability for emissions or activities which were not considered harmful at the time they occurred – the state-of-the-art defence.

5.19   One innovation is the ability of an environmental pressure group to take action under the Directive. This is explained by the twenty-fifth recital, which states:

> 'Persons adversely affected or likely to be adversely affected by environmental damage should be entitled to ask the competent authority to take action. Environmental protection is, however, a diffuse interest on behalf of which individuals will not always act or will not be in a position to act. Non-governmental organisations promoting environmental protection should therefore also be given the opportunity to properly contribute to the effective implementation of this Directive.'

5.20   The Directive will, therefore, when it comes into force, introduce a new type of regime in respect of the remediation of certain types of environmental harm that occur after it has entered into force. But its effect will be limited. Certainly it will not be of assistance to individuals seeking to recover for economic losses sustained as a result of damage inflicted on their environment.

CHAPTER 6

Product liability

INTRODUCTION

6.01 Where a person suffers injury or loss that is caused by a product, the manufacturer or supplier of the product may be liable for the harm caused. In environmental law there are three aspects of this: (1) damage caused by toxic substances released into the environment; (2) damage caused to a building or other property by environmental factors such as flooding; and (3) harm caused by genetically modified organisms. This chapter briefly examines the EC Product Liability Directive and the Consumer Protection Act 1987, and then looks at each of these three aspects.

THE PRODUCT LIABILITY DIRECTIVE

6.02 The Product Liability Directive[1] aims, in Article 1, to make the producer liable for damage caused by a defect in its product. The reason for this is that liability without fault on the part of the producer is the sole means of adequately solving the problem, peculiar to our age of increasing technicality, of a fair apportionment of the risks inherent in modern technological production.[2]

1   Dir 85/374.
2   Dir 85/374, second recital.

6.03 Article 2 of the Directive defines a 'product' as all moveables, including electricity. Initially it excluded liability for primary agricultural products, but this was altered by an amendment in 1999[1] which re-defines 'products' as all moveables even if incorporated into another moveable or into an immoveable. This was mainly done as a result of the BSE crisis and means that agricultural products come under the provisions of the Directive. The 'producer' of the 'product' is defined in Article 3 to include its manufacturer, miner, farmer etc or its importer or, where the producer cannot be identified, its supplier.

1   Dir 1999/34, Article 1.

6.04   Article 4 requires the injured person to prove the damage, the defect and the causal relationship between defect and damage. For these purposes the product is 'defective' when it does not provide the safety which a person is entitled to expect, taking all circumstances into account, including its presentation, the use to which it could reasonably be expected that it would be put and when it was put into circulation. However it will not be considered defective merely because a better version is subsequently issued.[1] Article 7 gives the producer some defences to an action under the Directive, while Article 8.2 allows a contributory negligence defence. However, its liability is not affected by any limitation of liability clauses.[2] 'Damage' is defined to include death or personal injury and damage to material goods of more than 500 ECU which the claimant used, and which ordinarily would be used, for private use or consumption.[3]

1   Dir 85/374, Article 6.
2   Dir 85/374, Article 12.
3   Dir 85/374, Article 9.

6.05   An action under the Directive should ordinarily be brought within three years of the day on which the claimant became aware, or should reasonably have become aware, of the damage, the defect and the identity of the producer.[1] Even if national law allows actions to be brought after this time, Article 11 provides a long stop of 10 years. After 10 years from the date the product was put into circulation, no action can be brought under the Directive, regardless of the reasons for the delay.

1   Dir 85/374, Article 10.

THE CONSUMER PROTECTION ACT 1987

6.06   The Product Liability Directive is implemented in Great Britain by Pt I of the Consumer Protection Act 1987 ('CPA 1987'). The amendment effected by Directive 1999/34 is implemented by the Consumer Protection Act 1987 (Product Liability) (Modification) Order 2000.[1] The limitation provisions of the Directive are contained in, and put into context by, Sch 1 to the Act. The time at which any loss or damage should be regarded as having occurred is dealt with in s 5(5)–(8).

1   SI 2000/2771.

6.07   The CPA 1987, s 2 provides for who is liable for damage caused by a defective product. Section 2(5) states that, 'Where two or more persons are liable by virtue of this Part for the same damage, their liability shall be joint and several.' This follows Article 5 of the Directive and its fifth recital which considers that in such a situation the consumer should be able to claim full compensation for the damage from any one of those persons. Thus, as long as the claimant can prove that the actions of the defendant materially contributed to his or her injury, the rule of apportionment between those who contributed to the illness in *Holtby v Brigham & Cowan (Hull) Ltd*[1] does not apply in claims under the CPA 1987, even if producers of other products might also be liable for the damage.

1   [2000] 3 All ER 421, CA.

6.08   The CPA 1987, s 3 sets out the meaning of 'defect'. It looks at three types of defect: (i) a design defect, (ii) a manufacturing or processing defect and (iii) a defect in supply such as failure to give proper warnings or instructions for use. This latter aspect is made clear in s 3(2)(a) which enables a court to consider all the circumstances in relation to a product including the 'manner in which, and the purposes for which, the product has been marketed, its get-up, the use of any mark in relation to the product and any instructions for, or warnings with respect to, doing or refraining from doing anything with or in relation to the product'. In assessing the position, it is irrelevant that the producer did not know of the defect before the damage complained of occurred.[1]

1   *Abouzaid v Mothercare (UK) Ltd* (2001) Times, 20 February, CA.

LIABILITY FOR HARMFUL SUBSTANCES

6.09   Take the example of a person who claims that he or she was injured by herbicide spray drift. The natural defendant here would be the sprayer of the chemical. The sprayer could be sued in negligence. The negligence might consist of failures in respect of the provisions of the Control of Pesticides Regulations 1986[1] or breaches of any relevant Code of Practice on the use of the chemical or spraying operations. Causation would be slightly different from other types of claim in that, in addition to showing that the chemical could cause the harm suffered, it would also be necessary to show that the spray – with the droplet size sprayed – could reach the place where the claimant says he or she was affected in the prevailing meteorological conditions.

1   SI 1986/1510 as amended by SI 1997/188.

6.10   It may be possible to sue the manufacturer of the chemical in product liability, on the basis of poor instructions to the sprayer or design defects. However, some caution has to be exercised here. If the chemicals drift further than they should, is this the fault of the manufacturer of the chemical or of the spray machinery?

6.11   Under the CPA 1987 the position is reasonably clear in a case of personal injury. The chemical is a 'product' for the purposes of s 1(2), its 'producer' will be its manufacturer and the claimant will have suffered 'damage' in accordance with s 5(1). The real question, assuming that questions of causation can be dealt with satisfactorily, will be whether the product was 'defective' for the purposes of s 3. The main difficulty for the claimant here is the need for pre-action disclosure under the Civil Procedure Rules 1998

('CPR'), r 31.16. In particular, the claimant will have to define clearly the issues that disclosure is required for.[1] These are likely to be 'the nature of the defect in the product' and the documents required would be Health and Safety data sheets and instructions for the use of the product. If there is reason to believe that there may have been a design defect, an expert should be consulted.

1   *Medisys plc v Arthur Andersen (a firm)* [2002] Lloyd's Rep PN 323.

LIABILITY IN RESPECT OF BUILDINGS

6.12   Where a building becomes damaged as a result of flooding or some other environmental cause, it may not be possible to bring an action against the person that enabled the flood to occur, such as a flood defence organisation. However, an action against the developer of the building may be possible if floor levels were too low in the light of a foreseeable risk or if there was some other fault in the property. Such an action can be brought against the developer,[1] architect[2] or surveyor.[3]

1   *Murphy v Brentwood District Council* [1991] 1 AC 398, HL.
2   *Baxall Securities Ltd v Sheard Walshaw Partnership* (2000) 74 Con LR 116.
3   *Alliance and Leicester Building Society v J & E Shepherd* (1995) unreported, Outer House.

6.13   In addition to a common law action, the Defective Premises Act 1972 ('DPA 1972') gives a right of action against builders, architects and others in respect of defective dwellings. Such an action can be brought where something is omitted from the building, such as a failure to raise floor levels to cope with likely flooding.[1] The DPA 1972, s 2 excludes a right of action where the property is covered by the National House-Building Council scheme. However, it may be that if the particular defect in the building is not encompassed by the scheme, then s 2 does not apply.[2] The DPA 1972, s 1(5) deems that the cause of action accrues at the time when the dwelling was completed. It may be that the courts will not extend the usual period of limitation under s 14A(1) of the Limitation Act 1980, as that provision is concerned with 'any action for damages for negligence'.

1   *Alexander v Mercouris* [1979] 3 All ER 305, CA.
2   DPA 1972, s 2(2)(b).

LIABILITY FOR GENETICALLY MODIFIED ORGANISMS

6.14   Provision for the 'contained' use of genetically modified micro-organisms ('GMOs') – use in a laboratory etc – is made in EC Directive 90/219 as amended by Directive 98/81. The Directive is implemented in Great Britain by the Genetically Modified Organisms (Contained Use) Regulations 2000.[1] These Regulations are made under the Health and Safety at Work Act 1974 and apply the civil liability provisions of s 47 of that Act to the regime for contained use.[2]

1   SI 2000/2831.
2   SI 2000/2831, reg 26(1).

6.15 'Living organisms, whether released into the environment in large or small amounts for experimental purposes or as commercial products, may reproduce in the environment. The effects of such releases on the environment may be irreversible'.[1] The EC Directive on Deliberate Release into the Environment of Genetically Modified Organisms ('GMOs') defines a 'deliberate release' as:

'Any intentional introduction into the environment of a GMO or a combination of GMOs for which no specific containment measures are used to limit their contact with and to provide a high level of safety for, the general population and the environment.'[2]

Thus a farmer planting a GMO-based crop is deliberately releasing the GMO into the environment. In addition, producers who place on the market GMOs or GMO products must comply with the requirements of Pt C of the Directive.

1   Dir 01/18, Recital 4.
2   Dir 01/18, Article 2(3).

6.16   In Great Britain, general provision is made in respect of GMOs by Pt VI of the Environmental Protection Act 1990 ('EPA 1990'). The Directive is implemented in England[1] by the Genetically Modified Organisms (Deliberate Release) Regulations 2002,[2] which amend the provisions of the EPA 1990, Pt VI where necessary to fall in line with the Directive. The regime set out in the Act and Regulations requires a risk assessment before GMOs are released, imported or marketed, imposes general duties on the importation, acquisition, keeping, release or marketing of organisms and requires the consent of the Secretary of State before any GMO is imported, acquired, released or marketed. Failure to comply with the provisions of the Act or Regulations is an offence. A public register of relevant information must be maintained by the Secretary of State under the EPA 1990, s 122.

1   For Wales see SI 2002/3188 and for Scotland see SSI 2002/541.
2   SI 2002/2443.

6.17   The offence provisions of the EPA 1990, s 118 make it doubtful that an action for breach of statutory duty could be brought in respect of damage arising from a failure either to comply with the general duties in s 109 or with consent conditions.[1] The only remedy the EPA 1990 provides is in s 120, which enables a court convicting a person of a relevant offence 'in respect of any matters which appear to the court to be matters which is in his power to remedy' order the person to take specified steps to remedy them. However, as private prosecutions are ruled out by s 118(10), this provision is of limited use and would need consent of relevant landowners before damage arising on lands outside the defendant's occupation could be remedied.

1   See Chapter 5.

6.18   It might be considered that the Consumer Protection Act 1987 ('CPA 1987') provides a remedy here. However, while the GMO would be a 'product' supplied by a 'producer', the real difficulty here is with the type of damage sustained. The most likely claimant is a farmer of organic crops that seeks damages because as a result of contamination with GMOs, the organic farmer's crops are no longer marketable. Even assuming that the farmer could show a defect in the product, the farmer's crops are unlikely to be 'property ordinarily intended for private use or consumption or intended for such use or consumption' for the purposes of the CPA 1987, s 5(3). Moreover, a gardener whose vegetables are intended for private use and consumption would need to achieve the £275 threshold required under the CPA 1987, s 5(4). Thus the CPA 1987 is unhelpful in these circumstances.

6.19   While the EC Directive on environmental liability may assist in this area, this is unlikely to be in force before 2006 at the earliest and is in any event targeted at remedying harm, not compensating loss. The Agriculture and Environment Biotechnology Commission ('AEBC') has a liability sub-group that is considering the way forward. At the moment, however, a potential claimant is left with his or her common law remedy, namely a nuisance/ negligence claim under the principles set out in *Leakey v National Trust*.[1] Any such case would be difficult to bring, involving as it would problems of causation, foreseeability of harm and the intricate interrelationships in ecosystems.

1   [1980] QB 485, CA.

CHAPTER 7

Criminal liability

INTRODUCTION

7.01 Criminal liability has traditionally been seen as a sanction of last resort in both health and safety and in environmental regulation. Even in cases where criminal proceedings have been brought, the defendant has usually been the company rather than the individual. The mood of both courts and the regulators is changing. Whilst thirty years ago judges could describe environmental crimes as offences which 'are not criminal in any real sense, but are acts which in the public interest are prohibited under a penalty', the courts are now willing to visit heavy financial penalties on companies, and imprisonment on officers of companies, where really serious consequences have occurred.

OFFENCES

Main criminal offences

7.02 The main criminal offences are:
- integrated pollution control and air pollution control – carrying on a prescribed process without, or in breach of, authorisation;
- depositing, recovering or disposing of controlled waste without a Waste Management Licence or in breach of its conditions;
- polluting controlled waters;
- abstracting water illegally;
- failing to meet packaging, recycling and recovery obligations or to register or to provide information under the Producer Responsibility Obligations (Packaging Waste) Regulations 1997;[1]
- failing to comply with a Remediation Notice in respect of a contaminated site.

1   SI 1997/648.

Integrated pollution control and air pollution control – carrying on a prescribed process without, or in breach of, authorisation[1]

7.03 Integrated pollution control[2] covers the more complicated processes, which often have the greatest potential for pollution. There are about 5,000 such processes. The Environment Agency ('the Agency') Inspectors who over-see them are scientifically qualified. These processes are generally, but not always, carried out in larger factories.

1 Environmental Protection Act 1990 ('EPA 1990'), s 23.
2 The regime for integrated pollution and control ('IPPC') and for air pollution control ('APC') in England and Wales is provided by the Pollution Prevention and Control (England and Wales) Regulations 2000, SI 2000/1973, which were made under the Pollution Prevention and Control Act 1999. This regime replaces that under the EPA 1990, Pt I (see Chapter 16), but existing 'authorisation' under the EPA 1990 continues in force for the time being.

7.04 Pollution control offences, on the other hand, are prosecuted by local authorities who are concerned with significant local air polluting industrial processes, including processes with a potential for serious nuisance impacts (especially odour) under the EPA 1990, Pt III (statutory nuisance).

7.05 The maximum penalty for the above offences is £20,000 and/or three months' imprisonment on summary conviction, and an unlimited fine and/or two years' imprisonment on indictment.

Depositing, recovering or disposing of controlled waste without a Waste Management Licence or in breach of its conditions[1]

7.06 The deposit and recovery of waste must be carried out under a Waste Management Licence and in accordance with its conditions. It must also be carried out in a manner not likely to cause pollution to the environment or harm to human health. Risks associated with waste which is not properly disposed of or recovered include ground and surface water pollution and soil contamination.

1 EPA 1990, s 33.

7.07 The maximum penalty is £20,000 and/or six months' imprisonment on summary conviction and an unlimited fine and/or two years' imprisonment on indictment. Where this offence is committed in relation to waste which is 'special waste' (broadly, any controlled waste which is classified as toxic, very toxic, harmful, corrosive, irritant or carcinogenic) the maximum term on indictment rises to five years' imprisonment.

Polluting controlled waters[1]

7.08 Controlled waters are coastal and territorial waters and any streams or rivers, and lakes or ponds attached to them. Polluted controlled waters can have a devastating effect on the flora and fauna and on the quality of water abstracted for drinking and other purposes.

1   Water Resources Act 1991 ('WRA 1991'), s 85.

7.09   The maximum penalty is £20,000 and/or three months' imprisonment on summary conviction and an unlimited fine and/or two years' imprisonment on indictment.

Abstracting water illegally [1]

7.10   Water abstraction is governed by a licensing system which ensures that only sustainable amounts are used. Over-abstraction can seriously harm the environment and flora and fauna dependent on it. Those who take water beyond their licensed quantity may put the public drinking water supply and other lawful users at risk. A reduction in the flow of streams may lead to an unacceptable concentration of pollutants from legitimate discharges, such as sewage treatment works.

1   WRA 1991, s 24.

7.11   The maximum penalty is £5,000 on summary conviction and an unlimited fine on indictment. This offence is not imprisonable.

Failing to meet packaging, recycling and recovery obligations or to register or to provide information [1] and the Producer Responsibility Obligations (Packaging Waste) Regulations 1997 [2]

7.12   This legislation requires businesses to achieve minimum levels of recycling and recovery of an equivalent amount of packaging waste in relation to the packaging or packed goods they sell. The environmental objective is to use waste more productively and reduce the use of landfills.

1   Environment Act 1995 ('EA 1995'), s 93.
2   SI 1997/648.

7.13   The maximum penalty is £5,000 on summary conviction and an unlimited fine on indictment. The offence is not imprisonable.

Failing to comply with a Remediation Notice in respect of a contaminated site [1]

7.14   This legislation permits either the Agency or the local authority to serve Remediation Notices on persons who caused or knowingly permitted the contamination and also (in certain circumstances) the owner or occupier for the time being of the site in question.

1   EPA 1990, Pt IIA as amended by the EA 1995.

7.15   The maximum penalty for this offence is £20,000 and/or three months' imprisonment on summary conviction and an unlimited fine and/or two years' imprisonment on indictment.

Offences by company officers

7.16   The acts of a company do not ordinarily give rise to personal responsibility for its directors, managers or shareholders. If X Co deposits controlled waste unlawfully, it is X Co that is liable, not its chairman, directors, officers or shareholders. However, the EPA 1990, s 157(1) provides that where an offence under the Act is committed by a company or other corporate body and is proved to have been committed with the consent or connivance of, or to have been attributable to any neglect on the part of, any director, manager, secretary or any similar officer of the company, that person, as well as the company, shall be guilty of that offence and liable to be proceeded against and punished accordingly.

7.17   In a pre-Act case, *Huckerby v Elliott*,[1] it was considered that a director 'consents' to a course of conduct for these purposes if the director is aware of what is going on and agrees to it. 'Connivance' means that the director is aware of what is going on but turns a blind eye to it, letting it continue: see *Huckerby*. 'Neglect' means a failure to perform a duty which a person charged knows or ought to know, that he or she should perform: *Re Hughes*.[2]

1   [1970] 1 All ER 189.
2   [1943] 2 All ER 269.

7.18   It is not every company manager who is an officer of the company. The provision is aimed at those who control the company, not middle management. In *R v Boal*[1] it was held that a temporary manager who was put in charge of a shop for a week was not a 'manager' of the company for the purpose of a provision of this kind.

1   [1992] 3 All ER 177, CA.

7.19   However, a middle manager who himself or herself causes and knowingly permits an offence to take place can be charged as an original offender with the company. To avoid unfairness it is a defence to a charge under the EPA 1990, s 33(1) that an employee 'acted under instruction from his employer and neither knew nor had reason to suppose that the acts done by him constituted an offence under Section 33(1)'. This defence does not appear in any other environmental statute.

7.20   Prosecution of directors under the EPA 1990, s 157(1) has occurred, and in a few cases directors have been sent to prison. It is also possible to prosecute shareholders since, by s 157(2), it is possible to prosecute 'a member of the company exercising management functions'. Thus, an individual or a company who is a shareholder, could be prosecuted for the acts or defaults as if a director of the company but only if found to be *exercising management functions*. We are not aware of any prosecution under s 157(2).

ENFORCEMENT AND PROSECUTION POLICY

7.21 The Agency, in common with other prosecuting authorities, seeks to be transparent about its enforcement and prosecution policy, and it is advisable to check its website[1] both for changes in enforcement and prosecution policies (which are continually evolving), and also for its database of cases on sentencing.

1   www.environment-agency.gov.uk

7.22 The Agency sees the main purpose of enforcement as being to protect the environment or secure compliance with the regulatory system, for example by Enforcement Notices, Works Notices, Prohibition Notices, Suspension of Licences, Variation of Licences and, as the ultimate sanction, Prosecution.

7.23 The principles adopted are the following:
- *Proportionality* – The Agency's reaction to an incident will be proportionate to the risk posed and the gravity of the incident.
- *Consistency* – Using a similar approach to similar circumstances.
- *Transparency* – Informing individuals as to why action is proposed; if remedial action is needed, why this is the case; discussing requirements before action but not if urgent action is needed; providing a written note after the event; and providing explanation as to statutory rights of appeal.
- *Targeting* – Efforts are to be directed at high-risk activity and deliberate criminality. High-hazard sites will be visited regularly.

7.24 So far as prosecution is concerned, the Agency follows the Code for Crown Prosecutors and, particularly, the criterion that no prosecution should commence unless there is sufficiency of evidence for a 'realistic prospect of conviction'. It states that public interest is a second hurdle to be surmounted: aspects to be considered include environmental effect, foreseeability, intent, history; attitude; detriment; and personal circumstances. Finally, whilst noting that companies should usually be prosecuted the Agency states in terms: 'But also senior officers if they consented, connived in the commission of the offence, or neglected their duties.'

7.25 Sometimes, either in deciding to prosecute or not to prosecute as the case may be, the Agency appears to depart from its own policy. We are not aware of any case where such a decision has been successfully challenged by way of judicial review. We think it highly improbable that the Agency would fail to be able, rationally, to justify a decision to take proceedings. In the case of a refusal to take proceedings, a private prosecution would be available.

INVESTIGATION OF OFFENCES

7.26   The Agency has powers to request information under the EPA 1990, s 71 and powers to gather information and to ask questions under the EA 1995, s 108 (which resembles materially the Health and Safety at Work Act 1974, s 20). These statutory provisions give the Agency wide powers to search premises, seize documents, ask questions, and take witness statements, photographs and samples.[1]

1   See Chapter 4 at paras **4.15–4.16**.

7.27   In our experience the taking of statements under the EA 1995, s 108 is almost always a prelude to a prosecution. Non-compliance with the section is a criminal offence and the Agency prosecution policy states in terms that they generally prosecute where this offence is committed.

7.28   There is no *right* to have a solicitor present. The prosecuting authority will normally allow the interviewee to have his or her own solicitor present. In the usual case, s 108 statements are being taken from *employees* when the target of the prosecution is likely to be the company and/or an officer of the company. It is not usual for the prosecuting authority to allow a company lawyer to be present when an employee is having a statement taken.

7.29   Attempts have been made to challenge the validity of powers to request information. In *R v Hertfordshire County Council, ex p Green Environmental Industries Ltd*[1] it was held that the powers to request information under the EPA 1990, s 71 are valid. The House of Lords said that it was up to the trial judge to decide whether the replies should be excluded from the evidence given at trial by exercising his powers under s 78 of the Police and Criminal Evidence Act 1984 ('PACE'). The Crown Courts are not used to evidence gathering in this way, and in our experience feel somewhat uncomfortable about it. It is reasonable therefore to seek to challenge admissibility of such evidence on such grounds as:

- if a PACE interview was an option, that is the one that ought to have been used;
- a s 108 interview should only be used (it may be argued) in the case of on-site emergencies or incidents where a party is being obstructive;
- in a non-urgent investigation there is no proper excuse for not using the PACE route;
- particular objections should be taken to use of these powers *after* the summons has been issued.

1   [2000] 2 AC 412, HL.

STRICT LIABILITY

7.30   Water pollution offences under the Water Resources Act 1991, s 85 and offences under the EPA 1990, Pt I are regarded as 'strict' in the sense that once the prosecution can establish *causation* any defence is exceedingly limited in scope, eg state of emergency.

7.31 The word 'cause' where it appears in s 85 had given considerable difficulty which has now been resolved by the House of Lords in *Environment Agency (formerly National Rivers Authority) v Empress Car Co (Abertillery) Ltd.*[1] In giving the leading judgment, Lord Hoffmann identified five principles relating to 'causing'. These principles can be summarised as follows:

(1)   The prosecution must identify what it says that the defendant did to cause the pollution.

(2)   The prosecution is not required to show that the defendant's actions were the immediate cause of the pollution. Maintaining the sewage systems is doing something even though the immediate cause of the pollution may be a lack of maintenance, a natural event, or the act of a third party.

(3)   Where the prosecution has established that the defendant did do something, the court must decide whether it 'caused' the pollution. To say that something else caused the pollution, for example an act of vandalism, is not inconsistent with the defendant having caused it as well.

(4)   Where the defendant claims that the pollution was caused by the act of a third party or a natural event, the court must consider whether the act or event is a normal fact of life or something extraordinary. An ordinary act or event will not negate the causal effect. An extraordinary event may break the chain of causation.

(5)   The distinction between ordinary and extraordinary is one of fact and degree and will be determined by the court applying their common sense and knowledge of what happens in the area.

1   [1999] 2 AC 22, HL.

7.32 Waste offences under the EPA 1990, s 33 are in some cases subject to a 'knowingly' element. In *Ashcroft v Cambro Waste Products*[1] it was held that this means knowledge of the facts, not knowledge that an offence has been committed; this was approved more recently in *Shanks v McEwan (Teesside) Ltd v Environmental Agency.*[2]

1   [1981] 1 WLR 1349.
2   [1997] Env LR 305.

7.33 The much used offence of dealing with waste in a manner likely to cause pollution under the EPA 1990, s 33(1)(c) is usually strict in that licence conditions are drafted in strict terms. There are, however, defences under s 33(7) including the defence that the defendant took 'all reasonable precautions and exercised all due diligence to avoid the commission of the offence'.

7.34 The 'remediation' offences under the EPA 1990, Pt IIA are based on the concept of 'caused or knowingly permitted' and this phrase has not yet been tested by the courts within that particular statutory framework. It may be assumed that liability for 'causing' is strict, but there are various circumstances (set out in the Guidance which is incorporated) where the person who caused can be excluded from liability; save only where such a person is the *only person* in his or her liability class, where the person will be responsible regardless of knowledge. In this particular context, the expression 'knowingly permit' is bound to cause difficulty and will need interpretation by the courts.

7.35   Offences of strict or nearly strict liability are difficult to defend. Culpability is relevant in the sentencing process and, for this reason, has a significant bearing on questions of plea bargaining.[1]

1   See paras **7.58–7.61** below.

DEFENCES TO ENVIRONMENTAL CRIMES

Overview

7.36   The rigour of some environmental offences has been softened by the inclusion in the statute which created such offences of specific defences to the particular charge (as with the 'due diligence' defence in the EPA 1990, s 33[1]). These vary from statute to statute. For example, there are no statutory defences to a charge under the EPA 1990, s 23(1)(a) of operating a prescribed process without authorisation to do so.

1   See para **7.33** above and paras **7.39–7.42** below.

7.37   Thus UK environmental law is ambivalent in its approach to providing defences to a charge. In some areas – for example, waste management, supplying unfit drinking water and dumping at sea – it will be a defence for the accused to show that he or she has taken all reasonable precautions and exercised all due diligence to avoid the commission of the offence (the 'due diligence' defence). For other offences – such as polluting control waters under the WRA 1991, s 85(1) – no such defence exists. There seems to be no logical pattern to this legislative process.

7.38   Where no defence is provided there may be common law defences available, such as the defences of necessity, act of God or act of a third party. However, there is, in reality, little scope for such defences in the case of environmental offences. The *Empress Car* case[1] shows, for example, that it will be very difficult successfully to deploy a defence of act by a third party.

1   [1999] 2 AC 22, HL. See para **7.31** above.

The 'due diligence' defence

7.39   The 'due diligence' defence places the onus on the accused to show that they acted without negligence. For example, in the case of an EPA 1990, s 33 waste management offence the court may look at the size of the business involved to determine the extent of the precautions they should have taken as against the risks the precautions are supposed to avoid. The 'risks' here are environmental pollution or harm to health. The 'precautions' will be based on those set out in the Code of Practice on the duty of care under s 34 of the EPA 1990. In addition, a court would look at Waste Management Papers. However, while a court may look at the size of a firm in determining the extent of precautions, it may well consider that, given the inherent risks, a small business should not be involved in the particular type of operation at all if it cannot fund the relevant precautions.

7.40 To establish the defence it will have to be shown that a system has been created that could rationally be said to be so designed that the commission of the offence would be avoided: *Tesco Supermarkets Ltd v Nattrass*.[1] The system can have two bases. It can be an enquiry to responsible persons, such as the Agency, as to whether a particular course of action would constitute an offence. As long as all relevant information is given to the Agency then, particularly for a small operator, the defence should succeed: see *Riley v Webb*,[2] although a defendant will not be allowed to shift responsibility for his or her actions to the Agency.

1 [1972] AC 153 at 180F, HL.
2 (1987) 151 JP 372.

7.41 Alternatively, the firm should establish its own system for compliance with the relevant legislation. It will have to be a thorough one that takes account of Government guidance and standards in the industry. Where, for example, sampling of incoming waste is required, the system will depend on checking the waste involved and its origin, but a court will expect it to be more than an occasional check unless the standard of waste is always the same. Once the system is established it should be properly supervised to ensure that it operates effectively. The best written procedures are no good if no one enforces them in practice.

7.42 If a company has established a proper system of control which fails because of the actions of an employee then, as long as they can show that the system was being operated properly and that they had exercised all due diligence in relation to it, they will succeed in making out their defence: see *Tesco*.[1] However, it is not an easy thing to do. In *Naish v Gore*[2] Lord Widgery said that justices examining a seller's defence under the Trade Descriptions Act 1968, s 24 should be meticulous in considering all the courses which the seller might have adopted to prevent the offence being committed. This line of argument is likely to be adopted by the courts in relation to environmental offences.

1 [1972] AC 153 at 180F, HL, at para **7.40** above.
2 [1972] RTR 102.

Emergencies

7.43 As the EPA 1990, s 33(7)(c) provides a defence where the defendant can show that the acts alleged which constitute the contravention were done in an emergency in order to avoid danger to the public and that, as soon as reasonably practicable, after they were done, particulars of them were furnished to the relevant authority. In *Larchbank v British Petrol*[1] an 'emergency' was considered to be 'a condition of things causing a reasonable apprehension of the near approach of danger'. However, if the emergency was caused as a result of the defendant's own negligence the defence may not be available, while the measures taken to deal with it must be proportionate to the risks involved. More recently in *Express Ltd (t/a Express Dairies Distribution) v Environment Agency*[2] the court looked at where the 'emergency' occurred in the chain of causation.

1   [1943] AC 299, HL.
2   [2003] Env LR 654.

CHALLENGING THE INDICTMENT

7.44   Culpability is of the greatest importance in sentencing. Where a strict liability offence has been committed, such that the defendant must plead guilty to something, it is important to establish the extent of the culpability. This can be approached by particularising the indictment or by establishing clearly the basis of the plea of guilty.

7.45   Prosecuting authorities, perhaps fearing criticism for having too many charges, sometimes use a charge that is so broad-brush that matters of importance are left unclear.

7.46   The Indictments Act 1915, s 3 requires that every indictment shall contain a statement of the specific offence or offences with which the accused person is charged together with 'such particulars as may be necessary for giving reasonable information as to the nature of the charge'. This is broadly repeated in the Indictment Rules 1971.[1]

1   R 5(1).

7.47   In *R v Warburton-Pitt*[1] the Court of Appeal said:[2]

'In our opinion, it is incumbent upon the prosecution, in such a case as this, to particularise the facts upon which they rely in support of their allegations of recklessness and negligence, so that the defence know at the outset what the case is that they have to meet ... where the prosecution fails to do this, it is always open to the defence to apply for such particulars and, if need be, for the trial judge to order that they should be provided before arraignment. Even without application from the defence, there may be cases where the trial judge himself should direct the prosecution to particularise their allegations. However it is done, the particulars should be reduced to writing so that there is no doubt in anyone's mind what the case is about.'

1   (1990) 92 Cr App Rep 136, CA.
2   At 139.

7.48   The proper time for making an application to quash an indictment for a defect is before the plea is made. In practical terms, however, an indictment will not be quashed; it will merely be cured by amending to supply such particularity as will enable the defence to know the case it has to meet (and perhaps also to enable the judge to know the basis upon which he will have to sentence).

SENTENCE

R v F Howe & Son (Engineers) Ltd

7.49   The principal case on sentencing for environmental offences is *R v F Howe & Son (Engineers) Ltd.*[1] In that case the Court of Appeal set out sentencing guidelines for health and safety financial penalties and broadly held that the relevant facts were as follows:
- In assessing the gravity, regard should be had as to how far short of the appropriate standard the defendant fell.
- Deliberately breaching legislation with a view to financial profit seriously aggravates the offence.
- The size of a company and its financial strength or weakness cannot affect the degree of care that is required.
- The degree of risk and extent of danger created by the offence.
- Whether the offence was an isolated incident or continued over a period of time.
- The resources of the defendant and the effect of the fine on its business.

1   [1999] 2 All ER 249.

7.50   In addition to the above, the Court of Appeal identified other aggravating features, including:
- a failure to heed warnings; and
- where a defendant had deliberately profited financially from a failure to take the necessary measures, or has run a risk to save money.

7.51   Particular mitigating factors included:
- a prompt admission of responsibility and a timely plea of guilty;
- steps to remedy deficiencies after they have been drawn to the defendant's attention;
- a good record.

The Sea Empress

7.52   In 1996 the 77,000 tonne tanker 'Sea Empress' struck mid-Channel rocks when attempting to enter the port of Milford Haven. The resultant oil spillage of some 70,000 tonnes was a catastrophe. There was a fishing ban in the area for months. There was a significant impact on the bird population. The total cost of the clean-up operation was estimated at £60 million and, as the trial judge, Mr Justice Steel, pointed out in sentencing Milford Haven Port Authority to a fine of £4 million, the figure (of £60 million) 'does not reflect the financial impact on tourism or commercial fisheries measured in total in further tens of millions of pounds'.

7.53   In February 2000 the Court of Appeal allowed the Port Authority's appeal against the fine and reduced it to £750,000. It was argued on behalf of the Port Authority that Steel J had erred in a number of important respects in setting the level of the fine at £4 million. In summary, the submissions that found favour with the Court of Appeal, may be set out as follows:

- The judge gave inadequate recognition to the relative lack of culpability of the Port Authority.
- The judge was wrong to deny the Port Authority full credit for its plea of guilty.
- The status of the Port Authority as a public trust was relevant to the issue of assessing the appropriate level of fine.
- The judge misunderstood the financial position of the Port Authority.

7.54   The Court of Appeal clearly found the argument that there had been no admission of fault on the part of the Port Authority convincing, although it did point out (as relevant to possible offences in the future):

'... Although the Port Authority is fully entitled to rely strongly on its relative lack of culpability – *and its position would be very much more vulnerable if it were unable so to rely* – it cannot reasonably hope to escape a very substantial financial penalty when its commission of an offence against the section has such serious results.'[1]

1   From Transcript. Emphasis added.

7.55   The Port Authority faced two counts on the Indictment. One was a count of public nuisance, which is fault-driven. The other was causing water pollution under the WRA 1991, s 85. In negotiating a plea bargain whereby the public nuisance count was not pursued the prosecution was effectively abandoning a case on *fault*. Therefore sentencing could only be based on *gravity of consequences*.

7.56   In March 2000 the Sentencing Advisory Panel issued advice to the Court of Appeal on sentencing in respect of environmental offences. In the *Sea Empress*[1] case the Court of Appeal explicitly declined to accept such guidance, stating that the guidance already set out in *Howe Engineers*[2] would be sufficient so long as it was borne in mind that health and safety and environmental offences are not completely analogous because, in the former, people are killed or seriously injured whereas in the latter only the environment is harmed.

1   *R v Milford Haven Port Authority* [2000] Env LR 632.
2   [1999] 2 All ER 249.

Summary

7.57   In short, it now appears that £750,000 is the maximum fine based on the gravity of the environmental damage caused. If the fine is to be significantly higher than this, the prosecution will need to establish a significant degree of culpability on the part of the defendant.

THE PLEA BARGAIN

7.58 The *Sea Empress* negotiations took months. In the end, prosecution and defence not only negotiated the plea of guilty to one offence and not guilty to the other, but also most of the factual averments that should be put before the court in the sentencing process.

7.59 Not only the issue of culpability, but all the *Howe Engineers*[1] issues, are capable of being controversial. The Court of Appeal has now held that in cases involving prosecutions under the Health and Safety at Work Act 1974 in which a guilty plea is entered, the parties must attempt to agree the relevant mitigating and aggravating features in writing so that there would be no doubt about the basis upon which the court was sentencing. If there is a disagreement of substance the court could then conduct a *Newton* hearing: *R v Friskies Petcare (UK) Ltd.*[1]

1   [1999] 2 All ER 249, CA. See para **7.49** above.
2   [2000] 2 Cr App Rep (S) 401, CA.

7.60 It now follows that in environmental cases, as in health and safety cases, the prosecuting authority will typically serve a so-called 'Friskies' statement of aggravating facts upon which it intends to rely, and which it intends to draw to the attention of the sentencing court. Where the defendant company responds that it contests an assertion – for example that the company acted deliberately, or that the company was putting profit before environment – then the prosecution will have to decide whether to pursue the assertion, in which case oral evidence will have to be heard in a mini-trial by the sentencing judge (called a '*Newton*' hearing), or whether it will drop it.

7.61 Practitioners should be on their guard, first, to be aware of averments which are really significant in the sense of influencing sentence; and second, to see that the proceedings, whether by means of the way in which the Indictment is drawn, or by means of 'Friskies' statements, are conducted so that the sentencing court is left in no doubt as to the factual basis on which the sentence is to be handed down.

THE DEFENDANT'S MEANS

7.62 In the *Howe Engineers*[1] case the Court of Appeal stated that where accounts or other financial information had deliberately not been supplied by the defendant, the court would be entitled to assume that the company is in a position to pay any financial penalty the court is minded to impose.

1   [1999] 2 All ER 249. See paras **7.49–7.51** above.

7.63   In other words, in a case where the defendant company's survival may be put at risk by a fine of the sort of size that may be in play, the defendant will have to prove that fact, and that means expert accountancy evidence and proper disclosure. The prosecuting authority is perfectly entitled to analyse this material, and if not served in advance of the hearing, could apply for an adjournment so as to conduct a proper analysis for the assistance of the court.

COSTS

7.64   A court normally makes an order for costs in favour of the prosecuting agency. Such an order reflects the costs of the investigation, together with file preparation and presentation costs, the benchmark being 'the sum which the prosecutor has actually and reasonably incurred'. Relevant principles are set out by the Court of Appeal in *R v Associated Octel Co Ltd*[1] and have been reviewed recently in *R v Northallerton Magistrates' Court, ex p Dove*.[2] According-ing to the latter case, the order for costs ordinarily should not be disproportion-ate to the level of fine imposed. It was held that the court should fix the level of the fine first, then consider awarding compensation, and then determine the costs. If the total sum exceeds the defendant's means, the order for costs should be reduced rather than the fine. Compensation should take priority over both the fine and costs.

1   [1997] 1 Cr App Rep (S) 435, CA.
2   [2000] 1 Cr App Rep (S) 136, DC.

DISQUALIFICATION

7.65   Practitioners should bear in mind that where a company officer is convicted, the court may wish to exercise its power to make an order to disqualify the defendant from acting as a company director for a specified period of up to 10 years.

PRIVATE PROSECUTIONS

7.66   The Prosecution of Offences Act 1985, s 6 provides that any person may institute and conduct any criminal proceedings save where a statute expressly limits this right. The point needs to be made that in all private prosecutions both the Attorney General and the Director of Public Prosecutions ('DPP') have a right to take over and either continue the prosecution themselves, or close down the prosecution.

7.67   An example of the DPP taking over a prosecution arose out of the Camelford water pollution incident in 1987. The Anglers' Co-operative Asso-ciation ('ACA') initiated a private prosecution in respect of damage to fish under the Salmon and Freshwater Fisheries Act 1975, s 4 and the Control of

Pollution Act 1974, s 32. The DPP took it over, added the public nuisance charge, and prosecuted South West Water to conviction. We do not know whether the DPP would have acted but for the ACA's initiative, but it is interesting to note that in the *Sea Empress* case,[1] Friends of the Earth publicly stated that if the prosecuting authority failed to take criminal proceedings it, Friends of the Earth, would bring a private prosecution. In the event, as stated above, the Environment Agency brought charges of public nuisance, and under the WRA 1991, s 85.

1   See paras **7.52–7.56** above.

7.68   Neither the EPA 1990 nor the WRA 1991 contains any express restriction on private prosecutions, but wherever a private prosecution is contemplated, it will be necessary to check the enactment. It is rare for there to be prohibition on private prosecution. Where it occurs, the restriction will normally involve seeking the consent of the DPP to the prosecution.

7.69   The first private prosecution for freshwater pollution appears to be that of *Wales v Thames Water Authority*[1] in 1987. There, a private prosecution was successfully instituted by the Anglers' Association under the Control of Pollution Act 1974, s 34(5) in respect of various breaches of the discharge consents from a sewage plant.

1   Unreported.

7.70   In 1991, the environmental protection group Greenpeace prosecuted Albright and Wilson, a chemical company, for breaches of its consent limits for zinc, chromium, copper and nickel (discharges into the Irish Sea). The defendant company vigorously contested this prosecution but on 31 August 1991 was convicted by the Whitehaven Justices and fined £2,000. It was further ordered to pay substantial costs.

7.71   There seem to be no cases on private prosecution in relation to air pollution and waste disposal.[1] There are, of course, numerous instances of private prosecutions in magistrates' courts for statutory nuisances, particularly noise.

1   See the specific offences outlined at paras **7.03** and **7.06** above.

7.72   A major difficulty in pursuing a private prosecution is that public funding is not available to prepare the case. It is, however, possible that legal expenses insurance may cover such a prosecution. In cases where funding is available to mount a prosecution, there are good reasons why this may be an appropriate route as part and parcel of the strategy of seeking redress for an environmental wrong.

● Interlocutory procedures involving discovery, particulars and interrogatories are not generally so cumbersome in prosecutions as can be the case in environmental civil litigation, with the result that criminal cases tend to come to trial sooner and are less expensive than civil proceedings.

- The second advantage is that there may be cases in which it is felt that it would be more desirable to have a jury considering the case than a judge. A jury will very rarely be available in a civil action, but where the justices commit a prosecution to the Crown Court in criminal proceedings, which is highly likely in any case of unusual gravity or complexity, then a jury will determine the verdict.
- A conviction can be relied upon in a civil claim.[1]

1   See para **7.73** below.

7.73   A conviction in a criminal court is admissible as evidence in a civil court and may therefore be used to advance a claim for damages in nuisance or negligence.[1]

1   See the Civil Evidence Act 1968, s 11.

7.74   The conviction is not conclusive of the issue in the civil proceedings, even where the issue is the same, but, unless the defendant can establish that the conviction was in some material sense irrelevant, or arrived at on the basis of irregularity (in which case the civil judge will expect it to have been successfully appealed), it is highly unlikely that the civil judge will arrive at a finding inconsistent with it, particularly taking into account that the standard of proof upon which the defendant has been convicted in the criminal court is significantly higher than the standard of proof in the civil court.

PART II

Practice and procedure

CHAPTER 8

Access to environmental information

INTRODUCTION

8.01 This chapter is concerned with access to information on the environment. The UK has a Freedom of Information Act 2000 for central government, however it is not yet in force, although one is in operation for local government.[1] The EU Directive on Freedom of Access to Information on the Environment,[2] as well as the most recent UK legislation referred to below, has started an irresistible move to confirm the right of the citizen, pressure group, company or state agency to know much more about the environment. The concept of a 'right' to environmental information is crucial because it improves environmental monitoring systems, increases the quality of environmental information which is gathered, and makes much of that information available to the public. These effects will, in turn, increase public participation in the procedures to control pollution, including the enforcement of environmental laws.

1 Local Government (Access to Information) Act 1985 ('LG(AI)A 1985').
2 The Directive was adopted by the Council of Ministers on 7 June 1990 (90/313/EEC OJ 1990 L158/56, 23 June 1990).

REGISTERS

8.02 The provision for the keeping of registers of environmental information which are available to the public is one now well established in English law. Thus local planning authorities are required to keep registers of all planning applications[1] and conditions imposed on planning permissions are registerable in the Local Land Charges Register.[2]

1 Town and Country Planning Act 1990, s 69.
2 Local Land Charges Act 1975, s 1(1)(b)(i). As to conditions imposed by planning permissions before 1 August 1977, see s 2(e).

8.03   Furthermore, what are now ss 100A–100K of the Local Government Act 1972 ('LGA 1972') (introduced by the LG(AI)A 1985) make minutes of committee decisions available to the public, together with reports and documents relating to the decision-making process. The Environmental Protection Act 1990 ('EPA 1990'), s 20 requires each local authority to set up a register giving details of all integrated pollution control ('IPC') and local authority air pollution controlled processes in its area. These must include prescribed particulars of applications, authorisations, notices, directions issued by the Secretary of State, revocations, appeal decisions, process data, convictions for certain offences and other particulars as prescribed by regulation of, or relating to, the matters set out in the Act.

8.04   Local authorities must also supply the information under their own control in respect of local authority air pollution control applications. Information relating to IPC processes is supplied to local authorities by the Environment Agency. The information is to be kept from the register only on grounds of national security or commercial confidentiality.[1] Information on noise data can also be obtained from local authority environmental health departments under the Control of Noise (Measurement and Registers) Regulations 1976[2] and the Control of Industrial Air Pollution (Registration of Works) Regulations 1989.[3] The EPA 1990, s 78R provides that each enforcing authority is required to keep a public register of information in relation to Pt IIA relating to contaminated land. Schedule 3 to the Contaminated Land (England) Regulations 2000[4] sets out the details of the information which is to be kept on the register. These include particulars of remediation statements, declarations and notices, appeals, convictions, notices in relation to special sites and information about remediation work notified to the authority although there is no official guarantee of compliance with remediation notices.

1   EPA 1990, ss 21–22; the Environmental Protection (Applications, Appeals and Registers) Regulations 1991, SI 1991/507; and GGN3 – Applications and Registers (DOE).
2   SI 1976/37.
3   SI 1989/318.
4   SI 2000/227.

8.05   The EPA 1990, s 20 also requires the Environment Agency to keep a register of all applications made under the EPA 1990, Pt I, as it is responsible for granting authorisations for the largest and most complex industrial plants. A local authority whose area adjoins that of a Port Health Authority must include in its register corresponding information contained in the Port Authority's register. So far as water discharges are concerned, the local authority's register must also contain prescribed particulars with such information as is contained in any register maintained by the Environment Agency as relates to the carrying on in the area of the local authority of a prescribed process in relation to which the Agency has functions under Pt I of the EPA 1990.

8.06   The Environment Agency has a duty to maintain registers containing prescribed particulars of abstraction and impounding licences, for the purposes of works discharges, details of persons and premises, prescribed particulars of water quality objectives, applications for consents, consents given and information produced by analysis of water samples, amongst other matters.[1]

1   Water Resources Act 1991 ('WRA 1991'), ss 189–191; Control of Pollution (Applications, Appeals and Registers) Regulations 1996, SI 1996/2971.

8.07   Waste regulation authorities are required by the EPA 1990, ss 64–66 to maintain a register containing prescribed particulars of or in relation to current or recently current applications to the authority along with modification applications, notices issued by the authority, appeals, certificates of completion, convictions for any offence under the EPA 1990, Pt II and various other matters. There are detailed provisions relating to the exclusion of information affecting national security and certain confidential information. There is a separate duty on each waste regulation authority to establish and maintain a register of carriers of controlled waste which is open to public inspection free of charge, and indexed and arranged in such a way as to enable members of the public readily to trace information contained in it.[1]

1   Controlled Waste (Registration of Carriers and Seizure of Vehicles) Regulations 1991, SI 1991/1624 as amended by SI 1998/605.

8.08   Sewerage undertakers are under a duty by the Water Industry Act 1991 ('WIA 1991'), s 196 to keep records about trade effluent discharge consents in respect of discharges into public sewers. Finally, every hazardous substance authority is under a duty to keep a register with prescribed particulars relating to hazardous substances consents.[1]

1   Planning (Hazardous Substances) Act 1990, s 28.

THE ENVIRONMENTAL INFORMATION REGULATIONS 1992

Introduction

8.09   The Environmental Information Regulations 1992[1] are designed to implement EC Directive 90/313/EEC.[2] They differ little from the draft Regulations sent out for consultation on 29 October 1992 (apart from widening the exemption relating to legal proceedings discussed below). The Regulations came into force on 31 December 1992 and apply to Great Britain only.

1   SI 1992/3240.
2   OJ 1990 L158/56, 23.06.90.

The effect of EU law

8.10   Before discussing the Regulations in detail it is important to bear in mind what effect EU law has on their application and construction. First, the courts must give effect to the EC Directive in construing the Regulations.[1]

Second, in any event the Directive may be directly applicable and an aggrieved person would have a separate cause of action against the UK Government under the Directive itself.[2] Finally, under EC law the UK Government is liable to pay compensation to an aggrieved party for its failure fully to implement an EC Directive.[3]

1   *Litster v Forth Dry Dock and Engineering Co* [1990] 1 AC 546, HL.
2   *Van Duyn v Home Office: 41/74* [1974] ECR 1337, ECJ.
3   *Francovich and Bonifaci v Italy: C-6, 9/90* [1992] IRLR 84, ECJ.

Application of Regulations

8.11   By reg 2(1) the Regulations apply to any information which:
(a)   relates to the environment;
(b)   is held by a relevant person in an accessible form and otherwise than for the purposes of any judicial or legislative functions; and
(c)   is not (apart from these Regulations) either:
      (i)   information which is required, in accordance with any statutory provision, to be provided on request to every person who makes a request; or
      (ii)   information contained in records which are required, in accordance with any statutory provision, to be made available for inspection by every person who wishes to inspect them.[1]

1   SI 1992/3240, reg 2(2).

8.12   Information relates to the environment if, and only if, it relates to any of the following, that is to say:
●   the state of any water or air, the state of flora or fauna, the state of any soil or the state of any natural site or other land;
●   any activities or measures (including activities giving rise to noise or any other nuisance) which adversely affect anything mentioned in paragraph (a) above or are likely adversely to affect anything so mentioned;
●   any activities or administrative or other measures (including any environmental management programmes) which are designed to protect anything so mentioned.

8.13   Regulation 2(1) is based on Article 2a of the EC Directive which defines 'information relating to the environment' as meaning:

'Any available information in written, visual, aural or database form on the state of water, air, soil, fauna, flora, land and natural sites, and on activities (including those which give rise to nuisances such as noise) or measures adversely affecting or likely so to affect these, and on activities or measures designed to protect these, including administrative measures and environmental management programmes.'

8.14   Although wide, this definition does not include climatic changes nor human conditions in the aftermath of an environmental disaster, for example, the Camelford water pollution case. It does, however, cover environmental damage which is likely to occur as well as that which has already occurred. It would not cover activities where there is no *adverse* impact, or where it is considered unlikely there will be an adverse impact. Furthermore, a literal reading of the listed media would exclude, for example, microbial and bacteriological life-forms which may not be regarded as fauna but whose functioning may be essential to the environment.

8.15 Regulation 2(1)(b) is amplified by reg 2(3) which defines relevant persons as:
(a) all such Ministers of the Crown, government departments, local authorities and other persons carrying out functions of public administration at a national, regional or local level as, for the purposes of or in connection with their functions, have responsibilities in relation to the environment; and
(b) any body with public responsibilities for the environment which does not fall within paragraph (a) above but is under the control of a person falling within that paragraph.

8.16 The word 'as' in the third line of reg 2(3) is assumed to be a misprint for 'and' which is the word used in the draft Regulations sent out for consultation.

8.17 Whilst paragraph (a) is clear, the same cannot be said for paragraph (b). This is provided to implement Article 6 of the EC Directive. The DOE Consultation Paper Annexe D listed a substantial number of 'public bodies' with responsibilities for the environment. There are some obvious omissions, for example, BNFL, and the privatised water and sewerage companies which are not *public* bodies but do have public environmental responsibilities. The water companies are also subject to considerable supervision by the Secretary of State and Ofwat. Other bodies are npower, PowerGen and British Gas. A literal interpretation of the phrases, 'any body with public responsibilities for the environment' and 'under the control of a person' within paragraph (a) means the exclusion of these bodies. In some cases the regulatory agency itself, for example, Ofwat and Ofgem, is included while the private bodies they regulate are not. Given the massive effect which the activities of the bodies named above can have on the environment it makes no sense at all to exclude them. Whether they are excluded is a matter for the courts.

8.18 Regulation 2(1)(c) is further amplified by reg 2(4) which provides:

'(4) In these Regulations—
"Information" includes registers, reports and returns, as well as computer records and other records kept otherwise than in a document; and
"statutory provision" means any provision made by or under any enactment.'

8.19 It is not clear whether this covers precisely the same ground covered by Article 2a,[1] but as the Regulations have to be interpreted to conform with the

EU Directive attempts to exclude, for example, visual or aural forms must be included within the word 'information'.

1   Set out at para **8.13** above.

The duty to make environmental information available

8.20   Every relevant person who holds any information to which the Regulations apply 'shall make that information available to every person who requests it'.[1] The duty is owed to the person requesting the information,[2] and it is that person who will have the legal interest to take proceedings to enforce the right.

1   SI 1992/3240, reg 3(1).
2   SI 1992/3240, reg 3(6).

8.21   That primary duty is made effective by reg 3(2), which imposes a further duty on every relevant person to make arrangements to give effect to the primary duty to ensure:
(a)   that every request made for the purposes of reg 3(1) is responded to as soon as possible;
(b)   that no such request is responded to more than two months after it is made; and
(c)   that, where the response to such a request contains a refusal to make information available, the refusal is in writing and specifies the reason for the refusal.

8.22   The Regulations themselves do not give any further guidance as to how these arrangements are to have effect in practice. The Guidance Notes issued by the DOE with the Regulations[1] say that such guidance is impossible to give in a way which will cover all situations. General guidance is given to the extent that each relevant person is advised to report what information is available by means, for example, of an annual report, and consideration should be given to publishing reports of information. The public register system is again commended[2] and the necessity for answering personal requests is emphasised.[3] However, if it is not known what information exists it is extremely difficult to know what information may be asked for!

1   'Guidance on the Implementation of the Environmental Information Regulations 1992 in Great Britain' (DOE, 21 December 1992).
2   Guidance Notes, para 26.
3   Guidance Notes, para 27.

8.23   Provision is made in reg 3 to enable the relevant person:
(a)   to refuse a request for information in cases where a request is manifestly unreasonable or is formulated in too general a manner;[1]
(b)   to include provision for the imposition of a charge in respect of the costs reasonably attributable to the supply of information;[2]
(c)   to make the supply of any information conditional on the payment of such a charge;[3] and

(d)   to make the information available in such form, and at such times and places, as may be reasonable.[4]

1   SI 1992/3240, reg 3(3).
2   SI 1992/3240, reg 3(4)(a).
3   SI 1992/3240, reg 3(4)(b).
4   SI 1992/3240, reg 3(5).

8.24   A literal interpretation of this provision could drive a coach and horses straight through the Regulations. If there is no clear published index of information on the environment by the relevant person concerned, how on earth can an interested person know what to ask for? The relevant person decides whether or not the request is 'manifestly unreasonable' or 'is formulated in too general a manner'. Such an administrative decision could only be challenged by political pressure or by way of judicial review.

Exceptions to disclosure

8.25   Regulation 4(3) lists the cases under which requested information must be treated as confidential. They are as follows:
(1)   The information is capable of being treated as confidential and its disclosure in response to a request would (apart from reg 3(7)) contravene any statutory provision or rule of law or would involve a breach of any agreement.[1]
(2)   The information is personal information contained in records held in relation to an individual who has not given his consent to its disclosure.[2]

1   SI 1992/3240, reg 4(3)(a).
2   SI 1992/3240, reg 4(3)(b).

8.26   The DOE Guidance Notes make it clear that personal information should not be withheld when there are provisions to the contrary, for example, information supplied under the Environmental Protection (Stray Dogs) Regulations 1992.[1] The DOE Guidance Notes go on to say that unless there is provision to the contrary, information containing the addresses of individual dwellings should be restricted in order to safeguard the property against possible blighting (the standard property information form used by solicitors tends to incorporate such information when it becomes publicly available). Examples would be radon tests (where householders are told the test results will not be released) and the quality of drinking water supplies serving single dwellings for domestic purposes only. In such cases it should be possible to release summary information or remove reference to the actual address and release the remaining information.

1   SI 1992/288.

8.27   (3) Another case is where information is held by the relevant person in consequence of having been supplied by a person who was not under, and could not have been put under, any legal obligation to supply it to the relevant person and has not consented to its disclosure.[1] The justification for this exception is that it would inhibit the 'present open and constructive discussion between environmental control authorities and industry and the gathering of information on which environmental studies are based'. It is difficult to see how the honest exchange of information and views between Government and industry can be inhibited by the publication of that kind of information.

1   SI 1992/3240, reg 4(3)(c).

8.28   (4) The final case is where the disclosure of the information in response to that request would, in the circumstances, increase the likelihood of damage to the environment affecting anything to which the information relates.[1] The examples given in the DOE Guidance Notes are non-contentious: information about the location of nesting sites, rare habitats, or endangered/protected species. Also included is information about possible Sites of Special Scientific Interest not being made available until a formal notice is served, thereby avoiding the risk of pre-emptive damage being caused to the site before it was protected. However, the phraseology of the exception would enable a much broader view to be taken by a relevant person in refusing to grant disclosure of information.

1   SI 1992/3240, reg 4(3)(d).

Information which may be treated as confidential

8.29   Regulation 4(2) sets out the following additional cases where requested information *may* be treated as confidential. These are:
(1)   information relating to matters affecting international relations, national defence or public security;[1]
(2)   information relating to, or to anything which is or has been the subject of, any legal or other proceedings (whether actual or prospective).[2] This definition is greatly extended by reg 4(5) which defines 'legal or other proceedings' as including

> 'any disciplinary proceedings, the proceedings at any local or other public inquiry and the proceedings at any hearing conducted by a person appointed under any enactment for the purpose of affording an opportunity to persons to make representations or objections with respect to any matters'.

1   SI 1992/3240, reg 4(2)(a).
2   SI 1992/3240, reg 4(2)(b).

8.30   Whilst there are clearly strong arguments in favour of some limitation on the disclosure of information in relation to prospective (particularly criminal) proceedings and proceedings which are actually taking place, it is difficult to see what justification there can be for refusing to release information which relates to proceedings which are completed. Even where proceedings have not yet been commenced it is difficult to see why, for example, a government department such as DEFRA should be entitled to refuse to disclose information which will assist one or either party in civil litigation in which DEFRA itself is not involved. Such information would be discoverable if DEFRA itself were a party to the litigation.

8.31 (3) Another case is information relating to the confidential deliberations of any relevant person or to the contents of any internal communications of a body corporate or other undertaking or organisations.[1] Under the Local Government Act 1972, ss 100A–100K, the public has rights of access to council, committee, and subcommittee meetings and to the papers and background papers relating to those meetings. The information relating to the confidential part of such meetings may be released by a local authority. No such rights of access exist in relation to central government. Internal communications cover a wide variety of matters and according to the DOE Guidance Notes could include classified documents, information passed between officials in the course of their duties, deliberations during the decision-making process, and advice on policy and recommendations given to ministers and members. It does not need much imagination to realise how much information could be kept secret under this exception.

1   SI 1992/3240, reg 4(2)(c).

8.32 (4) A further case is information contained in a document or other record which is still in the course of completion.[1] Again, it is difficult to see the logic of this exception. The DOE Guidance Notes say this:

'Bodies may carry out their own studies including inspection, testing, evaluation, monitoring and research; data may be collected in the process. It is reasonable that access to the documents and data should await the completion of the study so that analysis and interpretation can proceed *unhindered.*'[2]

1   SI 1992/3240, reg 4(2)(d).
2   Emphasis added.

8.33 Quite why the disclosure of data should impede its analysis is unknown to us. In the case of a major public inquiry into, for example, a nuclear power station or a road-widening scheme it is important that objectors have early access to the database upon which the proposer's case is based. Experience at such inquiries suggests that a proposer is often unwilling to provide early access to such information precisely because it undermines the case put forward. There is the added complication that a relevant person can always say that a document or record is still in the course of completion.

8.34 (5) The final case is information affecting matters to which any commercial or industrial confidentiality attaches or any intellectual property.[1] The DOE Guidance Notes suggest that there are two ways of proceeding when the information has been received from a third party under contract or statute: to classify information when it is received or to classify it when access is first requested. Some guidance is given as to the procedure to be followed when adopting either approach.

1   SI 1992/3240, reg 4(2)(e).

Existing rights to information

8.35   Regulation 5 deals with information which is not covered by these Regulations but which is required under any other statutory provision to be made available to any person. There is now a duty on any relevant person to make arrangements to implement such statutory duty so as to provide a similar procedure to that required for information covered by the Regulations so as to secure:

(1)   that every request for information relating to the environment which is made for the purposes of that provision is responded to as soon as possible;

(2)   that each request is responded to within two months of being made;

(3)   that, where the response to such a request contains a refusal to make information available, the refusal is in writing and specifies the reasons for the refusal; and

(4)   that no charge that exceeds a reasonable amount is made for making information relating to the environment available in accordance with that provision.

Rights of appeal

8.36   Where a relevant person refuses a request to make information available, the refusal must be in writing and specify the reason for the refusal.[1] Examples given in the DOE Guidance Notes are:

(1)   that the organisation does not consider itself a relevant person and thus subject to the requirements of the Regulations;

(2)   that the relevant person does not consider that the information requested is 'environmental' as defined by the Regulations;

(3)   that the information requested is not held by the person;

(4)   that the information is used by the person acting in its judicial or legislative capacity; or

(5)   that one of the exemptions apply.

1   SI 1992/3240, reg 3(2)(c).

8.37   There is no statutory right of appeal given by these Regulations. Any applicant dissatisfied with the refusal by a relevant person to make information available, or who considers that a request for information has been inadequately answered or delayed may seek a remedy through judicial or administrative review, for instance, by utilising an MP, local councillor or board member, or by way of complaint (in appropriate cases) to the local or parliamentary ombudsman. On a matter of European law it may ultimately be necessary to go to the European Court of Justice.

OTHER EU DEVELOPMENTS

8.38   There is a Code of Conduct on Public Access to Commission and Council Documents. The Code of Conduct is subject to a general principle that the public should have 'the widest possible access to documents held by the Commission and the Council', although there are mandatory and discretionary exemptions to the general disclosure rule. The European Court of Justice has held that although the Code of Conduct is a voluntary document, it is capable of conferring rights on third parties and the exception should be construed in a manner which does not override the general principle.[1] Each request for documents has to be assessed individually with specific reasons given for refusal for disclosure.[2]

1   Decision 94/90 ESSC EC, Euratom.
2   *WWF UK v EC Commission: T-105/95* [1997] Env LR 242, CFI.

8.39   The European Environment Agency has adopted a Code of Conduct on access to its documents which is similar to that referred to above. It also produces periodic reports on the state of the European environment which are available from its website.[1] The European Environment Agency is closely involved with the European Environment Information and Observation Network which connects national environmental information organisations within Member States and also includes some countries outside the EU and other organisations such as the European Free Trade Association.

1   www.eea.eu.int

ENVIRONMENTAL AUDITING

8.40   This section is concerned with a number of different kinds of audits all of which have implications for access to and dissemination of information on the environment.

Company audits

8.41   The 'company audit' has been defined as:

'Partly a management tool comprising a systematic, documented, periodic and objective evaluation of how well organisations, management and equipment are performing in the environmental area with the aim of helping to safeguard the environment by facilitating management control of environmental practices and assessing and verifying compliance with company policies which would include meeting regulatory requirements. It is also a risk assessment tool for use in negotiating updated consent conditions. It highlights issues – what is at stake. It helps to give quality assurance in TQM programmes by standard setting – what can be achieved. It is the audit of existing activities and can therefore be distinguished from the environmental assessment which is a kind of audit of proposed activities. It is much wider than the compliance audit which merely looks at a detailed operating facility; it identifies areas where environmental improvements may be achieved and savings made. It tests company performance as against company policy. It can review what competitors are doing. It is undertaken with reference to performance of personnel, technology, systems and documentation and how those relate to relevant standards of practice. It is quite different from a due diligence audit consisting of procedures which lawyers use on the acquisitions, disposal and merger of companies. It is also quite different from a property environmental audit which lawyers use in connection with the purchases and sales of property. It should also be distinguished from an environmental risk assessment which is often used in connection with insurance matters to assess a production process in order to identify potential liabilities. The Environmental Audit is therefore in the nature of a Corporate Policy Audit'.[1]

1   John R Salter *Corporate Environmental Responsibility: Law and Practice* (London, Butterworths, 1992), p 148.

8.42   Before an environmental audit can be commissioned there must be a corporate environmental policy in place and available. If not, then such a policy will need to be established first. Pre-environmental audit action requires the establishment of such corporate policies and procedures by identifying key policy areas and aims and objectives, the agreement of the scope of the audit, and a timetable, setting up legal measures to ensure confidentiality and the method of reporting. The audit questionnaire will need to be agreed and the audit team given as much information as possible about site operations and conditions before arriving on site. Part of pre-environmental audit action is a records review. This is a review not only of the legal position in fact but also of all compliance measures taken by the company including health and safety, training and insurance.

8.43   This chapter is not the place to consider best practice for the carrying out of an environmental audit. There is a wealth of information obtainable through the environmental audit process, which may cover many facets of a company's activities. Some of this information will be of use to competitors and some of it may be of use to individuals or pressure groups who object to the impact of a process or a product.

Eco-audit

8.44   EC Regulation 880/92 came into force on 2 May 1992 with formal compliance for Member States by 2 November 1992. The Regulation establishes a voluntary scheme for the award of eco-labels to products with reduced environmental impact, as assessed against uniform Community criteria. The scheme's objectives are to promote the design, production, marketing, and use of such products and to improve the information available on their environmental impact to consumers, without compromising product or worker safety or significantly affecting a product's essential useful properties.

8.45 Under the Regulation, manufacturers or importers may apply for the award of an eco-label to products which meet the scheme's basic objectives and EC health, safety and environmental requirements. Food, drink and pharmaceuticals are excluded. Products manufactured by processes likely to harm significantly humans and/or the environment are not eligible; neither are products which are classified as dangerous substances or preparations under Directives 64/548EEC or 88/379EEC. The eco-label may be awarded to products containing such a substance or preparation in so far as they meet the scheme's basic objective. In the UK the Eco-labelling Board was established in July 1992 and it is the UK's competent body under the scheme. It is to the Eco-labelling Board that applications for the eco-label are to be made by the manufacturer or importer. The Eco-labelling Board consults the registers of applications maintained by the EC Commission. If the product falls within an established product group, its environmental performance is assessed by reference to the scheme's general principles and relevant product group's criteria. If a competent body decides to award an eco-label it notifies the Commission of the full results and a summary of its assessment. The Commission circulates the decision and summary to all the competent bodies of the Community. If no objections are received within 30 days the Eco-labelling Board may award an eco-label. There are procedures within the Regulations for dealing with conflicts between Member States.

8.46 The information gained in the course of assessing applications must not be divulged, although after the award of an eco-label, the name of the product, its manufacturer or importer and the reasons for awarding the eco-label may not be kept secret. The Commission must publish the following information in the Official Journal:
(1) product groups and ecological criteria, with their periods of validity;
(2) a list of products awarded an eco-label, with their manufacturers or importers and expiry dates (to be published at least annually);
(3) names and addresses of all the competent bodies;
(4) a consolidated list of all products awarded an eco-label.

8.47 In addition, Member States are required to ensure that consumers and undertakings are informed about the eco-label award scheme. References to eco-labels in advertising may be made only after their award and only in relation to the specific products concerned. Fake or misleading advertising, or the use of a label or logo which leads to confusion with the EC eco-label is banned.

Acquisition audits

8.48 An acquisition audit is undertaken by lawyers and consists of procedures used on acquisitions, disposals or mergers of companies. Its main objective is to identify potential liability exposure problems. The result of such an audit should result in a well-drawn disposal or merger agreement containing warranties and indemnities covering likely environmental risks.

Property audits

8.49   These are audits carried out on the sale and purchase of land. They are quite specific, but otherwise procedures are very much the same except that a detailed questionnaire is put by way of preliminary inquiries to the vendor's solicitors. The Environmental Information Regulations 1992[1] discussed above[2] should give much greater access to environmental information to a prospective purchaser from bodies such as the Coal Authority which keeps information about mining under or in relation to a site and English Nature which publishes a range of ecological information about sites and their surrounds.

1   SI 1992/3240.
2   See paras **8.09–8.37** above.

Risk audits

8.50   A risk audit leads to an assessment of, for example, a production process, to identify potential liabilities and problems, and is linked to an action plan resulting from the audit. It examines impairment or claims arising from environmental pollution. Such an audit would include obtaining details of general liability insurance cover with copies of declarations made to the insurer; copies of environmental risk assurance cover; environmental reports; history of accidents; health and safety records under COSHH,[1] CIMAH[2] and the EPA 1990.

1   COSHH (SI 1988/1657).
2   CIMAH (SI 1984/1902). See also DOE Guidance Note, June 1991 and HS(R)21 (Rev) 1990.

Privilege and environmental audits

The scope of legal professional privilege

8.51   This may apply whether or not litigation is contemplated or pending. Advice privilege covers communications between a lawyer in his or her professional capacity and the lawyer's client if the communications are confidential and for the purposes of seeking or giving legal advice. Those purposes have to be construed broadly, and will include communications in 'the continuum aimed at keeping [solicitor and client] informed' and 'must include advice as to what should prudently and sensibly be done in the relevant legal context'.[1]

1   *Balabel v Air India* [1988] Ch 317 at 331, CA.

'Litigation' privilege

8.52 This covers confidential communications made after litigation is commenced or even contemplated, between (a) a lawyer and his or her client, (b) a lawyer and his or her non-professional agent or (c) a lawyer and a third party, for the sole or dominant purpose of such litigation (whether for seeking or giving advice in relation to it, or for obtaining evidence to be used in it).[1]

1   *Wheeler v Le Marchant* (1881) 17 Ch D 675 at 681, CA; *Re Highgrade Traders Ltd* [1984] BCLC 151, CA; *Ventouris v Mountain* [1991] 3 All ER 472 at 475–6, CA.

8.53 The test as to whether litigation is contemplated is simply whether litigation is 'reasonably in prospect'.[1] It should be noted that the contemplated litigation need not be the particular litigation in which the discovery is being sought, but may be other litigation, involving different parties and subject-matter.[2]

1   *Waugh v British Railways Board* [1980] AC 521 at 544A, CA.
2   *Bullock v Corry* (1878) 3 QBD 356.

8.54 Given that an eco-audit may contain potentially sensitive information about, say, a company's compliance record, it is clearly important that companies are aware of how eco-audits fit into the framework of legal professional privilege.

8.55 The general principle is that documents embodying communications (including reports) between a solicitor and a non-professional servant, agent or third party are privileged if and only if coming into existence for the purposes of obtaining legal advice in existence or anticipated proceedings.[1]

1   *Seabrook v British Transport Commission* [1959] 1 WLR 509.

8.56 In *Wheeler v Le Marchant*, Jessell MR held that documents communicated to the solicitor by third parties who are not agents of the clients seeking advice:

> '... are protected where they have come into existence after litigation commenced or in contemplation, and when they have been made with a view to such litigation, either for the purpose of obtaining advice as to such litigation, or of obtaining evidence to be used in such litigation, or of obtaining information which might lead to the obtaining of such evidence. But it has never hitherto been decided that documents are protected merely because they are produced by a third person in answer to an inquiry made by the solicitor.'[1]

And Brett LJ said this:

> 'This applies to information such as a surveyor's report obtained by a solicitor with a view to giving his client legal advice, and such information is not privileged unless obtained with a view to contemplated or existing litigation.'[2]

1   (1881) 17 ChD 675 at 680–1, CA.
2   (1881) 17 ChD 675 at 683, CA.

8.57   Similarly, in *Price Waterhouse (a firm) v BCCI Holdings (Luxembourg) SA*,[1] reports prepared by bank accountants in the course of investigating problem loans were held not to be protected as (a) such were not communications between a bank and its legal advisers and (b) were not documents produced in contemplation of litigation.

1   [1992] BCLC 583.

Summary

8.58   The following propositions state the current position:
(1)   an environmental report prepared by a third party (eg an environmental consultant) will not be covered by legal advice privilege;
(2)   an environmental report prepared by a *solicitor* based on information obtained directly from the client may be covered by legal advice privilege if the report was prepared for the purposes of giving legal advice; and
(3)   an environmental report prepared by a third party (eg an environmental consultant) may be covered by litigation privilege if it was prepared after litigation is commenced or contemplated, for the sole or dominant purpose of such litigation.

Structuring eco-audits with a view to privilege

8.59   Clearly it is desirable to hive off contentious matters to an eco-audit which is not susceptible to disclosure (eg a legal eco-audit). The legal advice and the documents on which it is based should be prepared by the solicitor using information taken directly from the client. It is imperative that the purpose of the report is to obtain legal advice and that unrelated matters are not incorporated. Any non-sensitive auditing (ie matters not related to compliance with regulations/assessing exposure to third-party claims) should be carried out by independent auditors in a separate report to avoid the suggestion that the purpose of the legal eco-audit is other than to obtain legal advice. If litigation is pending or contemplated, a more comprehensive eco-audit can be carried out by a third party (eg an environmental consultant) which would then, provided it was carried out for the sole or dominant purpose of litigation, be privileged.

COMPANIES

8.60   In the UK at present the shareholders of a company – who are best placed to influence a company's policy – have no legal right to be informed of its safety and environmental record. One obvious place for publication of such information would be in the annual report. Unfortunately, few companies actually do this. Even when environmental information is included in the annual report it is often selective and inadequate.

CHAPTER 9

Using environmental experts

WHAT IS EXPERT EVIDENCE?

9.01   At common law the opinion of an expert is admissible where the subject is one upon which competency to form an opinion can only be acquired by a course of special study or experience. Expert evidence is admissible in civil cases where the Civil Evidence Act 1972 ('CEA 1972') and the Civil Procedure Rules 1998 ('CPR') apply. In criminal cases the relevant legislation is the Police and Criminal Evidence Act 1984 ('PACE') and the Criminal Justice Act 1988 ('CJA 1988').

9.02   Where the opinion of the expert is based on reports of fact, those facts, unless within the expert's own knowledge, must be proved independently. An expert's evidence is based on his or her training and experience, both of which involve the acceptance of hearsay information. However, an expert can give an opinion on the basis of such hearsay provided it relates to specific matters of which the expert does have personal knowledge or of which admissible evidence will be given by another party. An expert cannot give evidence of any particular transaction if the expert has no personal knowledge of it, but the expert can refer to such transaction as the basis of his or her opinion.[1]

1   *R v Abadom* [1983] 1 WLR 126, CA (experts could give opinion evidence based on statistics collected by others).

9.03   An expert witness is treated in exactly the same way as a witness of fact. An expert's evidence is given on oath and the expert may be cross-examined on it. It is essential to remember that the expert owes an overriding duty to the court.

9.04   Experts who give evidence theoretically do not decide the issue in the case. However, this is often unavoidable particularly where the expert evidence of one side is unchallenged. In civil cases an expert may testify on an ultimate issue subject to any common law discretion a court has to exclude particular questions.[1]

1   CEA 1972, s 3(1).

9.05 Where the issue involves other elements besides the purely scientific, an expert must confine himself or herself to scientific matters and not give his or her opinion upon the legal or general merits of the case. However, where the issue is one of science or skill, the expert, if the expert has himself or herself observed the facts, may be asked the question which the court has to decide. If the expert's opinion is based merely upon facts proved by others, then such facts should be put to the expert hypothetically but not en bloc, and the expert should be asked to assume one or more of them to be true and to state his or her opinion. Where the facts are not in dispute, then there is no practical difficulty about asking for an opinion on the issue which the court has to decide. In criminal cases, an expert opinion is inadmissible as to material which is not before the court or which has been merely reported to the expert by hearsay. It is necessary to distinguish between the issues on which the expert's opinion is sought and theories or generalisation by reference to which the expert forms his or her opinion: these may be based on data provided by others.

9.06 The results of experiments made either out of court with special reference to trial or even before the court itself may be given in evidence in corroboration, illustration or rebuttal of the opinion.

9.07 An expert may refer to textbooks or learned journals to refresh his or her memory or to correct or confirm his or her opinion. Such books or articles are not evidence as such, even though the expert describes such passages as representing his or her views, but they may be read as part of the expert's own evidence. However, a trial judge may not form an opinion based upon part of a book not referred to in evidence. Counsel may not read out particular passages as part of his or her address.

EXPERT EVIDENCE IN CIVIL PROCEEDINGS

9.08 Expert evidence is governed by Pt 35 of the CPR subject to the Overriding Objective in Pt 1. Expert evidence should be restricted to that which is reasonably required to resolve the proceedings.[1] The operation of Pt 35 must also be read with the Pre-Action Protocol and the Practice Directions. In summary form, the position is as follows:

(a) the concept of an expert is defined;[2]

(b) expert witnesses have an overriding duty to the court to which they may apply for directions. They must show that they have conformed with certain standards of objectivity;[3]

(c) the primary source of written evidence is written reports which may be supplemented by the answers to written questions directed to them by another party. The rules lay down a template for admissible reports. In general, an expert may not be called to give evidence, nor may an expert's evidence be relied on unless his or her report is disclosed. Once it has been disclosed it may be relied upon by another party;[4]

(d) the court has general control over the use of expert evidence;[5]

(e)   that control may involve:
   (i)   limiting both the scope and cost of expert evidence;[6]
   (ii) requiring disclosure of information by one party to another where the former but not the latter has already access to it;[7]
   (iii) directing that meetings take place between experts for the purpose of narrowing the dispute;[8]
   (iv) requiring that the expert evidence is to be given by a single joint expert (selected by the parties) or, in default of agreement, by the court;[9] or

(f)   appointing an assessor appointed to assist the court.[10]

1   CPR Pt 35 r 1.
2   CPR Pt 35 r 2.
3   CPR Pt 35 rr 3, 14 and 10.
4   CPR Pt 35 rr 5–6, 10–11, 13.
5   CPR Pt 35 r 4, Pt 27 r 4, Pt 28 rr 3 and 7, Pt 29 rr 2, 4–5.
6   CPR Pt 35 r 4, Pt 27 r 4, Pt 28 rr 3 and 7, Pt 29 rr 2, 4–5.
7   CPR Pt 35 r 9.
8   CPR Pt 35 r 12.
9   CPR Pt 35 r 7.
10 CPR Pt 35 r 15.

EXPERT EVIDENCE IN CRIMINAL PROCEEDINGS

9.09   The duties of an expert in a criminal case are those laid down by the common law. In practice they are not very different to those which the CPR has imposed in civil cases, and we must expect them to be assimilated more and more to those standards. The duties of an expert in civil cases were clearly set out by Cresswell J in *The Ikarian Reefer*.[1] Those duties were as follows:

(a)   Expert evidence presented to the court should be, and should be seen to be, the independent product of the expert uninfluenced as to form or content by the exigencies of litigation.

(b)   An expert witness should provide independent assistance to the court by way of objective unbiased opinion in relation to matters within the expert's expertise. An expert witness in the High Court should never assume the role of an advocate.

(c)   An expert witness should state the facts or assumptions upon which his or her opinion is based. An expert should not omit the material facts which could detract from the expert's concluded opinion.

(d)   An expert witness should make it clear when a particular question or issue falls outside his or her expertise.

(e)   If an expert's opinion is not properly researched because the expert considers that insufficient data is available, then this must be stated with an indication that the opinion is no more than a provisional one. In cases where an expert witness who has prepared a report could not assert that the report contained the truth, the whole truth and nothing but the truth without some qualification, that qualification should be stated in the report.

(f)   If after exchange of reports, an expert witness changes his or her view on a material matter having read the other side's expert's report or for any other reason, such change of view should be communicated (through legal representatives) to the other side without delay and when appropriate to the court.

(g)   Where expert evidence refers to photographs, plans, calculations, analyses, measurements, survey reports or other similar documents, these must be provided by the opposite party at the same time as the exchange of reports.

1   *National Justice Compania Naviera SA v Prudential Assurance Co Ltd* [1993] 2 Lloyd's Rep 68 at 81–82.

9.10   In magistrates' courts, the position is that expert evidence must be disclosed in advance of a hearing.[1] In any environmental case where expert evidence is considered necessary then we recommend that a Pre-Directions Hearing take place at which (amongst other things) provision can be made for the service and exchange of expert evidence on fixed timescales.

1   Magistrates' Courts (Advanced Notice of Expert Evidence) Rules 1997, SI 1997/705.

9.11   In the Crown Court, the position is regulated by the Crown Court (Advance Notice of Expert Evidence) Rules 1987[1] which provides for the disclosure of reports of experts who are to be called to give expert evidence. The prosecution and the defendant are treated in the same way. The rules provide that 'as soon as practicable' after the accused has been committed for trial, a party who wishes to adduce expert evidence must serve certain documents on all other parties (so that all co-accused must be served). The documents to be served are:

(a)   a written statement of the expert evidence intended to be adduced;

(b)   a copy of 'the record of any observation, test, calculation or other procedure of which such finding or opinion is based' carried out by an expert;[2]

(c)   the written statement of the expert evidence must always be served; the records of tests etc must only be served where there is a written request for it. In that case the defendant is able to satisfy the Rules by offering the other party 'a reasonable opportunity to examine them' if it appears more practicable. The benefit of the rule may be waived either wholly or by accepting an oral notification.[3] Furthermore, r 4 provides that 'if a party has reasonable grounds for believing' that there is a risk of intimidation of a witness or of any other type of interference of the course of justice, he or she is exonerated from the requirement of advance disclosure. In such a case the party must give written notice that he or she is withholding the expert evidence and the reason that he claims to be entitled to do so. Failure to comply with these rules results in there being no right to adduce that evidence although the trial judge has power to permit it to be given. The duty of disclosure also lies on the forensic scientist who prepares reports for the prosecution and in such a case there is a positive duty to disclose experiments which tend to disprove the prosecution case.[4]

1   SI 1987/716.
2   SI 1987/716, r 3(1).
3   SI 1987/716, r 3(2).
4   *R v Maguire* [1992] QB 936, CA; *R v Ward* (1992) 96 Cr App Rep 1, CA.

9.12   Hearsay evidence of expert opinion is admissible whether or not the expert is called to give oral evidence.[1] The evidence must be in the form of a written report prepared by a person properly qualified to give expert testimony. It is admissible for the purpose of proving any fact or opinion which the maker of the report could have given in oral evidence. Leave of the court is required to adduce the report without calling the maker. In deciding whether or not to give such leave the judge must have regard to the following matters:

(a)   the contents of the report;
(b)   the reasons why it is supposed that the person giving the report should not give oral evidence;
(c)   any risk, having regard in particular to whether it is likely to be possible to controvert statements in the report if the person making it does not attend to give oral evidence, that its admission or exclusion will result in unfairness to the accused or, if there is more than one, to any one of them;
(d)   any other circumstances that appear to the court to be relevant.

1   Criminal Justice Act 1988, s 30(1).

THE COMPETENCY OF THE EXPERT WITNESS

9.13   Whether the expert is competent to give evidence or not is a preliminary question for the judge. The expert does not have to have acquired his or her knowledge professionally; that goes to weight and not to admissibility. However, the expert must be 'skilled by special study or experience'.[1] The fact that an expert adopts an approach which will be unacceptable to the majority of experts in that field again does not mean that the expert is incapable of giving expert evidence about the topic, provided that the expert can demonstrate that his or her case is a rational one backed up by intelligent study and relevant formal qualifications.[2]

1   *R v Somers* [1963] 3 All ER 808, CCA.
2   *R v Robb* [1991] 93 Cr App Rep 161, CA.

THE VALUE OF EXPERT EVIDENCE

9.14   The expert is to furnish the judge or jury with the necessary scientific criteria showing the accuracy of his or her conclusion so as to enable the judge or jury to form their own independent judgment by the application of these criteria to the facts proved in evidence. Thus the specimen direction for circuit and High Court judges in criminal cases relating to expert evidence states that although the decision is that of the jury, they will wish to give due weight to any expert evidence given to them; they must not reject it in favour of their own intuition.

CHAPTER 10

Remedies: injunctions

INTRODUCTION

10.01 Apart from damages, there is also a remedy by way of injunction to prevent the commission of torts which are threatened or anticipated or, in cases of continuing injury, to restrain them being continued. The basic principle is that the injury to be inflicted is to be of such a character that the claimant could not practically be compensated in damages. The injunction may be a mandatory injunction, e g where the defendant has created a permanent source of injury such as the obstruction of a right of way or the continuance of a smell or water pollution by a method of work. Such an injunction orders the defendant to restore the claimant to his or her right by removing the obstruction or other source of damage.

10.02 The High Court and the county court have power to grant an injunction in cases falling within their jurisdiction. Injunctions may be granted in all cases in which it appears to the court to be 'just or convenient' to do so, but the discretion must be exercised in a judicial manner. Breach of a statutory obligation which is supported by criminal sanctions does not give rise to a tortious claim unless the court considers that such was the intention of Parliament; where no such inference is drawn (and no other private tort is made out) the court may not grant an injunction to a private individual in respect of the breach.[1]

1   A very recent example is *Worcestershire County Council v Tongue* [2003] 39 LS Gaz R 39. Neuberger J (breach of an order made by a magistrates' court disqualifying the defendant from having custody of an animal).

10.03 As we have indicated, the grant of an injunction is always discretionary and the discretion is that of the trial judge. On appeal, the Court of Appeal may not substitute its own views on the merits of the case but may intervene only 'if the judge misdirected himself in law, took into account irrelevant matters or failed to take into account relevant matters'.[1] However, it should be noted that the principles differ depending on the injunction sought. Where an injunction is sought to restrain the continuation of a wrongful act (ie a prohibitory injunction) then, absent special circumstances, the claimant is entitled to an injunction 'as of course'. The best that a defendant could ask for is a suspension of the operation of an injunction to enable him or her to take steps to bring the nuisance to an end. However, the grant of a mandatory injunction requiring the defendant to take some specific action involving, eg, the carrying out of certain works on the other hand can never be 'as of course'. It depends upon a number of factors which will be examined below.[2]

1   *Duport Steels Ltd v Sirs* [1980] 1 WLR 142 at 171, HL per Lord Scarman.
2   See para **10.05** below.

PROHIBITORY INJUNCTIONS

10.04   What happened in the past is not sufficient to entitle the claimant to obtain an injunction from the court. The court must be satisfied that the interference with the claimant's right is continuing or that it is likely to be repeated unless restrained. Unless special circumstances exist then the claimant is entitled to an injunction 'as of course'. Actual damage is not necessary as long as an actionable interference with proprietary rights is shown.[1] It is impossible to give a complete list of 'special circumstances which prevent the claimant of his prima facie right to have a prohibitory injunction'. A list of the main factors would include the following:

(a)   The claimant's own conduct is a relevant factor, eg if he or she has given consent to the acts complained of (at least until withdrawn).

(b)   The triviality of the harm suffered by the claimant may be a factor although the authorities conflict.

(c)   It is arguable that a reason for refusing an injunction would be that compliance by the defendant would be impossible or illegal. However, there is very little authority to support this argument.[2]

(d)   The social and economic effects on third parties. Here again there is conflicting authority in the Court of Appeal, but in our view the court may decide to suspend an injunction because of harm to third parties which might otherwise result.[3]

1   *Monson v Tussauds Ltd* [1894] 1 QB 671, CA.
2   *Pride of Derby, etc Ltd v British Celanese Ltd* [1953] Ch 149, CA.
3   Compare *Miller v Jackson* [1977] QB 966, CA with *Kennaway v Thompson* [1981] QB 88, CA.

MANDATORY INJUNCTIONS

10.05   A mandatory injunction is never issued 'as of course' and is *always* at the discretion of the court. In the leading case of *Redland Bricks Ltd v Morris*[1] Lord Upjohn set out the following principles governing the exercise of the court's discretion:

(a) A mandatory injunction can only be granted where the claimant shows a very strong probability that grave damage will accrue to him or her in the future if the intervention of the court is denied. The power to issue mandatory injunctions, though it should be exercised unhesitatingly in a proper case, must be used sparingly and with caution and only in cases 'in which extreme, or at all events, very serious damage' will ensue if the injunction is withheld.

(b) The damage which will follow a refusal of an injunction must be such that the damages awarded in respect of it would not be a sufficient remedy.

(c) Relief will be refused where compliance by the defendant would be illegal. Moreover the cost to the defendant of compliance with a mandatory injunction must be taken into account. However, considerations of cost are irrelevant if the defendant has acted wantonly or unreasonably in relation to the claimant's rights or has tried to steal a march on the claimant or on the court.

(d) If, in the exercise of its discretion a court decides that the case is a proper one for the issue of a mandatory injunction, then the court must be careful to see that the defendant knows exactly what he or she has to do, not just as a matter of law but as a matter of fact, so that in carrying out the order of the court the defendant can give his or her contractors the proper instructions.

1   [1970] AC 652 at 665–666, HL.

QUIA TIMET INJUNCTIONS

10.06 Normally the claimant cannot apply to the court for an injunction before the cause of action has accrued. Thus damages cannot be awarded where no damage has actually occurred yet. However, the court does have the power in certain circumstances to issue a Quia Timet injunction to restrain conduct which, if permitted, would almost certainly lead to substantial damage to the claimant. The power to grant a Quia Timet injunction extends to both prohibitory and mandatory injunctions but is exercised rarely and only where the possibility of damage is very high. The rule has been expressed by different courts in different ways, thus the damage must be 'imminent' or there must be a 'real possibility' that damage would result to the claimant's property 'in time'. The authorities[1] appear to give the court considerable discretion in granting a Quia Timet injunction in order to do justice between the parties having regard to the factual circumstances of the particular case.

1   *Hooper v Rogers* [1975] Ch 43, CA. But see *Lemos v Kennedy Leigh Development Co Ltd* (1961) 105 Sol Jo 178, CA; *Fletcher v Bealey* (1885) 28 Ch D 688.

INTERIM INJUNCTIONS

10.07 Both prohibitory and mandatory injunctions may be granted on an interim application. Often the application is made when the legal validity of the claim or the factual basis for it may be uncertain. The granting of an interim injunction is a matter for the court's discretion and there are well-known guidelines for the grant of an interim injunction. In the *American Cyanamid* case[1] Lord Diplock held that, provided there was a 'serious question' to be tried, the application should be decided on the balance of convenience and the following principles should be applied in determining which way the balance of convenience lies; the court should consider the adequacy of the claimant's and the defendant's respective remedies in damages either at the trial, if the injunction be refused and the claimant finally succeeds, or on the claimant's undertaking in damages if it be granted and the defendant finally succeeds. If these considerations leave the matter in doubt, various factors depending on the nature of the case must be taken into account to see where the balance of convenience lies. These include:

(a) the difficulty in framing the injunction in clear and fair terms;
(b) the degree of injury to each party if the application is not granted but that party succeeds at the trial;
(c) whether either party would enjoy an unfair advantage if matters were left open until the trial;
(d) that the defendant is unarguably committing a legal wrong so the only arguable defence is that the claimant is not the person entitled to complain of that wrong;
(e) delay by the claimant in seeking the injunction;
(f) only if the uncompensatable disadvantage to each party caused by the grant or refusal of the injunction, as the case may be, would not differ widely, then the court can take into account the relative strengths of each party's case as revealed by the affidavit evidence;
(g) where other factors are evenly balanced 'it is a council of prudence to take such measures as are calculated to preserve the status quo';
(h) finally, 'there may be other special factors to be taken into consideration in the particular circumstances of individual cases'.

1   [1975] AC 396, HL.

10.08 Subsequent case law provides some assistance as to these special factors. They are as follows:

(a) One special factor is where a trial is unlikely to take place because the grant of an injunction effectively puts an end to the action. Whilst this principle has obvious application in the case of a trade union that wishes to call a strike, it would seem to have little applicability in environmental law.
(b) It may be appropriate to take account of public interest, for example, where the defendant is a local authority carrying out public duties or where the defendant is in the process of committing acts which are close to becoming criminal.
(c) Interim injunctions should not be issued in a libel action where the defendant raises a defence, whether of justification, fair comment on a matter of public interest or privilege unless the defence would obviously fail at trial. The effect of the Human Rights Act 1998 on, eg, anti-hunt

demonstrators trespassing on private land has not yet been fully tested in the courts to see whether this principle would apply there.

(d)   The principles of the *American Cyanamid* case do not apply where there is only a dispute as to the law and not a factual dispute or where there is no arguable defence to the claim.

(e)   Neither do the principles of *American Cyanamid* apply where the interim injunction sought is mandatory and not prohibitory. Here again the correct principle is not clear but the Court of Appeal has held that a mandatory injunction will be issued at an interlocutory stage only in a clear case, that is where there is a high degree of assurance (higher than that appropriate for a prohibitory injunction) that at the trial it would appear that the injunction had rightly been granted.[1] However, in *Films Rover International Ltd v Cannon Film Sales Ltd*[2] Hoffmann J (now Lord Hoffmann) took a different view. He granted an interim mandatory injunction even though the claimant could not establish a strong prima facie case.

1   *Locabail International Finance Ltd v Agroexport* [1986] 1 WLR 657, CA.
2   [1987] 1 WLR 670.

INJUNCTIONS AGAINST THE CROWN

10.09   The Crown Proceedings Act 1947, s 21 provides as follows:

'... where in any proceedings against the Crown any such relief is sought as might in proceedings between subjects be granted by way of injunction or specific performance, the court shall not grant an injunction or make an order for specific performance, but may in lieu thereof make an order declaratory of the rights of the parties ...'.

10.10   What this means is that an injunction cannot be directly ordered against the Crown, but an injunction (including an interim injunction) can be granted against an officer of the Crown when sued in his or her personal capacity and, in judicial review proceedings (to which s 21 does not apply), when sued in his or her official capacity.[1]

1   *Re M* [1994] 1 AC 377, HL.

10.11   Alternatively, the claimant will often be satisfied with a declaration against the Crown and there is now power to award an interim declaration.[1]

1   Civil Procedure Rules 1998 ('CPR'), r 25.1(1)(b).

UNDERTAKING AS TO DAMAGES

10.12   As we have explained, an interim injunction freezes the situation and prevents the defendant from taking some action, which at trial, may prove to be lawful. Such an injunction may cause the defendant to suffer substantial loss and will not normally be granted unless it is accompanied by an undertaking from the claimant to the court to pay the defendant such damages as it is just the defendant should receive if the issue of the injunction should turn out to have been unjustified. While the rule also applies to the Crown at least in the protection of its own proprietary interests, such an undertaking would not be required from the Crown or other public authorities seeking interim injunctions to enforce the law.[1]

1   *Kirklees Metropolitan Borough Council v Wickes Buildings Supplies Ltd* [1993] AC 227, HL.

LOCAL AUTHORITY PROCEEDINGS

10.13   The Environmental Protection Act 1990, s 81(5) permits a local authority to take proceedings in the High Court to secure the abatement, prohibition or restriction of a nuisance where it is of the opinion that a prosecution would not be an adequate remedy. The application may be made irrespective of whether the local authority has or has not suffered damage.[1] In *City of London Corpn v Bovis Construction Ltd*[2] the local authority applied for an injunction under s 222 of the Local Government Act 1972 in respect of repeated contraventions of a Notice issued under s 60 of the Control of Pollution Act 1974. The High Court considered injunctive relief was appropriate where necessary to prevent damage not preventable by proceedings before Justices, or, where criminal sanctions are otherwise insufficient or technically deficient, or where unlawful activity will continue unless restrained by an injunction.[3]

1   *Hammersmith London Borough Council v Magnum Automated Forecourts Ltd* [1978] 1 WLR 50, CA.
2   (1988) 86 LGR 660, CA.
3   See also *Camden London Borough Council v Alpenoak Ltd* [1985] NLJ Rep 1209 (contempt proceedings for breach of an injunction).

10.14   Section 187B of the Town and Country Planning Act 1990 provides that injunctive relief may be applied for either in the county court or the High Court where the local planning authority consider it necessary or expedient for actual or apprehended breaches of planning control, whether or not other enforcement powers are to be used. It is clear from the wording of the section that the power to apply for injunctive relief is a wide and flexible one.[1]

1   *Croydon London Borough Council v Gladden* [1994] JPL 723, CA and *Harwood v Runnymede Borough Council* [1994] JPL 723, CA.

SEARCH ORDERS AND FREEZING INJUNCTIONS

10.15   A search order was previously known as an 'Anton Piller' order and a freezing injunction was formerly known as a 'Mareva' injunction. We do not know of an environmental case where such orders have been sought and they would seem to us to be outside the scope this book. The reader is therefore referred elsewhere to the standard books on the subject.[1]

1   I Goldrein QC et al *Commercial Litigation: Pre-emptive Remedies* (4th edn, 2002, Sweet & Maxwell); S Gee QC *Mareva Injunctions and Anton Piller Relief* (1998, Sweet & Maxwell).

CHAPTER 11

Remedies: damages

INTRODUCTION

11.01 Generally damages are awarded in the form of a lump sum which is the assessment of all losses flowing from the tort. The exceptions to this are for interim payments in proceedings relating to personal injury and death claims, and more recently the payment of provisional damages in certain personal injury cases. Mention should also be made of the development of the structured settlement. Statute has intervened and the Damages Act 1996, s 2 provides that a court awarding damages for personal injury or death may, with the consent of the parties, make an order for the damages to be in the form of periodical payments.

11.02 Damages are normally unconditional. The two exceptions to this are:
(a) where the damages are received by a person under a disability where the court can issue directions relating to the investment or other dealings with the money;[1]
(b) in some personal injury cases involving assistance rendered by a third party, damages have been awarded on the condition that the claimant pays them over to, or holds them on trust for, the third party.[2]

1 Civil Procedure Rules 1998 ('CPR'), r 21.11.
2 *Hunt v Severs* [1994] 2 AC 350, HL.

11.03 We must initially distinguish between 'general' and 'special' damages. 'General' damages are what the law presumes to flow from the tort complained of and need not be specially pleaded in the Particulars of Claim, although it should be averred that such damage has been suffered. 'Special' damage means particular damage which results from the facts of the case and these must be specifically pleaded. The CPR states that 'The claimant must attach to his Particulars of Claim a Schedule of details of any past and future expenses and losses which he claims'.[1]

1 CPR, r 16.2(1)(d), 16PD-001.

GENERAL PRINCIPLES

11.04 The object of an award of damages is to compensate the claimant for the losses, both financial and non-financial, sustained as a result of the defendant's wrongdoing. The aim is to put the party who has been injured or who has suffered financial loss in the same position as if he or she would have been if he or she had not sustained the wrong for which that party is now getting compensation or reparation. Three comments should be made here. First, the principle of restitution is clear where the loss is financial, but in a case of personal injury or death, the principle of restitution becomes one of compensation. Hence the detailed tariff found in the standard books on the subject. Second, where property has been damaged, the courts do not always apply the restitution principle literally by awarding the cost of restoring the property to its original state: they may instead assess the damages on the diminished value of the asset. Third, in some exceptional cases exemplary damages may be awarded. The object here is to punish the defendant rather than to compensate the claimant.

11.05 It is necessary to say something about causation and remoteness. The principle is that the loss for which compensation is claimed must be caused by, and be not too remote a consequence of, the defendant's wrongdoing. The same principles apply to the test of causation and the effect of overlapping, concurrent and cumulative causes. In cases involving injury to the person or property, the cause of action is established by showing that the kind of injury was a reasonably foreseeable consequence of the defendant's conduct. However, in order to determine the extent of the recoverable loss flowing from the injury, it is not necessary for a defendant reasonably to foresee the full extent of the injury caused by his or her conduct which must be reasonably foreseeable not the ultimate consequences to the claimant.

11.06 A claimant is under a duty to mitigate the losses resulting from the defendant's wrongdoing. Damages are not recoverable for such losses as the claimant has avoided by taking action subsequent to the tort. The general principle of compensation means that a claimant can only recover for losses actually sustained. Thus, for example, the owner of a car damaged by acid rain from a nearby factory might recover only the cost of purchasing a near equivalent on the market where this was cheaper than having his or her own model repaired. The accepted rule is that the onus is on the defendant to show that the claimant failed to mitigate his or her loss and much will depend on what the court regards as being 'reasonable' in the circumstances. Our experience is that judges are reluctant to impose excessive demands on claimants. Finally, it should be noted that a claimant may not increase the damages claimed by his or her own unnecessary acts subsequent to the wrongdoing. But where an act is reasonably done with a view to minimising any possible future damage, it is not therefore extraneous to any subsequent loss and such expenses should be recoverable. An obvious example is where a farmer's cattle have become ill as a result of drinking polluted water from neighbouring land and the obvious necessity to call in veterinary or other assistance.

11.07 Finally, consideration needs to be given to the extent to which the losses pleaded must be certain and how a court can take account of future contingencies. Special damages such as expenses and the loss on a contract or contracts must be pleaded and proved exactly. Some elements in general damages, such as pain and suffering, are inferred or presumed and little evidence is normally required here but that of the claimant. Financial elements in the general damages will not normally be presumed and should thus be supported by evidence.

11.08 Leaving aside claims which are too small to permit recovery (the so called 'de minimis' principle), there is no bar to recovery for loss of a chance and damages are assessed in proportion to that chance. A classic example in personal injury law is where a claimant is awarded damages for disadvantage in the labour market following an accident for which the employer is liable.[1] In this sort of situation there are two questions. First, how does the injury adversely affect the claimant's future and second, what would have been the claimant's prospects if the injury had not occurred? Thus in the case of a person who is injured at work the court must have regard to the security of that person's employment prospects in the future.

1   *Moeliker v A Reyrolle & Co Ltd* [1977] 1 WLR 132, CA.

11.09 There are other uncertainties. It is common in a personal injury claim for the court to make a deduction for the possibility that the claimant may recover earlier than anticipated, or that a surgical operation might have been unsuccessful even if performed at the right time. Similarly a deduction may be made for the possibility that part of the future loss would have been suffered even if the tort had not been committed, eg future unemployment or illness.

DAMAGES FOR PERSONAL INJURIES

11.10 A claimant in a personal injury action normally suffers financial and non-financial loss. *Financial loss* is that which is susceptible of money assessment and includes such matters as loss of earnings, actual and prospective, and out-of-pocket expenses. *Non-financial loss* includes such elements as pain and suffering and loss of amenity or enjoyment of life.

Financial loss

11.11 In respect of financial losses, a claimant may recover any medical or related expenses (such as hospital, nursing or special accommodation costs) that the claimant has reasonably incurred or will reasonably incur as a result of his or her injuries. The claimant cannot recover as part of his or her damages the capital cost of acquiring special accommodation for the claimant retains the capital in question in the form of the accommodation. However, the claimant can recover 3% per annum on the cost of the purchase as the cost of the capital. Mitigation through the possibility of making use of the facilities of the National Health Service ('NHS') is to be disregarded.[1] However, if a claimant does take advantage of those facilities then the claimant is not entitled to recover what he or she would have to pay if he or she contracted for them privately. A similar deduction will be made where it is clear that a claimant cannot obtain all of the nursing services that he or she requires privately and will eventually have to enter an NHS hospital. The same principle applies for a deduction on domestic expenses from an award made to a person who is dependent on institutional care, whether private or under the NHS.[2] The claimant should normally be able to recover for all other non-remote expenses that have been or will reasonably be incurred as a result of the injury. An obvious example is the cost of employing domestic help.

1   Law Reform (Personal Injuries) Act 1948, s 2(4).
2   *Lim Poh Choo v Camden and Islington Area Health Authority* [1980] AC 174, HL (private care); Administration of Justice Act 1982, s 5 (NHS care).

11.12 Loss of earnings for which damages can be recovered includes wages, salaries, professional fees, a share in company or partnership profits, prize money, or perquisites such as a company car. Deduction is made for income tax, National Insurance contributions and compulsory contributions to an Occupational Pension Scheme that would have been paid from the claimant's earnings. Loss of earnings accrued to the date of trial can normally be calculated by reference to the claimant's pre-accident earnings and the period of disability, but such a calculation depends upon the assumption that, but for the accident, the claimant would have continued to earn at the same rate. If this assumption is incorrect, then a deduction must be made accordingly. After the date of trial the assessment of prospective loss of earnings becomes potentially more speculative. This is because of the uncertainty over the period of the claimant's future incapacity (if any), his or her future employment prospects and the normal hazards of life. The starting point for calculating the multiplicand (the net annual loss) is what the claimant would have been earning at the time of trial. This figure is then adjusted to meet the claimant's prospects of promotion and thus of an increase in the real value of his earnings. Where the claimant's working capacity has not been totally destroyed, an allowance must be made for such income as the claimant is likely to earn in the future.

11.13 The starting point for the multiplier is the number of years during which the loss, represented by the multiplicand, is likely to endure and thus typically, the remaining period of the claimant's working life. This figure is then reduced to account not only for the elements of uncertainty contained in the prediction (eg unemployment, redundancy or sickness), but also for the fact that the claimant receives a lump sum which he or she is expected to invest. Where the injury has reduced the claimant's life expectancy, the multiplier is calculated according to the claimant's pre-accident working life expectancy, with a deduction for the living expenses that the claimant would have incurred during those 'lost years'.

11.14 The appropriate discount rate (for receiving the capital sum of damages, which can be invested, earlier than the lost income), is the rate of return on Index-Linked Government Stock ('ILGS').[1]

1   *Wells v Wells* [1999] 1 AC 345, HL. The same decision approved the use of the Ogden Tables as giving the appropriate multiplier for a particular rate of discount.

11.15 Various deductions also have to be made in assessing the damages payable to the claimant. In summary form they are as follows:

(a)   The claimant's liability to tax on the earnings for the loss of which the claimant claims compensation must be taken into account in assessing the damages payable by the defendant.[1]

(b)   The defendant must reimburse the State for the total amount of listed Social Security benefits received by the claimant during the relevant period in respect of the injury or disease.[2] The relevant period is five years, or if shorter, the period to a final settlement payment from the date following the accrual of the cause of action. The list of Social Security benefits is extensive.[3] It follows that the defendant may deduct the amount of benefits from any compensation payable to the claimant because they must be reimbursed to the State.

(c)   Where the statute does not apply, the receipt of other benefits is governed by the common law principle that the claimant should not recover any more than he or she has actually lost. Thus a defendant should not have to pay where the claimant's loss has been diminished in whole or in part by a benefit received from a collateral source. Such collateral benefits do not include insurance payments and any charitable payment made to the claimant by a third party. However, the defendant may make a deduction where the claimant is entitled to sick pay, sickness benefit or the continuation of wages under the claimant's contract of employment.

1   *British Transport Commission v Gourley* [1956] AC 185, HL.
2   Social Security (Recovery of Benefits) Act 1997, s 6.
3   Social Security (Recovery of Benefits) Act 1997, s 29, Sch 2.

Non-financial loss

11.16 Non-financial losses are more difficult to quantify. As we have indicated above they include pain and suffering and loss of faculty and loss of amenity. Reference should be made to the standard textbooks on this subject.[1]

1   See, eg, Gordon Exall *Damages for Personal Injuries and Death* (11th edn, 2003, Butterworths); Michael Jones *Law of Damages* (2003, Butterworths); Brian Langstaff and others *Personal Injury Schedules – Calculating Damages* (2001, Butterworths); Rodney Nelson-Jones *Butterworths Personal Injury Damages Statistics* (2001, Butterworths); Rodney Nelson-Jones *Multipliers* (1998, Butterworths).

Interest

11.17 The Supreme Court Act 1981, s 35A and the County Courts Act 1984, s 69 provide that a court may include in any sum for which judgment is given simple interest on all or any part of the damages for which judgment is given or for which payment is made for judgment; and, in the case of a judgment for damages for personal injuries or death exceeding £200, such interest shall be included unless the court is satisfied that there are special reasons to the contrary. The court has a discretion to fix the period for which interest is payable, within the limits of the date when the cause of action arose until the date of judgment, or, in the case of a sum paid out before judgment, the date of that payment. The rate of interest is also at the discretion of the court. The CPR provides that a Pt 36 offer (an offer to settle) or a Pt 36 payment (a payment into court) is taken to include any interest payable, unless the contrary is indicated.[1] The detail of the law relating to interest is outside the scope of this book.

1   CPR, r 36.22.

DESTRUCTION AND DAMAGE TO GOODS

11.18   Where goods are destroyed by the wrongful act of the defendant, the claimant is entitled to their value at the time of destruction. That value is normally the sum of money which the claimant would have to pay in the market for identical or essentially similar goods plus, in an appropriate case, damages for loss of use during the period of full replacement. A claimant with only a limited interest in the goods will normally not be allowed to recover more than the value of that interest.[1]

1   Torts (Interference with Goods) Act 1977, s 708.

11.19   In the case of damaged goods, the normal rule is that the claimant is entitled to recover damages to the extent of which the value of the goods have been reduced. This is normally the cost of repair.[1] The cost will be determined at the time it was reasonable in the circumstances of the case for the claimant to have the chattel repaired.[2] It should be noted that the repairs do not have to be carried out at the date of the trial or, even if they are never carried out at all, eg, if the damaged goods are lost before repair. However, if it is unreasonable as between the parties for the goods to be repaired rather than replaced, eg where the cost of the repair greatly exceeds the value of the goods themselves, then the claimant cannot recover more than the value of the goods.[3] Damages for reinstatement may nevertheless be awarded where the court considers that it is reasonable to have the property reinstated, eg because the claimant is resident there and this is the claimant's intention: *Dodd Properties (Kent) Ltd v Canterbury City Council*.[4] The onus is on the defendant to establish that the diminution in value is less than the cost of repair. The normal rule is that the value of a damaged chattel is less by the cost of repair than the value would have had if the damage had never been done. Thus the defendant is not entitled to credit for the fact that, by reason of the use of new materials in the course of repair, the goods are in better condition after repair than they were before the damage was caused.[5] However, if the claimant proves that the value of the chattel has diminished because it has had to be repaired, then the claimant may recover damages over and above the cost of the repair.[6]

1 *The London Corporation* [1935] P 70, CA.
2 *Dodd Properties (Kent) Ltd v Canterbury City Council* [1980] 1 WLR 433, CA.
3 *Darbishire v Warran* [1963] 1 WLR 1067, CA. The same principle applies to damaged buildings: *Farmer Giles Ltd v Wessex Water Authority* [1988] 2 EGLR 189.
4 [1980] 1 WLR 433 at 456–457 per Donaldson LJ.
5 *Bacon v Cooper (Metals) Ltd* [1982] 1 All ER 397.
6 *Payton v Brooks* [1974] RTR 169, CA.

11.20   Apart from having to pay the cost of repair for damaged goods, the owner would normally be entitled to damages for the loss of use during the period needed for their repair. A court has to ask itself the question: What is the use which the damaged goods are put to? Where the goods have a commercial use then any loss of profit may be recovered providing it is the defendant's wrongdoing which has caused the loss of use and not, eg, other necessary repairs. The claimant may avoid a loss of profits by hiring a substitute during the period of repair and the claimant is thus entitled to recover the cost of hire as damages for loss of use. The hiring of a substitute must be reasonable in the circumstances. Furthermore, the hire of a substitute must be strictly pleaded and proved as special damage. If the cost of hiring a substitute exceeds the profits which could have been earned, then only the profits which could have been earned are recoverable. Additional profit must be set against any loss claimed.

11.21   Even where goods are non-profit earning, a claimant may still be entitled to damages for loss of use. If a substitute has been hired then the cost of a substitute can be recovered provided that the substitute actually hired and the sum paid for the hire were both reasonable. Otherwise the assessment of damages for non-profit-earning goods is dependent on the facts of the case. Many of the cases in this area relate to shipping law, but the principles are of general application.

AGGRAVATED DAMAGES

11.22   Aggravated damages are awarded where the manner of the commission of the tort is such as to injure the claimant's proper feelings of dignity and pride. They will be higher than ordinary general damages.[1] While aggravated damages have been awarded for several different types of tort, they have featured most typically in defamation cases. They are likely to be of little relevance in environmental law, although they have been awarded in cases of trespass to land.[2] They are not recoverable in a negligence or nuisance claim.

1 *Rookes v Barnard* [1964] AC 1129 at 1221, HL, per Lord Devlin.
2 *McMillan v Singh* (1984) 17 HLR 120, CA.

EXEMPLARY DAMAGES

11.23   Finally, mention should be made of exemplary damages. In the leading case of *Rookes v Barnard*[1] the House of Lords set out the categories of case in which exemplary damages should be awarded unless expressly authorised by statute (irrelevant in the context of environmental law). The categories are as follows:

(a)   '*Oppressive, arbitrary or unconstitutional action by the servants of the government*' – 'The government' for these purposes includes local government but not a nationalised corporation or a privatised utility. Thus in *Gibbons v South West Water Services Ltd*[2] exemplary damages were refused against a nationalised corporation in contaminating drinking water and failing to warn the public properly of this.

(b)   '*Cases in which the defendant's conduct has been calculated by him to make a profit for himself which may well exceed the compensation payable to the plaintiff*' – Thus tortious interference with the claimant's business (eg by sabotaging the claimant's water supply by trespassing on his land and polluting it) would enable exemplary damages to be recovered.[3]

1   [1964] AC 1129, HL.
2   [1993] QB 507, CA.
3   *Bell v Midland Rly Co* (1861) 10 CBNS 287.

11.24   Finally, it should be noted that it is not possible to recover exemplary damages except for a tort for which exemplary damages had been awarded prior to 1964. If this were not so, no exemplary damages can be awarded even if the case fell within one of the categories set out above: *Gibbons v South West Services Ltd*.[1] In that case there was a claim for exemplary damages for the tort of public nuisance in supplying contaminated drinking water to the inhabitants of Camelford in Cornwall. It was struck out as a public nuisance was not a tort for which exemplary damages had been awarded prior to *Rookes v Barnard*.[2] The same principle applied to alternative claims in negligence and for liability under the Consumer Protection Act 1987. It follows that exemplary damages cannot be awarded for breach of European Community law.[3]

1   [1993] QB 507, CA.
2   [1964] AC 1129, HL.
3   *R v Secretary of State for Transport, ex p Factortame Ltd (No 5)* [1997] Eu LR 475.

PART III

Substantive practice areas

CHAPTER 12

Personal injury claims

INTRODUCTION

12.01   This chapter does not deal with the general law of personal injury. Rather, it deals with the two aspects of personal injury litigation which are most challenging where pollution is alleged to cause injury: causation and evidence. *Causation* can be a daunting hurdle where both the law and the facts are complex. A considerable body of jurisprudence has now developed, particularly in relation to workmen's dust disease claims which, in respect of the issue of causation, and apportionment, is of general applicability. This chapter then goes on to consider questions of *evidence* which are particularly relevant to personal injury claims arising in environmental pollution actions.

CAUSATION

Test of causation

Overview

12.02   It is clear that the 'but for' test is too crude to be regarded as a universal test of causation. The House of Lords has recently held that there is no uniform causal requirement for liability in tort. Instead, there are varying causal requirements depending upon the basis and purpose of liability. One cannot separate questions of liability from questions of causation: they are inextricably connected. One is never simply liable; one is always liable for something and the rules which determine what one is liable for are as much part of the substantive law as the rules which determine which acts give rise to liability: see *Kuwait Airways Corpn v Iraqi Airways Co (Nos 4 and 5)*.[1]

1   [2002] UKHL 19, [2002] 2 AC 883.

12.03   In particular, it seems that the test of causation is in part dependent upon the mechanism of the disease/injury complained of, eg whether it is a traumatic injury, a cumulative injury or a 'one off' exposure taking place in the context of multiple exposures. Each type of injury has implications for whether medical causation can be established; for whether *legal* causation (ie whose breach of duty caused the injury/disease) can be established; and to what extent (apportionment).

Traumatic injuries

12.04   Traumatic injuries are ones that occur as a result of a single or instantaneous event. For instance, a car crash, a trip, a slip or a fall or a malfunction of machinery.

Cumulative injuries

12.05   Cumulative injuries are injuries caused by stress, strain, damage or exposure over a longer period of time. The injuries are caused by an accumulation of damage or insult over time rather than something which occurs immediately before the instant the injury appears. In cumulative injury cases:
(a)   all exposure contributes to taking the claimant to the point of his or her threshold for developing the disease;
(b)   once that threshold has been reached, all exposure contributes equally to exacerbating the disease.

12.06   Diseases considered cumulative include asbestosis and silicosis, dermatitis, deafness, vibration white finger, carpal tunnel syndrome, asthma, repetitive strain injury and certain back injuries.

12.07   Medical science cannot always explain how and why exposure to certain substances or activities causes disease. It can say that the chances of developing the disease increase proportionately with dose or exposure (the result of epidemiological research). However, it cannot say how much exposure is needed to cause the disease or exacerbate it. Even if medical science can answer the question of how much exposure is needed to cause an injury, it is generally impossible for claimants to demonstrate how much dust, fibre, chemical, noise, stress or vibration they were exposed to at any particular time or over any particular period.

12.08   Furthermore, for different injuries, different rules will apply. In asbestos cases, all exposure that takes place more than 10–15 years before the injury develops will be considered to have contributed to the injury. Any exposure within 10 years can be discounted as it occurred too recently to have caused any injury. There is a very long latent period in asbestos cases (10 to 60 years) between exposure which contributes to an injury and that injury developing.

Accordingly, asbestosis will develop and continue to exacerbate (become worse) many years after the exposure ceases. By contrast, with dermatitis, asthma and allergy cases, all past exposure fills up the claimant's reservoir of resistance. However, if exposure ceases before it overflows, then no injury will result. Once the injury has started, it will only exacerbate with continued exposure. If exposure ceases, the injury cannot get worse. In deafness cases no exposure can be discounted and all noise exposure is considered to contribute equally to the injury.

'One off' cases

12.09 Before dealing with legal causation in disease cases, it is worth noting that not every injury is either traumatic or cumulative. There are cases in which medical experts believe that the injury is caused by a single event taking place in the context of multiple events. An example might be a rambler shot at by 10 farmers with shotguns; one lead pellet passes through the rambler's heart, killing him.

12.10 The disease examples of this type of injury are typically cancers. Of all the cancers that can be caused by workplace exposure, only mesothelioma is litigated with any regularity. Medical experts believe that mesothelioma can be caused by a single asbestos fibre triggering a cancer. However, the chance of this occurring is increased in direct proportion to exposure, ie the chances of a person inhaling 1 million asbestos fibres and developing mesothelioma is 1 million times greater than for a person inhaling one asbestos fibre. Accordingly, mesothelioma cannot be considered a cumulative injury. Although the risk increases with exposure, each exposure cannot be said to have contributed to the injury (as it would in a cumulative injury case).

12.11 A pharmaceutical example is Creutzfeldt-Jakobs Disease ('CJD') as a consequence of receiving human growth hormone ('HGH') treatment contaminated with the CJD virus. The HGH treatment, consisting of injections, was given on a regular basis over a period of time. The preponderance of medical opinion was that medical causation was by a single injection or dose. There was no issue of cumulative cause nor of idiosyncratic susceptibility.

Legal causation and disease cases

12.12 The seminal decision on the law relating to causation in disease cases was the judgment of the House of Lords in the pneumoconiosis case of *Bonnington Castings Ltd v Wardlaw*.[1] The claimant was exposed to dust from metal grinders. The medical experts were satisfied that the claimant developed pneumoconiosis as a result of this workplace exposure (medical causation). The defendant was found in breach of duty for failing to reduce the claimant's exposure to silica dust. However, in neither case did the court find that the defendants should have avoided all exposure. That is, even if there had been no breach of duty ('guilty dust'), there would still have been exposure to silica ('innocent dust') and therefore a risk of pneumoconiosis. The claimant could not show that 'but for' the additional exposure to guilty dust, he would not have developed the disease. However, the claimant could show, because the disease was cumulative in effect, that the guilty dust contributed to his disease. The House of Lords recognised that it was never possible for claimants to satisfy the 'but for' test in this sort of case and demonstrate that their injuries were caused solely by dust present due to the defendant's breach of duty (guilty dust). But, as the claimant had shown that the guilty dust had made a 'material contribution' to his disease, he was entitled to recover in full.

1   [1956] 1 All ER 615.

12.13   That line of reasoning was upheld in *McGhee v National Coal Board*,[1] a case concerning causation in dermatitis cases. The House of Lords held that if a claimant could show that a defendant's breaches of duty had made a material contribution to the disease, then that had the same effect as proving that the defendant had caused the whole injury. In *McGhee*, the court found that the claimant's exposure to dust between 9am and 5pm was not negligent (innocent dust). But his dust exposure when he cycled home from work without having first showered was negligent (guilty dust).

1   [1973] 1 WLR 1.

12.14   Neither case differentiated between cumulative injuries and 'one off' exposure cases. It should be added that at the time of *McGhee*, the medical experts did not know whether dermatitis was cumulative or 'one off'. It is now widely considered to be due to cumulative exposure.

Legal causation and mesothelioma: Fairchild

12.15   The story starts with the judgment of Mr Justice Phillips in 1988 in *Bryce v Swan Hunter Group plc*.[1] Mr Bryce developed and died from mesothelioma. He worked in the same shipyard from 1937 to 1975 and was exposed to a lot of asbestos. The shipyard changed hands a number of times while he was there and so there were many potential defendants, of which his estate sued three. The judge found that all three defendants were in breach of duty for the whole period. However, he found that their breaches were that they did not 'reduce' the amount of asbestos to which Mr Bryce was exposed. He did not find that they were under a duty to avoid all exposure to asbestos. Even if the defendants had complied with their duties, Mr Bryce would still have been exposed to a significant quantity of asbestos. Further, two other non-defendant employers had also exposed Mr Bryce to asbestos. Whilst the judge found that the breaches of duty by the three defendants caused a significant increase in the total volume of asbestos to which Mr Bryce was exposed, it was less than half his total exposure to asbestos dust (ie the innocent exposure exceeded the guilty exposure). The next question was the role the guilty exposure played in causing the mesothelioma. Phillips J stated:[2]

'It is not possible for the [claimant] to prove on the balance of probabilities that the additional fibres inhaled by Mr Bryce as the result of breaches of duty by either defendant were a cause of his mesothelioma.'

1   [1988] 1 All ER 659.
2   At 665h.

12.16   Phillips J, after considering the case law, approved the principle of *McGhee* as identified by Mustill LJ in *Wilsher v Essex Area Health Authority*[1] (a clinical negligence case) as follows:[2]

'If it is an established fact that conduct of a particular kind creates a risk that injury will be caused to another or increases an existing risk that injury will ensue and if the two parties stand in such a relationship that the one party owes a duty not to conduct himself in that way and if the other party does suffer injury of the kind to which the risk related then the first party is taken to have caused the injury by his breach of duty, even though the existence and extent of the contribution made by the breach cannot be ascertained.'

1   [1986] 3 All ER 801, CA.
2   At 669j.

12.17   Applying (and simplifying) the above, Phillips J concluded:[1]

'The defendants' breaches of duty ... increased the risk of his developing mesothelioma. He developed mesothelioma. Each of the defendants must accordingly be taken to have caused the mesothelioma by its breach of duty.'

1   At 671h.

12.18   The real problem is whether a claimant can recover damages when all he or she can show is that the asbestos fibre came from one of the three claimant's employers, but was unable to show which one, nor whether it was due to negligent or non-negligent exposure.

12.19   The House of Lords has now held that a claimant can recover damages in cases such as the above if the claimant could show that:
(a)   the claimant was employed by the defendant(s);
(b)   the defendant(s) were subject to a duty to prevent the claimant inhaling asbestos because of the known risk of mesothelioma (existence of a duty);
(c)   the defendant(s) breached that duty causing the claimant to inhale excessive asbestos (breach of duty);
(d)   the claimant developed mesothelioma (injury);

(e)   the mesothelioma was developed as a result of exposure at work (medical causation);
(f)   the risk of the claimant developing mesothelioma was increased by the breach of duty by the defendant(s) (legal causation).

See *Fairchild v Glenhaven Funeral Services Ltd.*[1]

1   [2002] UKHL 22, [2003] 1 AC 32.

Lord Rodger's speech

12.20   If the foregoing pre-conditions for liability were definitive, they would have little applicability in pollution cases because pollution cases rarely involve employees. However, according to Lord Rodger's speech in *Fairchild*, the approach in *McGhee* (ie proving that a material increase of risk will be taken in law to have proved material contribution) is not restricted to an occupational context. Lord Rodger stated that the principle in *McGhee* is designed to resolve the difficulty that arises where it is inherently impossible for the claimant to prove exactly how his or her injury was caused.

12.21   Lord Roger lists the following pre-conditions of the application of the principle:[1]
(a)   Where the claimant has proved all that he or she possibly can, but the causal link could only ever be established by scientific investigation and the current state of the relevant science leaves it uncertain exactly how the injury was caused and, so, who caused it.
(b)   Part of the underlying rationale of the principle is that the defendant's wrongdoing has materially increased the risk that the claimant will suffer injury. It is therefore essential not just that the defendant's conduct created a material risk of injury to a class of persons but that it actually created a material risk of injury to the claimant himself or herself.
(c)   That the defendant's conduct must have been capable of causing the claimant's injury.
(d)   The claimant must prove that his or her injury was caused by the eventuation of the kind of risk created by the defendant's wrongdoing. In *McGhee*, for instance, the risk created by the defenders' failure was that the pursuer would develop dermatitis due to brick dust on his skin and he proved that he had developed dermatitis due to brick dust on his skin. By contrast, the principle does not apply where the claimant has merely proved that his or her injury could have been caused by a number of different events, only one of which is the eventuation of the risk created by the defendant's wrongful act or omission; *Wilsher*[2] is an example.
(e)   This will usually mean that the claimant must prove that his or her injury was caused, if not by exactly the same agency as was involved in the defendant's wrongdoing, at least by an agency that operated in substantially the same way. A possible example would be where a worker suffered injury from exposure to dust coming from two sources, the dusts being

particles of different substances each of which, however, could have caused the worker's injury in the same way.

(f)   The principle applies where the other possible source of the claimant's injury is a similar wrongful act or omission by another person, but it can also apply where, as in *McGhee*, the other possible source of the injury is a similar but lawful act or omission of the same defendant.

1   At 118E.
2   *Wilsher v Essex Area Health Authority* [1988] AC 1074 at 1087 and 1090, HL.

Summary of causation

12.22   In *Fairchild*[1] when considering the correct test for legal causation, Lord Hoffmann stated:

'The causal requirements for liability often vary, sometimes quite subtly, from case to case. And since the causal requirements for liability are always a matter of law, these variations represent legal differences, driven by the recognition that the just solution to different kinds of case may require different causal requirement rules.'

1   [2002] UKHL 22, [2003] 1 AC 32 at [72D].

12.23   Thus far there seem to be different tests for different cases as follows:
(a)   in traumatic injury cases, the traditional 'but for' test applies;
(b)   in cumulative injury cases, the claimant need only show that the defendant's breach of duty made a material contribution to the injury (ie caused part of the injury);
(c)   in 'one off' cases such as mesothelioma, the claimant need only show that the defendant's breach of duty increased the risk that the claimant might suffer the identified injury.

Apportionment

12.24   Apportionment is the reduction in a claimant's damages where the defendant's evidence establishes that:
(a)   the guilty exposure made a material contribution to or caused some of the claimant's injury;
(b)   the evidence also shows that the guilty exposure does not cause all of it and/or not X% of it.

The case law suggests (so far) three situations whereby damages have been reduced by apportionment. Before considering them it is worthwhile considering the principle.

The principles of apportionment

12.25   In *Allen v British Rail Engineering*[1] the Court of Appeal stated five points of principle as follows:

(1)   The employee will establish liability if he or she can prove that the employer's tortious conduct made a material contribution to the employee's disability.

(2)   There can be cases where the state of the evidence is such that it is just to recognise each of two separate tortfeasors as having caused the whole of the damage of which the claimant complains; for instance where a passenger is killed as the result of a head-on collision between two cars each of which was negligently driven and in one of which the passenger was sitting.

(3)   However, in principle the amount of the employer's liability will be limited to the extent of the contribution which the employer's tortious conduct made to the employee's disability.

(4)   The court must do the best it can on the evidence to make the apportionment and should not be astute to deny the claimant relief on the basis that the claimant cannot establish with demonstrable accuracy precisely what proportion of his or her injury is attributable to the defendant's tortious conduct.

(5)   The amount of evidence which should be called to enable a judge to make a just apportionment must be proportionate to the amount at stake and the uncertainties which are inherent in making any award of damages for personal injury.

1   [2001] EWCA Civ 242, [2001] PIQR Q10.

12.26   In *Holtby v Brigham & Cowan (Hull) Ltd*[1] Stuart-Smith LJ states:

'The claimant will be entitled to succeed if he can prove that the defendant's tortious conduct made a material contribution to his disability. But strictly speaking the defendant is liable only to the extent of that contribution.'

1   [2000] 3 All ER 421, CA.

The three situations where apportionment has been made

12.27   These are all cases where it is possible on the evidence to show a real and arguable separation between the injury caused by the defendant's breach of duty and some other factors. They may be summarised as follows:

(1)   pre-date of knowledge exposure (ie, injury caused by exposure to substances before a defendant knows or should have known of the link);

(2)   injury caused by a different employer employing the claimant at a different time; and

(3)   injury caused by the claimant's own conduct.

PRE-DATE OF KNOWLEDGE INJURY

12.28   In *Thompson v Smiths Shiprepairers (North Shields) Ltd*,[1] the High Court recognised that the defendants should have been acting on the risk of deafness from exposure to noise at work by 1963. Accordingly, claimants exposed before 1963 could not succeed. Those exposed after 1963 succeeded in full. However, the complication was for claimants exposed both before and after 1963. For such claimants, they would only recover for the proportion of their industrial deafness caused after the date of knowledge (1963), even where the court had to guess at the apportionment. The matter was fairly simple in a deafness case since all exposure was considered to contribute to the eventual deafness. Accordingly, apportionment was made on a simple *pro rata* basis to exposure.

1   [1984] QB 405.

12.29   In the *Creutzfeldt-Jakobs disease litigation, Groups A and C plaintiffs*[1] the claimants had received injections of a human growth hormone ('HGH') both before and after 1 July 1977, the relevant date of knowledge. Accordingly pre-July 1977 was 'innocent exposure' and post-July 1977 was 'guilty exposure'. It was not possible on the basis of expert evidence to say whether any given claimant had received the 'one off' contaminated dose before or after that key date. The trial judge held that any such claimant would succeed on causation where it could be shown that the claimant received the majority of doses after 1 July 1977.

1   (1998) 54 BMLR 111.

Non-defendant exposure

12.30   In *Holtby v Brigham & Cowan (Hull) Ltd*,[1] the Court of Appeal allowed a defendant to reduce the extent of liability by 25% in an asbestosis case on the grounds that another employer had exposed the claimant to a substantial amount of asbestos at an earlier time and must therefore have contributed to the asbestosis. The defendant was, in effect, found to be severally liable for the claimant's disease and not jointly liable for the whole disease. The defendant was liable in full under *McGhee* principles.[2] But, if the evidence established that another party was responsible for part of the injury, then there would be a reduction. The fact that this was an asbestosis case helped this defendant as all exposure occurring more than 10 to 15 years before the onset of symptoms contributed equally to the injury and apportionment could be made on a *pro rata* basis to exposure.

1   [2000] 3 All ER 421.
2   See para **12.13** above.

Claimant's conduct

12.31   In *Allen v British Rail Engineering*[1] the trial judge reduced the damages on account of the claimant's own conduct. He held as follows:

> 'In my view, if the first defendants had complied with their duty to him, Mr. Allen would probably have changed jobs within BREL by 1975 or

would soon afterwards have moved to a job which entailed less use of vibrating tools. The likelihood is that, whether he moved within BREL or away from it, he would still have used his manual skills and would have used some vibrating tools. Doing the best I can, and bearing in mind that Mr. Allen's exposure during the last 11 years with BR was not in any event very high, I conclude that if the first defendants had complied with their duty of care towards him, he would, between 1976 and 1987, have been exposed to a reduced level of vibration, of the order of a half to two thirds of the level to which he was actually exposed.'

1   [2000] CLY 454.

12.32   The trial judge reduced the damages by 50%. The Court of Appeal[1] in dismissing the appeal stated:

'There was however no evidence that non-vibratory work was available for which Mr Allen was suitable. The judge found that there was vibratory work involving lower doses of vibration and that if this had been offered Mr Allen would have taken it; if it had not been offered he would have found such work elsewhere.'

1   [2001] EWCA Civ 242, [2001] PIQR Q10.

12.33   *Smith v Wright and Beyer*[1] was a case where the trial judge made no reduction, but on quite similar facts. He found as follows:

'Had the defendants, whether in 1977 or 1980, issued warnings, then, no doubt, the claimant in the early 1980s would have realised what was happening and then, no doubt, the defendants would have reorganised work patterns so that Mr Smith could work without enduring further symptoms. Alternatively, if that were not possible, they would have, no doubt, dismissed him. As it was, the claimant continued until and after his symptoms had reached a stage where damage was irreversible.

Further, the defendants in 1977 or 1980, had they done their duty, would have reorganised their working practice so as to reduce exposure to vibration and hence the claimant may not ever have reached a stage when he would have experienced symptoms.

Put shortly, the pain and suffering and loss of amenity which this claimant feels is entirely, in my judgment, due to the fault of these defendants and if I am wrong in not deducting something for symptom-less damage occurring before the date of knowledge then, in my judgment, the deduction must be minuscule. In other words, hardly worth deducting.'

The Court of Appeal dismissed the defendant employer's appeal.[2]

1   (1 November 1999, unreported), HH Judge Tetlow, Manchester County Court.
2   [2001] EWCA Civ 1069.

12.34 In both cases the decisions were based on facts and not on legal principle, but the importance of pleading the apportionment case properly and therefore ensuring that the relevant evidence is before the court is very clear.

EVIDENCE

The burden of proof

12.35 The starting point is the burden of proof. In *Bonnington Castings Ltd v Wardlaw*[1] Lord Reid said:

> 'It would seem obvious in principle that a pursuer or plaintiff must prove not only negligence or breach of duty but also that such fault caused or materially contributed to, his injury ... In my judgement the employee must, in all cases, prove his case by the ordinary standard of proof in civil actions: he must make it appear at least that, on a balance of probabilities, the breach of duty caused, or materially contributed to, his injury.'

1   [1956] 1 All ER 615 at 618, HL.

12.36 The claimant has to establish a positive case. It is not good enough to say that a particular cause cannot be excluded as the origin of the injury. In *Sydney County Council v Furner*[1] Hope A-JA said:

> '... To find that a particular cause cannot be excluded as the cause of the relevant injury does not establish that on the probabilities it was the cause of that injury; it may have been "the" or "a" cause. In other words, to establish that medical evidence supports a conclusion that the cause could not be excluded as a cause of an injury does not establish, without more, that particular cause in fact resulted in or caused the injury.'

1   (1991) 7 NSWCCR 210 at 214.

12.37 It has been suggested that where there are a number of defendants and it can be shown that each of them has caused some of the claimant's harm, the burden of proof shifts to the defendants to show what portion of the harm they caused. However the Court of Appeal in *Holtby*[1] by a majority, rejected this view. A claimant's burden of proof does not shift in such circumstances, the claimant must prove his or her case against each defendant and, strictly speaking, a defendant is only liable to the extent of his or her contribution to the claimant's harm. Thus the claimant has to show that each defendant is responsible for the whole or a part of the harm caused.

1   *Holtby v Brigham & Cowan (Hull) Ltd* [2000] 3 All ER 421, CA.

12.38 However, the evidential burden may shift in cases involving a pre-existing condition. In *Purkess v Crittenden*[1] it was held that:

> '... where a [claimant] has ... made out a prima facie case that incapacity has resulted from the defendant's negligence, the onus of adducing

evidence that his incapacity is wholly or partly the result of some pre-existing condition or that incapacity, either total or partial, would in any event, have resulted from a pre-existing condition, rests upon the defendant.'

1   (1965) 114 CLR 164.

12.39 More difficult is the question of alternative causes. Suppose, for example, the claimant says that injury was due to exposure to benzene. The defendant argues that the claimant was also exposed to, say, toluene during the course of enjoying a hobby activity at home and this is the cause of the injury. On whom does the burden lie to prove or disprove the toluene theory? In *McGhee* Lord Wilberforce considered that:

'... where a person has, by breach of a duty of care, created a risk and injury occurs within the area of that risk, the loss should be borne by him unless he shows that it had some other cause. Secondly, from the evidential point of view, one may ask, why should a man who is able to show that his employer should have taken certain precautions, because without them there is a risk, or an added risk, of injury or disease, and who in fact sustains exactly that injury or disease, have to assume the burden of proving more, namely that it was the addition to the risk, caused by the breach of duty, which caused or materially contributed to the injury? In many cases ... this is impossible to prove just because honest medical opinion cannot segregate the causes of an illness between compound causes. And if one asks which of the parties, the workman or the employers, should suffer from this inherent evidential difficulty, the answer as a matter of policy or justice should be that it is the creator of the risk who, ex hypothesi must be taken to have foreseen the possibility of damage, who should bear its consequences.'

12.40 A later House of Lords criticised this statement (*Wilsher v Essex Area Health Authority*[1]) as a minority opinion that should be rejected. In *Wilsher* there were five competing causes for the injury and the claimant could not point to one particular one as *the* cause. Thus despite Lord Wilberforce, the evidential burden here will remain with the claimant. Nevertheless, the claimant can go a long way effectively to shift the burden. It is for the defendant to raise an alternative cause in the pleadings. The issue must be properly put before the court.[2] *Holtby* (which considered that strictly speaking such a matter need not be pleaded[3]) was decided under the old rules. The defendant must properly particularise his allegation. Properly addressed requests for further information will go a long way towards making the defendant justify the allegation that the claimant's injury was caused by another substance. The same applies to apportionment: see *Hatton v Sutherland*.[4]

1   [1988] AC 1074 at 1087 and 1090, HL.
2   [2000] 3 All ER at 428j; Civil Procedure Rules 1998, r 16.5.
3   [2000] 3 All ER at 428j; Civil Procedure Rules 1998, r 16.5.
4   [2002] EWCA Civ 76, [2002] 2 All ER 1 at [20d].

The standard of proof

12.41 A claimant in a civil case only has to prove his or her claim on the balance of probabilities. In other words, the claimant has to show that it was more probable than not that the defendant's act or omission caused the claimant's harm. In percentage terms that equates to 51%; 50% is not enough. 'The law never gives judgment in favour of a [claimant] when the only finding is equally consistent with liability and non-liability': *Moriarty v Evans Medical Supplies Ltd*[1] per Lord Denning. It is reaching the standard that creates most difficulty for a claimant. Usually a case can easily be brought to show that it is *possible* that the defendant caused the harm complained of. But this is no good. The claimant must show that it was *probable* that his or her harm arose from the defendant's wrong.

1   [1958] 1 WLR 66 at 91, HL.

Conjecture v inference

12.42 A *conjecture* is speculation, a guess. An *inference*, on the other hand, is the forming of a conclusion by reasoning from facts. A judge is entitled to draw inferences from the facts. A judge is not entitled to base a decision on conjecture. There is a fine dividing line between the two thought processes. The difference was recently dealt with by Spigelman CJ in *Seltsam Pty Ltd v McGuiness*:[1]

'(85)   Lord Macmillan in *Jones v Great Western Railway Co* (1930) 47 TLR 39, in the context of stating that a possibility that a negligent act caused injury was not enough, said, at 45:

"The dividing line between conjecture and inference is often a very difficult one to draw. A conjecture may be plausible but is of no legal value, for its essence is that it is a mere guess. An inference in the legal sense, on the other hand, is a deduction from the evidence, and if it is a reasonable deduction it may have validity as legal proof. The attribution of an occurrence to a cause is, I take it, always a matter of inference."

(86)   After referring to this passage, Sir Frederick Jordan in *Carr v Baker* (1936) 36 SR (NSW) 301 said, at 306:

"The existence of a fact may be inferred from other facts when those facts make it reasonably probable that it exists; if they go no further than to show that it is possible that it may exist, then its existence does not go beyond mere conjecture. Conjecture may range from the barely possible to the quite possible."

(87)   As Lord Wright put it in a frequently cited passage in *Caswell v Powell Duffryn Associated Collieries Ltd* [1940] AC 152 at 169–170:

> "Inference must be carefully distinguished from conjecture or speculation. There can be no inference unless there are objective facts from which to infer the other facts which it is sought to establish. In some cases the other facts can be inferred with as much practical certainty as if they had been actually observed. In other cases the inference does not go beyond reasonable probability. But if there are no positive proved facts from which the inference can be made, the method of inference fails and what is left is mere speculation or conjecture."

(88)   The test is whether, on the basis of the primary facts, it is reasonable to draw the inference …'

1   (7 March 2000, unreported), NSW CA at paras 85–88.

The net of causation

12.43   When the court has assembled its primary facts, it then needs to assess them to see if there are a number of causes and if so which is 'the' cause. In *Alphacell Ltd v Woodward*[1] Lord Pearson adopted Lord Shaw's approach to this aspect of causation as set out in *Leyland Shipping Co v Norwich Union Fire Insurance Society*[2] where Lord Shaw said:

> 'To treat as proxima causa as the cause which is nearer in time is out of the question. Causes are spoken of as if they were distinct from one another as beads in a row or links in a chain, but – if this metaphysical topic has to be referred to – it is not wholly so. The chain of causation is a handy expression, but the figure is inadequate. Causation is not a chain but a net. At each point influences, forces, events, precedent and simultaneous meet; and the radiation from each point extends infinitely. At the point where these various influences meet it is for the judgment as upon a matter of fact to declare which of the causes thus joined at the point of effect was the proximate and which was the remote cause.'

1   [1972] 2 All ER 475, HL.
2   [1918] AC 350 at 353, HL.

12.44   Lord Pearson went on to adopt Lord Simon LC's approach in *Yorkshire Dale Steamship Co Ltd v Minister of War Transport, The Coxwold*:[1]

> 'Most results are brought about by a combination of causes, and a search for "the" cause involves a selection of the governing explanation in each case.'

1   [1942] AC 691 at 698, HL.

12.45 Another way of looking at this is to regard causation as a rope made up of a number of strands of cord. In *R v Exall*[1] Pollock CB, rejecting the chain analogy said:

'It is more like the case of a rope comprised of several cords. One strand of the cord might be insufficient to sustain the weight, but three stranded together may be quite of sufficient strength.'

1   (1866) 4 F & F 922 at 929.

12.46 But whichever simile is adopted – a net of causation or the strands in a rope – what the court is doing at this stage in combining the facts in the case to draw its inferences as to whether or not the alleged cause was in fact 'the' cause.

The common sense approach

12.47 In assessing the evidence the court adopts a common sense approach. In *The Coxwold*[1] Lord Wright said:

'This choice of the real or efficient cause from out of the whole complex of the facts must be made by applying commonsense standards.'

1   [1942] AC 691 at 706, HL.

12.48 This was approved in *Stapley v Gypsum Mines Ltd*[1] where Lord Reid pointed out that a court must consider these questions broadly and on a common sense basis. In *Wilsher v Essex Area Health Authority*[2] Lord Bridge said:

'But where ... the layman is told by the doctors that the longer the brick dust remains on the body the greater the risk of dermatitis, although the doctors cannot identify the process of causation scientifically there seems to be nothing irrational in drawing the inference, as a matter of common sense, that the consecutive periods when brick dust remained on the body probably contributed cumulatively to the causation of dermatitis.'

1   [1953] AC 663, HL.
2   [1988] AC 1074 at 1088, HL.

12.49 This approach has also been upheld by the Supreme Court of Canada in *Snell v Farrell*[1] where it was said that the principle promoted 'a robust and pragmatic approach to the facts to enable an inference of negligence to be drawn even though medical or scientific expertise cannot arrive at a definitive conclusion'.

1   (1990) 72 DLR (4th) 289.

12.50 In *McKenzie v Harper*[1] the approach of Rich ACJ in *Adelaide Stevedoring Co Ltd v Forst*[2] was adopted:

'I do not see why a court should not begin its investigation, i.e., before hearing any medical testimony, from the standpoint of the presumptive inference which this sequence of events would naturally inspire in the mind of any common-sense person uninstructed in pathology.'

1   Supreme Court of NSW 7 September 1995.
2   (1940) 64 CLR 538 at 563.

12.51   This approach is of considerable importance in pollution cases. Often the defendant will say that because the precise nature of the way in which the claimant's injuries cannot be shown he or she cannot succeed. But the claimant is not required to show precisely how his or her injury occurred. In *Kay v Ayrshire and Arran Health Board*[1] Lord Keith said[2] that if there is acceptable medical evidence that (the action of the defendant would increase the risk to the claimant) 'it would be immaterial that medical science was unable to demonstrate the precise mechanism whereby the risk was increased'.

1   [1987] 2 All ER 417, HL.
2   At 421b.

12.52   See also per Mason P *Bendix Mintex Pty Ltd v Barnes*:[1] 'The inability to call lay or expert evidence that shows the precise way in which something has happened is not fatal.'

1   (1997) 42 NSWLR 307 at 317E.

The evidence before the court

12.53   Ideally in this type of case the evidence before the court will be such that it can definitely be shown that the alleged cause was responsible for the injury. However, in real life this rarely happens. Such cases tend to settle. More often the court is left to apply its common sense approach to complex questions of science that are vigorously disputed between the parties.

12.54   Evidence can be direct, hearsay or circumstantial. Direct evidence is either the testimony of a witness as to what the witness heard, felt or saw or the production of a document or other article. Hearsay evidence is likely to have less weight than direct evidence but is admissible under the Civil Evidence Act 1995 in accordance with the provisions of that Act.

12.55   Proof on the balance of probabilities may be established by circumstantial evidence. Circumstantial evidence is evidence of circumstances surrounding an event from which a fact in issue may be inferred. In *Belhaven and Stenton Peerage*[1] Lord Reid said:

'My Lords, in dealing with circumstantial evidence, we have to consider the weight which is to be given to the united force of all the circumstances put together. You may have a ray of light so feeble that by itself it will do little to elucidate a dark corner. But on the other hand, you may have a number of rays, each of them insufficient, but all converging and brought to bear upon the same point, and, when united, producing a body of illumination which will clear away the darkness which you are endeavouring to dispel.'

'It is no derogation of evidence to say that it is circumstantial': per Lord Hewart CJ *R v Taylor, Weaver and Donovan*.[2]

1   (1875) 1 App Cas 278 at 279, HL.
2   (1928) 21 Cr App Rep 20 at 21, CCA.

Conclusion on nature of evidence

12.56   The position as to possibility was summed up by Herron CJ in *EMI (Australia) Ltd v Bes*:[1]

'Medical science may say in individual cases that there is no possible connection between the events and the death, in which case, of course, if the facts stand outside an area in which common experience can be a touchstone, then the judge cannot act as if there were a connection. But if medical science is prepared to say that it is a possible view, then, in my opinion, the judge after examining the lay evidence may decide that it is probable. It is only when medical science denies that there is any such connection that the judge is not entitled in such a case to act on his own intuitive reasoning. It may be, and probably is, the case that medical science will find a possibility not good enough on which to base a scientific deduction, but courts are always concerned to reach a decision on probability and it is no answer, it seems to me, that no medical witness states with certainty the very issue which the judge himself has to try.'

1   [1970] 2 NSWR 238 at 242.

12.57   This was cited with approval by Spigelman CJ in *Seltsam Pty Ltd v McGuiness*[1] where he said:

'The courts must determine the existence of a causal relationship on the balance of probabilities. However, as is the case with all circumstantial evidence, an inference as to the probabilities may be drawn from a number of pieces of particular evidence, each piece of which does not itself rise above the level of possibility.'

1   (7 March 2000, unreported), NSW CA at para 98.

12.58   In a pollution case, therefore, a claimant should be wary of the defendant's attempts to make the claimant prove the case to an unnecessarily high standard. Nevertheless, the claimant must still call reliable evidence to show, on the balance of probabilities, that the defendant's wrong caused the injury.

The scope of the evidence

12.59   What is proof of causation in a pollution case? In some states of the US (see *James v Bessemer Processing Co*[1]) medical causation consists of proof 'that the plaintiffs' injuries were proximately caused by exposure to the defendant's product; this means the plaintiff must show that:

(a)   the exposure to each defendant's product was a substantial factor in causing or exacerbating the disease;

(b)   factual proof of the plaintiff's frequent, regular and proximate exposure to a defendant's products;

(c)   medical and/or scientific proof of a nexus between the exposure and the plaintiff's condition.

1   714 A 2d 898 at 899/900 (1998).

12.60   In the UK this standard may be adopted. Paragraph (a) reflects *Bonnington Castings*. Paragraph (b) is also in line with contemporary UK practice. Even paragraph (c) would be in line with *Kay v Ayrshire and Arran Health Board*[1] – the precise nexus does not have to be shown.

1   [1987] 2 All ER 417, HL.

12.61   There may be four main categories of evidence that establish causation in a pollution case:

(1)   *Historical evidence* – By which is meant the claimant's history of what occurred, the symptoms suffered and the effects. This may be enhanced by documents from discovery, police or regulatory authority witnesses and other witnesses of fact.

(2)   *Toxicological evidence* – Evidence concerning the substance concerned and its effects on humans.

(3)   *Medical evidence* – This to an extent overlaps with toxicology but concentrates on the physical and mental condition of the claimant.

(4)   *Epidemiological evidence.*

12.62   In any case the evidence must be reputable. In the US the courts will act as an assessor of the expert evidence and may dismiss it at an intermediate stage if it does not comply with r 702 of the Federal Rules of Evidence. Here if expert evidence falls within the general rules the court will accept it and the way in which the report was compiled will simply go to the weight to be given to it.

12.63   Nevertheless, the US approach to expert evidence is instructive. In *Daubert v Merrell Dow Pharmaceuticals Inc*[1] the Supreme Court laid down rules as to the admissibility of expert evidence. They said that for expert evidence to be admissible a court should examine – in a flexible way – these non-exclusive factors:

●   whether the theory can be (and has been) tested according to the scientific method;

●   whether the theory or technique has been subjected to peer review and publication;

- in the case of a particular scientific technique, the known or potential rate of error;
- whether the theory is generally accepted.

1   509 US 579 (1993).

12.64   In pollution cases there may be theories at the boundaries of science that enthusiasts of the theory will be keen to promote.[1] The legal adviser should be careful of such theories and ensure that the evidence will stand up to what is inevitably going to be rigorous cross-examination.

1   See *Kay* at para **12.51** above and para **12.72** below.

Historical evidence

12.65   The evidence of the history of the events leading up to the claim cannot be gathered too soon. Once the claimant has been accepted by the solicitor, the claimant should be asked to provide a detailed statement of the events. In particular the claimant should give information about the weather at the time, what he or she saw, his or her initial symptoms and any subsequent symptoms. The claimant should be asked about any other likely witnesses, whether the emergency services were involved and if any other regulatory body took a part in the matter. It is also important to get details of any contact the claimant may have had with the defendants.

12.66   The Fire Brigade or the police should be contacted for any information they may have. Fire Services, for example, keep logs of incidents and will usually provide them for a fee. Other regulatory bodies vary in their approach. The Environment Agency may resist providing information – despite the Environmental Information Regulations 1992 – on the basis that they don't have to supply information if there is a pending court case. However, they do have to register certain actions on the public registers held under, for example, s 64 of the Environment Protection Act 1990 (waste sites). Thus some material may become available.

12.67   Police, local government and regulatory authority witnesses will usually not attend court to give evidence unless required to do so under a witness summons issued under CPR, r 34.2. This is not them being awkward, but rather done for budgetary reasons. They may also refuse to supply a statement. Whilst the claimant could apply for them to make a deposition under r 34.8, usually this is not necessary. A witness attending under an order can be examined in chief in the usual way.

12.68   In some cases there may be a local inquiry into the incident; in serious cases, perhaps a public inquiry. The reports themselves should be treated with caution. A court is unlikely to accept the findings as evidence. However the statements of witnesses to the inquiry can be very useful.

Toxicological evidence

12.69　Toxicology evaluates the relationship between an exposure to a potentially hazardous substance and the onset of certain illnesses. Toxicological evidence can be divided into three parts:

(1)　Is the substance in question capable of causing the particular illness complained of?

(2)　What exposure to that substance is necessary to cause such illness?

(3)　What was the exposure of the claimant to that substance?

12.70　Establishing the basic substance to which the claimant was exposed is not usually a problem. In product liability cases the substance can be identified from the label. In workplace incidents health and safety data will be available. In incidents affecting the public, emergency services will usually be provided with the relevant information.

12.71　The substance concerned must be properly identified. For example, dioxins are said to be harmful. So they are, some of them. There are 210 dioxins. The most harmful is a known carcinogen; others are not. To prove injury from dioxins it will be necessary to show to which dioxin the claimant was exposed. Similarly with bacteria. There may be exposure to EColi, but it will be necessary to show which strain of EColi caused the claimant's illness – there are over 700.

12.72　If the substance concerned is not capable of causing the particular illness at all, the claim will fail. In *Kay v Ayrshire and Arran Health Board*[1] a young child went to hospital with meningitis. Unfortunately while there he was given an overdose of penicillin. He recovered but was found to be deaf. The claimant sued the Board to recover for his son's deafness. However, since according to the expert evidence, an overdose of penicillin had never caused deafness, the son's deafness had to be regarded as resulting solely from the meningitis.

1　[1987] 2 All ER 417, HL.

12.73　In *Seltsam Pty Ltd v McGuiness*[1] the issue was whether asbestos exposure caused or contributed to the claimant's renal cell carcinoma. It was held (by a majority) that whilst asbestos exposure could be shown to cause lung cancer, there was not sufficient evidence to show it could cause cancer in the kidneys.

1　(7 March 2000, unreported), NSW CA.

12.74　A guide to the toxicity of a substance should be found in chemical cases in the Health and Safety Guidance Notes for that chemical or group of chemicals. It may only be a guide however because it may reflect administrative caution, rather than evidence supported on the balance of probabilities. Thus whilst these Notes are a good first step to show a possible nexus – and should be adequate to get over any applications to strike out pursuant to CPR Pt 24 on the basis of toxicology – they need to be reinforced at trial by the evidence of a toxicologist to raise the standard of proof to probable.

12.75 The Health and Safety Executive Guidance Note may set out an Occupational Exposure Level. Usually this will be to so many units (often in parts per million) over a period of time. There may also be a Maximum Exposure Level. However, this level may be for the concentrated material. Environmental exposure will be to dilute material. Thus an estimate may need to be made of the amount of substance to which the claimant was exposed. It is unlikely that such an estimate will get beyond the 'possible', but even so it will give the court a useful 'strand in the rope'.

12.76 Alternatively it can be argued that given the claimant's symptoms the exposure must have been excessive. In some states of the United States a claimant need only

'prove exposure of sufficient frequency, with regularity of conduct, and with product in close proximity and such factors should be balanced ... focussing on cumulative effects of exposure. The test is a fair balance between the needs of the Plaintiff, recognising difficulty of proving contact, and Defendants, protecting against liability predicated on guess-work; however courts may rely on circumstantial proof of sufficiently intense exposure to warrant liability, especially in bystander cases, where proof of direct contact is almost always lacking'.[1]

1   *Sholtis v American Cyanamid Co* 586 A 2d 1196 (1989).

Epidemiological evidence

12.77 Epidemiology is the study of the distribution and determinants of disease in human populations. It is based on the assumption that a disease is not distributed randomly in a group of individuals. Accordingly, sub-groups may be identified which are at increased risk of contracting particular diseases. Epidemiological evidence identifies associations between specific forms of exposure and the risk of disease in groups of individuals. It looks at 'general causation' – ie, whether or not the particular factor is capable of causing the disease. Specific causation is left to the medical evidence. Most epidemiological studies identify the strength of an association by a measure called relative risk ('RR'). RR is defined as the ratio of the incidence of disease in exposed individuals compared to the incidence in unexposed individuals. If the relative risk equals 1:0, the risk in exposed individuals is the same as the risk in unexposed individuals. If the relative risk is greater than 1:0, the risk in exposed individuals is greater then the risk in unexposed individuals.

12.78 In *Seltsam Pty Ltd v McGuiness*[1] it was considered that epidemiology only provides evidence of a possible connection. Pointing out[2] that US cases generally require a RR of 2:0 before ascribing probative value to an epidemiological study the court went on to say:[3]

'In Australian law, the test of actual persuasion does not require epidemiological studies to reach the level of a Relative Risk of 2:0, even where that is the only evidence available to a court. Nevertheless, the closer the ratio approaches 2:0, the greater the significance that can be attached to the studies for the purposes of drawing an inference of causation in an individual case. The "strands of the cable" must be capable of bearing the weight of the ultimate inference.'

1   (7 March 2000, unreported), NSW CA.
2   At para 121.
3   At para 137.

12.79   In the UK the main authority on the use of epidemiological evidence is *Reay v British Nuclear Fuels plc*.[1] In that case French J[2] set out the basis of such evidence. In particular he adopted the criteria that should apply to such evidence – the *Bradford-Hill* criteria. The key criteria are, briefly:

● *The strength of the association found by the study.*
● *Biological gradient* – Consistency of dose with response in a dose–response relationship (ie, if the risk of disease rises with increasing exposure, a causal interpretation of the association is more plausible).
● *Temporal relationships* – Particularly the exposure must precede the onset of the disease.
● *The consistency of the result of the study with other similar studies concerned with the same subject matter.*
● *Biological plausibility* – Is it plausible that the substance can cause the relevant illness?
● *Experimental evidence* – Laboratory tests as a back-up.

1   [1994] 5 Med LR 1.
2   At 10–14.

12.80   There is usually considerable controversy over any epidemiological study. A typical area of dispute lies in the use of 'controls' – people who are as similar as possible to those who have the disease but either do not have it or have not been exposed to the alleged causal mechanism. As French J[1] said: 'Great care must be exercised in the selection of controls and in the obtaining of data concerning the cases and the controls.' Thus while epidemiological evidence can be useful, it should be treated with caution. If such evidence is to be the mainstay of the case then it would be wise to have the study independently tested before offering it as evidence.

1   *Reay v British Nuclear Fuels* [1994] 5 Med LR 1 at 11.

Medical evidence

12.81   The medical evidence will set out the initial and subsequent diagnosis, a history of treatment for the illness and a prognosis. In general it will differ little from the usual evidence in personal injury cases. However, it will be important to carry out a differential diagnosis. This is a determination of which two or more diseases with similar symptoms is the one from which a patient is suffering, based on analysis of the clinical data. Whilst doctors do this all the time, for the purposes of evidence it will be necessary to adhere rigorously to the protocols for doing such a diagnosis. Any errors are bound to be exploited by the defendant.

12.82   Where the claimant's character is said to have changed as a result of the exposure, it will be necessary to call people who knew the claimant well before the incident to give 'before and after' testimony.

12.83   Sometimes a conclusion may be sought to be drawn from animal studies. These should be treated with caution. The effects of chemicals on the animals concerned – rats, hens, rabbits etc – may be very different from the effect of the same chemical on humans. At best animal studies give an indication of the type of effect that may be expected but should not be advanced as definite evidence of causation.

12.84   Not every person reacts in the same way to a given exposure to a particular chemical. Some people are more susceptible to it than others. This may be genetic or as a result of lack of particular enzymes or in some other way. It is not always possible to test for susceptibility, but if it is possible then this should be done.

CONCLUSION

12.85   The following extract from Turner J's summary of judgment in the *British Coal Respiratory Disease Litigation*[1] is relevant here.

'119.   The cases of *Bonnington* and *McGhee* make it clear that the identification of the pathological route from tortious exposure to causation is not a pre-requisite to recovery. It is tempting at this stage to resort to robustness and pragmatism to find the answer to the problem under consideration. Having listened to evidence over many days, in part anecdotal from miners themselves, in part epidemiological, it would be easy to accept the intuitive solution and arrive at the general conclusion that exposure to mine dust is a cause of the breathlessness suffered by miners with respiratory disability, whether they had been smokers or not. But the temptation should be resisted. The same result can, however, be reached by a jurisprudential and analytical approach which stands up to examination. This can most efficaciously be done by formulation of a number of propositions, always mindful that the feature which unites all present cases, other than the asthmatics, is that they are a selection of men who have all suffered both loss of lung function and have been exposed to tortious mine dust to greater or lesser extent. At its most favourable to British Coal's case ... [His Lordship then discussed the relevant criteria in that case.]

120.   In narrative terms, then, where an individual miner can prove that he has been exposed to tortious as well as non-tortious mine dust and suffers from breathlessness the law will not demand more by way of proof than that the breathlessness has been, at least in part, caused by his exposure. In this way the common law demonstrated how it has been able to adapt to modern conditions where circumstances, such as those which occur in cases of occupational hygiene, have arisen and were not foreseen when the origins of tort based recovery were developed.'

1   23 January 1998 (available from the Court Service website: www.courtservice.gov.uk).

12.86 The formulation of such propositions – based on the historical, toxicological, epidemiological and medical criteria set out above – will go a long way to solve the difficulties arising in the proof of causation in pollution cases.

CHAPTER 13

Noise

INTRODUCTION

13.01 Noise is the nuisance which generates most complaints to Environmental Health Officers. The statutory framework to meet the challenge of noise pollution is sophisticated and has largely displaced common law. The practitioner must not only know the applicable statute law, but must also understand expert evidence as to how noise is measured. The first part of this chapter seeks to demystify some of the science of noise, before proceeding to summarise the law.

DEFINITION

13.02 We all know what noise is, but for the purposes of controlling it, English law has consistently failed to provide a satisfactory definition. The legal controls discussed below ask a series of questions about the science of noise.

13.03 Sound is not simply an individual element but rather a combination of ingredients which shape and form what the human ear records. Sound itself can be defined as a periodic fluctuation of air pressure. The sound pressure is the amount by which the air pressure changes during the period of fluctuation. The frequency of sound is dictated by the rate at which the air pressure fluctuates. In common parlance frequency might be referred to as pitch. Therefore the higher the frequency the higher the rate of air pressure fluctuation and the higher the pitch. The inverse is true.

13.04 It is important to be able to express scientifically the level of pitch. This is achieved by reference to *hertz (Hz)*. The human ear responds to frequencies between 18Hz and 18,000Hz. Therefore, should the rate of air fluctuation be either very slow or very fast it may fall outside the range of the human ear. Although the hertz level of a sound is a useful component in assessing the character of a sound it does not express the 'loudness' of a sound. Indeed, without scientific reference, 'loudness' is a meaningless term. This is why, in our experience, a noise nuisance action has never succeeded on the base of anecdotal evidence alone; such evidence always needs technical support by *measurement* of sound. However, in *Lewisham London Borough Council v Hall*,[1] it was held that in a noise nuisance case brought under the Environmental Protection Act 1990 ('EPA 1990'), there was no requirement for acoustic evidence. This contrasts with the position under the Noise Act 1996 ('NA 1996') where such evidence is required.

1   [2003] Env LR 4.

13.05   Given that sound is created by a fluctuation in air pressure, the greater the change in air pressure, the greater the degree of noise. The *decibel* (*dB*) is a unit of measurement which expresses the ratio between two levels of sound pressure. The higher the decibel level the greater the sound. We have noted that the human ear responds only to a given range of hertz; and it has been established that the human ear is more receptive at some frequencies than others. It is therefore usual when making noise measurements to incorporate an electronic filter in the measuring system in order to give a response similar to that of the human ear. The filter that is most frequently used is *A-weighting* and noise measured using this weighting is expressed *dB*(*A*). As well as filtering out those frequencies to which the human ear is less sensitive and which cannot therefore be intrusive, noise measurement needs to take account of any fluctuations in noise level *over time*. In other words, it may be *time weighted*. The fact that noise level at any particular point will probably vary from time to time makes it difficult to arrive at a figure for the 'level' of noise. In an attempt to arrive at a figure that reflects the variable nature of a noise a number of noise metrics have been developed.

13.06   The maximum decibel level recorded over a given measurement period is called *LAMAX*. This will be a useful measurement for intermittent intense noise against an otherwise quiet background level, for example a cock crowing at dawn.

13.07   On the other hand, where the noise is steadier, albeit fluctuating, such as in the case of construction-site noise, the *average* noise level over a given period of time is typically used. This is called *LAEQ* (pronounced L.ee.q). This is defined in the British Standard 7445: Pt 1 (1991) as:

> 'the value of the A-weighted sound pressure level of a continuous, steady sound that, within a specified time interval, has the same mean square sound pressure as a sound under consideration whose level varies with time'.

13.08   It will be immediately apparent that the choice of approach to measurement greatly influences the result. If the LAEQ approach is used in the case of the overflying Concorde, then assuming the timeframe is hours rather than minutes, the 'averaged' result will be quite misleading as to the noise effect suffered.

13.09 Another method, particularly appropriate in the case of a *variable* noise level, is expressed as *LA10* and *LA90*. Both of these parameters express a given noise level, eg 75dB(A), which is exceeded over a given measurement period, eg one hour. LA90 would mean that for 90% of the measurement period, ie 54 minutes, the noise level would exceed 75dB(A). For the remaining period the level would be less than 75dB(A). This six-minute period therefore reflects the 'quiet' phase of activity during the measurement period. In contrast LA10 is used to express situations in which the noise level is exceeded for only 10% of the time. This method finds favour where industrial noise is likely to be intermittent.[1]

1   For example, see BS4142 at para **13.12** below.

13.10 Some familiar situations and their relevant noise levels are contained in Table 1.

Table 1: Noise levels

Peak Sound Level in dB(A) (Decibels)	Event
140	Threshold of pain
130	Jet aircraft on ground; pneumatic road breaker
125	Noise under supersonic flight path within five miles of take-off
120	Jet take-off at 100 metres; loud motor horn at three feet
110–125	Broadcast pop music
115	Noise under jet flight path within five miles of take-off; riveting machine in sheet-metal works
100	House near airport; inside a moving underground train
90–92	Train; inside a moving bus
88–92	Heavy lorry
81–91	Sports car
77–83	Motor cars
80	Major road with heavy traffic at peak level
75	Average street corner noise
70	Conversational speech
65	Residential road with local traffic

Peak Sound Level in dB(A) (Decibels)	Event
60	Business office
50	Livingroom in a suburban area with distant traffic noise
40	Library
30	Quiet bedroom at night
25	Rustling leaves
20	Broadcasting studio
10	Threshold of hearing

This table is derived from D Hughes *Environmental Law* (Butterworths, 4th edn, 2002) pp 580–581.

13.11 Changes in noise levels are particularly important. A change in the average level of fluctuating sound such as traffic noise needs to be of the order of 3dB(A) before becoming definitely perceptible to the human ear. A change in sound level of 10dB(A) seems to the listener a very substantial change of the order of a doubling or halving of loudness. Expressed mathematically, the decibel scale is not linear but logarithmic.

GUIDANCE ON NUISANCE NOISE LEVELS

13.12 There is no overarching guidance on noise levels which constitute nuisance, even at night. The court will hear technical evidence concerning the relation of the sound levels to various British Standards relating to noise. Whilst compliance does not confer immunity, and non-compliance is not conclusive as to culpability, the court will certainly pay attention to them. Examples are as follows:

● In a case concerning noise from the dehumidifying equipment of a municipal swimming-pool, the court was influenced by BS8233 which gave a recommended maximum of 30–40dB(A) for intrusive noise. It concluded from the measurements that the noise from the dehumidifying equipment fell well below that level.[1]

● The WHO Guidance (1980) indicates (night time) disturbance of sleep threshold at about 35db(A), and it held that the court was entitled to take this into account in dismissing a nuisance claim.[2]

● The 'permitted levels' for night hours (11pm–7am) under the NA 1996 are defined as follows:

    (i) where the background noise level is less than 25dB, the permitted level should be 35dB;

    (ii) where the background level exceeds 25dB, the permitted level shall be 10dB in excess of the background level.

- Another British Standard of importance is BS4142: 1997 (3rd edn); 'Method for rating industrial noise affecting mixed residential and industrial areas'. The method involves subtracting measured background noise level from the noise level of the source under investigation. A difference of around 10dB or more indicates 'that complaints are likely'. Again, there is no reported case where the application of this British Standard for noise measurement has been very influential.

1   *Botross v Hammersmith and Fulham London Borough Council* (1994) 27 HLR, 179.
2   *Murdoch v Glacier Metal Co Ltd* [1998] Env LR 732, CA.

EVIDENCE

13.13   When bringing a complaint about the level of noise, the starting point will always be the collation of good anecdotal evidence. The following categories of evidence will be needed:
(a)   anecdotal evidence of the complainant;
(b)   anecdotal evidence of others, e g neighbours;
(c)   a noise notebook/diary should be kept by the complainant and by neighbours, detailing the time, date, duration and source of the noise and indicating its character and the perceived loudness;
(d)   where the character or pattern of the noise is important, a tape recording of the noise should be obtained. It should be emphasised that a tape recording cannot be used as evidence of the loudness of the noise which is the province of the decibel meter. Tape recorders may be useful to give some idea of the character of the noise, e g where it has a particularly irritating pattern;
(e)   if the loudness of the noise is to be measured objectively, a decibel meter must be used. It is important to record not just the measured level of noise, but also to note the point at which the reading was taken;
(f)   once the primary evidence has been obtained, an expert should be instructed to prepare a report which addresses the level of noise experienced by the complainant and sets out the level which the complainant alleges would be reasonable.

COMMON LAW CASES

13.14   There have been few successful common law noise nuisance actions in recent years. In part, this results from the increased effectiveness of Environmental Health Departments in bringing statutory nuisance claims. Noise is by far the most frequent environmental complaint received by local authorities, and the response in most cases has been properly to equip well-trained staff to investigate such complaints and, where appropriate, prosecute for statutory nuisance. Reported cases have generally been failures.[1]

1   *Murdoch v Glacier Metal Co Ltd* [1998] Env LR 732, CA; *Blackburn v ARC Ltd* [1998] Env LR 469 (on noise, but succeeded on litter and smell); *Milka v Chetwynd Animal Biproducts* ENDS, February 2000, p 56 (on noise, but succeeded on smell).

13.15   However, a notable recent success is the case of *Dennis v Ministry of Defence*[1] where the claimants succeeded in obtaining an award of £950,000 damages in compensation for noise nuisance from the defendant's Harrier jets overflying on training missions. The defendant relied upon public interest, maintaining that the training activities should be immune because of the need to maintain a state-of-the-art strike force and to train pilots. Whilst the judge held that, in appropriate circumstances, public interest might give rise to a defence in relation to an activity which would otherwise constitute an actionable nuisance (provided that no conflict arose under the European Convention on Human Rights), he found that the defence was not made out where the claimants suffered 'severe and frightening' noise disturbance on a daily basis as a result of the Harrier jets overflying their property. However, the judge ruled that it was permissible to take into account public interest at the *remedy* stage, and therefore refused an injunction, awarding damages instead.

1   [2003] EWHC 793 (QB), [2003] 19 EG 118 (CS), [2003] Env LR 741.

THE STATUTORY FRAMEWORK RELATING TO NOISE

Statutory nuisance

13.16   The EPA 1990, Pt III largely replaces the noise control provisions of the Control of Pollution Act 1974 ('COPA 1974'). It is dealt with in general terms in Chapter 3. The following paragraphs are particularly relevant to noise.

13.17   Two specific noise nuisances are defined in the EPA 1990:
(a)   s 79(1)(g) 'noise emitted from premises so as to be prejudicial to health or a nuisance';
(b)   s 79(1)(ga) 'noise that is prejudicial to health or a nuisance and that is emitted from or caused by a vehicle, machinery or equipment in a street'.[1] It does not apply to noise made by traffic or by demonstrations. 'Equipment' includes musical instruments.[2]

1   Thus overruling the case of *Tower Hamlets London Borough Council v Manzoni and Walder* (1983) 148 JP 123.
2   EPA 1990, s 79(7).

13.18   In addition, noise may also be crucial to another kind of statutory nuisance, viz 'any premises in such a state as to be prejudicial to health or a nuisance'.[1] In *Southwark London Borough Council v Ince*,[2] it was held that council flats were premises which constituted a statutory nuisance by virtue of the fact that road and railway noise had penetrated their walls because of inadequate insulation and was prejudicial to the tenants' health.[3]

1   EPA 1990, s 79(1)(a).
2   (1989) 21 HLR 504.
3   Cf *Baxter v Camden London Borough Council* [1999] 4 All ER 449, HL (no nuisance where noise caused by other tenants and no sound-proofing).

Procedure in the magistrates' court

13.19   An *individual* may make a complaint to a magistrates' court under the EPA 1990, s 82. A *local authority* may serve an Abatement Notice under s 80.

Local authorities: the Abatement Notice

13.20   Where a local authority is satisfied that a nuisance exists, or is likely to occur or reoccur in their area, they *must* by virtue of the EPA 1990, s 80(1) serve an Abatement Notice: *R v Carrick District Council, ex p Shelley*.[1] This, principally and where possible, is to be served on the 'person responsible' for the nuisance.

1   [1996] Env LR 273.

13.21   The 'person responsible' is defined in the EPA 1990, s 79(7). It means generally the person to whose act, default or sufferance the nuisance is attributable. However, in respect of machinery or equipment, it includes any person who is for the time being the operator of it.

13.22   Where a person responsible cannot be found, or if the nuisance is anticipated, the local authority should serve the Notice in a different way. In the case of noise emitted from premises, it should be served on the owner or occupier of the premises. Where the nuisance is noise from a street and arises from a vehicle, machinery or equipment, the Notice should be served by affixing it.[1] Such a Notice will require the abatement of the noise, or the prohibition or restriction of its occurrence or recurrence, or require the execution of such works or the taking of such steps as may be necessary. Where a nuisance is likely to recur, a permanent prohibition on its recurrence can be imposed.[2]

1   See EPA 1990, ss 80(2) and 80A.
2   See *R v Birmingham City Justices, ex p Guppy* (1987) 152 JP 159.

13.23   Under the EPA 1990, s 80(3) an appeal against a Notice may be made to a magistrates' court within 21 days of service. The grounds of appeal are contained in the Statutory Nuisance (Appeals) Regulations 1995.[1] They include the following:

(a)   that the Abatement Notice is not justified by the EPA 1990, s 80 (summary proceedings for statutory nuisances);

(b)   that there has been some informality, defect or error in, or in connection with, the Abatement Notice;[2] or in, or in connection with any copy of, the Abatement Notice served under s 80A(3) (certain notices in respect of vehicles, machinery or equipment);

(c)   that the time (or where more than one time is specified, any of the times) within which the requirements of the Abatement Notice are to be complied with, is or are not reasonably sufficient for the purpose.

1   SI 1995/2644.
2   In *Myatt v Teignbridge District Council* [1994] Env LR 78, a Notice was challenged on the ground that it did not make the source of the alleged nuisance clear. The Notice required that its recipient 'cease the keeping of dogs'. The court held that in the circumstances it was clear what the problem was, and that was the important issue.

13.24   An offence is committed by a person if, without reasonable excuse, that person contravenes or fails to comply with any requirements or prohibitions imposed by a Notice served on him or her. The offence is punishable by a fine or a series of fines for each day the nuisance continues after conviction. Moreover, where the offence is committed on industrial, trade or business premises, a fine of up to £20,000 is payable.[1]

1   EPA 1990, s 80(4), (5).

13.25   A number of defences are available for nuisances falling under the EPA 1990, s 79(1)(g) and (ga), including the state-of-the-art defence of 'best practicable means';[1] and that of 'reasonable excuse'[2] for failure to comply with any requirements or prohibitions of any Notice served. A lack of finance for carrying out abatement works, however, does not constitute a reasonable excuse. The High Court recently considered the defence of best practiceable means and provided guidance on its application.[3] The defendant, who was being prosecuted for transmitting music and voice-overs in breach of a s 80 notice, sought to rely on certain actions of the local authority as grounds for his defence. The High Court found no defence, rejecting the suggestion that the local authority's failure to assist the claimant in setting the appropriate level on a sound compressor could assist in establishing that he was using best practicable means to prevent noise.

1   EPA 1990, s 79(9).
2   EPA 1990, s 80(4).
3   *Tewkesbury Borough Council v Deacon* [2003] EWHC 2544 (Admin), ENDS December 2003 (No 347), p 66.

13.26   Instead of prosecution, a local authority may commence an action in the High Court to secure the abatement, prohibition or restriction of a statutory noise nuisance by way of injunction. This power arises under the EPA 1990, s 81(5) and is to be exercised when summary proceedings would provide an inadequate remedy. It is an important power because fines, after a successful prosecution, may well prove to be an inadequate deterrent. The figures laid down for fines are maxima rather than standard sums, so that the levels vary. Instead, the breach of an injunction can be treated as contempt of court.

13.27   Although local authorities are under a duty to inspect and investigate complaints relating to statutory nuisances,[1] they have tended to interpret these duties inconsistently. Environmental Health departments are often under-staffed. The most that some departments do is to send out a standard letter to the noise polluter or, aware of the costs of litigation, they will try exhortation or conciliation with the noise creator.

1   EPA 1990, s 79(1).

13.28 To obtain the most out of an Environmental Health department, it is prudent to adduce as much evidence as possible that a nuisance is occurring or likely to occur, thus increasing the pressure on the local authority to take action. Complaints to local councillors may also help.

Individuals in the magistrates' courts

13.29 In the event that a local authority is unwilling or unable to act, an 'aggrieved' individual can take proceedings in a magistrates' court.[1] Such a course of action will only be available when noise has occurred. Where the magistrates' court is satisfied that a nuisance exists, or that although abated it is likely to recur, they may make an order akin to an Abatement Notice. The breach of this will constitute an offence.

1   EPA 1990, s 82.

13.30 This type of proceeding will probably prove cheaper and quicker than a civil action. Moreover, not only can an abatement order be sought, but also an order for compensation for those affected by the nuisance.[1] However, the defence of best practicable means may be available to the defendant, and the burden of proof on the prosecution will be the criminal standard of proof even in relation to noise nuisances.[2]

1   *Botross v Hammersmith and Fulham London Borough Council* (1994) 27 HLR 179.
2   *Botross* above; *Lewisham London Borough v Fenner* [1996] 8 ELM 11 (Knightsbridge Crown Court).

13.31 Alternatively, redress may be sought against the local authority through the default powers of the Secretary of State contained in the EPA 1990, Sch 3, para 4. The Secretary of State is empowered to make an order declaring that the authority has failed to exercise its duties to inspect an area for nuisances, or to serve an Abatement Notice. The Secretary of State may make an order directing them to comply with their duties. Should the authority fail to obey such an order, the Secretary of State may take two courses of action: he may seek a mandatory order or make an order transferring the relevant functions of the local authority to himself.

NOISE ABATEMENT ZONES

Designation by local authorities

13.32 The COPA 1974, s 57 places a duty on every local authority to cause its area to be inspected from time to time to decide how to exercise powers concerning noise abatement zones. The purpose of designating a noise abatement zone is to prevent an increase in noise levels by registering current levels found at premises within the zone and imposing criminal sanctions if they are exceeded. Failure to carry out this duty is enforceable by the default powers of the Secretary of State under the COPA 1974, s 97.

13.33 The COPA 1974, s 63(1) empowers a local authority to designate all or any part of its area a noise abatement zone.[1] The order must specify the classes of premises to which it applies and the order may be revoked or varied by any subsequent order made by the local authority. The COPA 1974, Sch 1 sets out the procedure to be followed. Before making a noise abatement order, or before revoking or varying it, the local authority must:

(a) serve on every owner, lessee and occupier (other than tenants for a month over any period less than a month) of any of the premises within the area of a class to which the order will relate; and

(b) publish in the *London Gazette* and once at least in each of two successive weeks in a local newspaper,

a notice which complies with the requirements of the COPA 1974, Sch 1, para 2. Those requirements are:

(a) a statement that the local authority intends to make that order and its general effect;

(b) stating where a copy of the order and a copy of any map or plan referred to on it may be inspected by the public free of charge for at least six weeks from the last newspaper publication of the notice;

(c) a statement that objections may be made in writing within a period of six weeks from the last newspaper publication of the notice.

1 An authority is not required by law to make an inspection of the area prior to making an order or in connection with the making of it: *Morganite Special Carbons Ltd v Secretary of State for the Environment* (1980) 256 Estates Gazette 1105.

13.34 If an objection is made to the noise abatement order then the local authority must consider any such objection before making the order unless it is satisfied that it is unnecessary to do so having regard to:

(a) the nature of the premises to which the order will relate; or

(b) the nature of the interests of the person making the objection (it is not at all clear what this means but it cannot allow a local authority to disregard the views of eg conservation groups).

Where the order varies or revokes a previous order, the local authority may also disregard any objection to the order which is the same as an objection to the initial order.[1]

1 COPA 1974, Sch 1, para 3.

13.35 A noise abatement zone becomes operative on the date specified in the order, which must be at least one month from the date on which the order was made, except in the case of an order revoking or modifying a previous abatement order.

1 COPA 1974, Sch 1, para 4.

Measurement and registration of noise levels

13.36 Once a noise abatement order comes into effect, the local authority is required to measure noise levels from premises within the zone which are subject to the noise abatement order.[1] The procedure for measuring and calculating noise levels is set out in the Control of Noise (Measurement and Registers) Regulations 1976.[2] The COPA 1974, s 64(3) requires the local authority to record the measured levels in a register, but there is no time period within which this must be done. Copies of the entry are to be sent to the owner and occupier of all premises, and all owners and occupiers so served have a right of appeal to the Secretary of State within 28 days of the date of service. The register is open to the public free of charge and copies of entries must be provided at reasonable charge.[3]

1   COPA 1974, s 64(1).
2   SI 1976/37.
3   COPA 974, s 64(7).

13.37 Unless the local authority gives its consent in writing, it is an offence for the owner or occupier of premises to exceed the level recorded in the noise level register. The COPA 1974 itself does not provide any specific statutory defence. Where the owner or occupier of premises wishes to exceed the level of noise recorded in the noise level register, it may apply to the local authority for consent to do so. Such an application may be granted, with or without conditions, or refused. If it is granted, either by the local authority or by the Secretary of State, the consent must be recorded in the noise level register.[1]

1   COPA 1974, s 65(2).

13.38 The Control of Noise (Appeals) Regulations 1975,[1] Pt 3 sets out the procedure relating to appeals to the Secretary of State against the recorded noise level for premises, refusal to consent to exceed the registered noise level or against conditions attached to a consent. Within seven days of giving notice of appeal (or such longer period as the Secretary of State may at any time allow) the appellant must send to the Secretary of State the following documents:
(a)   the application, if any, made to the local authority;
(b)   any relevant plans and particulars submitted to the local authority;
(c)   any relevant record, consent to termination, notice or other notification issued by the authority;
(d)   all other relevant correspondence with the local authority;
(e)   a plan of the premises concerned.

The Secretary of State may require further written evidence either from the appellant or the local authority and has discretion to hold a local inquiry. There are no specific statutory grounds for appeal.

1   SI 1975/2116.

Offences

13.39 The COPA 1974, s 65(5) and (6) makes it a criminal offence to exceed the registered noise level, or to breach a condition attached to a consent, or to fail to comply with a court order to undertake works. Consent to exceed the registered noise level does not of itself provide a defence to proceedings relating to statutory nuisance under the EPA 1990, s 82 but it is a defence to proceedings for failure to comply with the local authority Abatement Notice under the EPA 1990, s 80.[1]

1   See the COPA 1974, s 65(8) and EPA 1990, s 80(9)(a).

NOISE LEVEL DETERMINATIONS FOR NEW BUILDINGS

13.40   Where it appears to the local authority:
(a)   that a building is going to be constructed and that a noise abatement order will apply to it when it is erected; or
(b)   that any premises will, as a result of any works, become premises to which a noise abatement order applies,

the local authority may, on the application of the owner or occupier of the premises or a person who is negotiating to acquire an interest in the premises, or on its own initiative, determine the level of noise which will be acceptable as that emanating from the premises.[1] That noise level must then be recorded in the noise level register.[2]

1   COPA 1974, s 67(1).
2   COPA 1974, s 67(2).

13.41   The local authority is required to give notice of its view of the application or of a decision on its own initiative to the owner or occupier of the premises, and that person has a right of appeal to the Secretary of State within a three-month period from the date of notification. The provisions relating to appeal are those laid down in the Control of Noise (Appeals) Regulations 1975,[1] Pt 3 and are the same as those relating to registration of noise levels generally in noise abatement zones.

1   SI 1975/2116.

Offences

13.42   The same provisions as those relating generally to the registration of noise levels in noise abatement zones apply. It should be noted that it is a defence in proceedings for non-compliance with a local authority Abatement Notice under the EPA 1990, s 80 to show that the noise did not exceed the level registered under this procedure.[1]

1   EPA 1990, s 80(9)(c).

NOISE REDUCTION NOTICES

13.43 If it appears to the local authority:
(a) that the level of noise emanating from any premises to which a noise abatement order applies is not acceptable, having regard to the purposes for which the order was made; and
(b) that a reduction in that level is practicable at reasonable cost and would afford a public benefit,

the local authority may serve a noise reduction notice on the person responsible.[1]

1   COPA 1974, s 66(1).

13.44 The notice must contain the following:
(a) a requirement to reduce the level of noise emanating from the premises to such level as may be specified in the notice;
(b) a prohibition on any subsequent increase in the level of noise emanating from the premises without the consent of the local authority;
(c) a specification of works as may be necessary to achieve (a) and (b);[1] and
(d) a specification of the time within which the noise level is to be reduced and within which any required works are to be completed. This must be at least six months or, for new building, three months.[2]

1   COPA 1974, s 66(2).
2   COPA 1974, ss 66(3) and 67(5).

13.45 In addition, a noise reduction notice may specify particular times or particular days within which the noise level is to be reduced, and may require the noise level to be reduced to different levels for different times or days.[1] A noise reduction notice may be served whether or not the local authority has consented to a higher level of noise.[2] The noise reduction notice must be recorded in the noise level register.[3]

1   COPA 1974, s 66(4).
2   COPA 1974, ss 65 and 66(7).
3   COPA 1974, s 66(6).

Appeal

13.46 A person served with a noise reduction notice may appeal to a magistrates' court against the notice within a three-month period.[1] The procedure for such appeals is set out in the Control of Noise (Appeals) Regulations 1975,[2] Pt 2, reg 7. The grounds of appeal include the following:
(a) that the notice is not justified by the COPA 1974, s 66;
(b) that there has been some material informality, defect or error in, or in connection with, the notice;
(c) that the local authority has refused unreasonably to accept compliance

with alternative requirements or that the requirements of the notice are otherwise unreasonable in character or extent, or are unnecessary;

(d)   that the time allowed to comply with the notice is not reasonably sufficient;

(e)   that the noise is caused in the course of a trade or business and that the best practicable means have been used for preventing, or for counteracting the effect of, the noise;

(f)   that the notice should have been served on some other person in substitution for or in addition to the appellant.

1   COPA 1974, s 66(7).
2   SI 1975/2116.

Offences

13.47   It is an offence for a person to contravene a noise reduction notice without reasonable excuse.[1] Thus it is a defence to prove that best practicable means have been used. 'Practicable' is defined in the COPA 1974, s 62 as meaning reasonably practicable having regard, among other things, to local conditions and circumstances, to the current state of technical knowledge and to the financial implications.[2] The 'means' to be employed include the design, installation and maintenance of plant and machinery, the manner and periods of operation of plant and machinery and the design, construction and maintenance of buildings and acoustic structure.[3] The test of best practicable means is to apply only so far as is compatible with any duty imposed by law and with safety and safe working conditions, and with the exigencies of any emergency or unforeseeable circumstances.[4] Regard shall be had to any provision of an approved code of practice.[5]

1   COPA 1974, s 66(8).
2   COPA 1974, s 72(2).
3   COPA 1974, s 72(3).
4   COPA 1974, s 72(4), (5).
5   COPA 1974, s 72(6).

13.48   Where proceedings are for non-compliance with the local authority Abatement Notice under EPA 1990, s 80, it will be a defence to show that the noise level at the time did not contravene the requirements of any noise reduction notice under this procedure.[1]

1   EPA 1990, s 80(9)(b).

NOISY NEIGHBOURS

13.49   The Noise Act 1996 ('NA 1996') provides a means of controlling night noise in private dwellings that is disturbing neighbours.[1] Section 1 provides that a local authority may resolve to apply the Act to its area. If it does not do so, the Secretary of State is empowered to make an Order requiring the authority to apply the Act. In local authority areas to which the NA 1996 applies, s 2 places a duty on the local authority to take reasonable steps to investigate any complaint that excessive noise is being emitted from a dwelling during 'night hours' above the 'permitted level' as measured from the complainant's dwelling. 'Night hours' are between 11pm and 7am. The 'permitted level' is defined in the Annex to DETR Circular 8/97 as being the following:

(a) in any case where the underlying level of noise does not exceed 25dB, the permitted level shall be 35dB;

(b) in any case where the underlying level of noise exceeds 25dB, the permitted level shall be 10dB in excess of that underlying level of noise.

1   See DETR Circular 8/97 and Neighbour Noise Working Party: Review of the Effectiveness of Neighbourhood Noise Controls, DETR 1995.

13.50 Where a local authority's officer considers that excessive noise above the permitted level is being emitted, the officer may issue a warning notice under the NA 1996, s 3. If the notice is not respected, the person responsible for the continuation of the noise without reasonable cause will be guilty of an offence under s 4. That person may be prosecuted summarily. Alternatively, a fixed penalty may be given, following the issuing of a fixed penalty notice.[1] Where a prosecution occurs, provision is made for the production of evidence as to the measuring of noise.[2]

1   NA 1996, s 8.
2   NA 1996, s 7.

13.51 The NA 1996, s 10 gives a local authority officer powers to enter a dwelling from which there is reason to believe excessive noise is being emitted and to seize and remove equipment which it appears is causing the noise. These powers only exist where there is reason to believe that a warning notice has been issued and that excessive noise is still being emitted from the dwelling. Where entry is refused or refusal is apprehended, and where a request to enter would defeat the object of the entry, a magistrates' warrant may be issued authorising entry, by force if necessary. Subsection 10(7) provides that the power of a local authority to abate a statutory nuisance which takes the form of 'noise emitted from premises' includes the power to seize and remove the noise-making equipment. It is an offence to obstruct a local authority officer who is exercising his or her powers of entry, seizure and removal.

AUDIBLE INTRUDER (BURGLAR) ALARMS

13.52 The disturbance of ringing burglar alarms[1] is provided for in the Noise and Statutory Nuisance Act 1993 ('NSNA 1993'), s 9. The section empowers a local authority, after consulting the relevant chief officer of police, to resolve to apply the provisions of Sch 3 to the Act within its area.[2] Schedule 3 provides that any person who installs a burglar alarm must ensure that it complies with any requirements in regulations made by the Secretary of State and further must notify the local authority within 48 hours of having installed the alarm.

The failure to do so without reasonable excuse is a criminal offence which is punishable following summary conviction by a fine not exceeding level 5 on the standard scale where the alarm does not comply with prescribed requirements, and by a fine not exceeding level 2 on the standard scale in any other case.

1   Provided that the alarms are on or in residential or commercial premises.
2   NSNA 1993, s 9(1).

13.53   The occupier of the premises in which the alarm is situated must also not permit the alarm to be operated without:
(a)   complying with any prescribed requirements;
(b)   the police having been notified of the names, addresses and telephone numbers of the two current keyholders to the premises;
(c)   the local authority having been notified of the address of the police station to which the details of the keyholders have been provided.

13.54   Failure to comply without reasonable excuse is a criminal offence punishable by fine. Further, if an alarm has been operating continuously for a period of one hour and is giving annoyance, an authorised officer of the local authority has a power of entry, in certain circumstances by force under a magistrate's warrant, to turn the alarm off. The local authority may in certain circumstances recover expenses when exercising its power of entry. Although the majority of the provisions of the NSNA 1993 have been in force since January 1994, the rather draconian powers of s 9 are as yet not in force.

13.55   Further, there is a 1982 Code of Practice on Noise from Audible Intruder Alarms made under the COPA 1974, s 71, which has been approved by statutory instrument.[1] In London, the London Local Authorities Act 1991, s 23 makes provision on a similar basis to that contained in s 9 above for the control of burglar alarms. The provisions of s 23 are in force. A failure to control the noise emitted from a burglar alarm can be a statutory nuisance.

1   SI 1981/1829.

STREET NOISE

13.56   The COPA 1974, s 62(1) makes it an offence to operate a loudspeaker in the street between 9pm and 8am for any purpose, and at any other time for the purpose of advertising any entertainment, trade or business. 'Street' is defined as meaning 'a highway and any other road, footway, square or court which is for the time being open to the public'.[1]

1   COPA 1974, s 62(1).

13.57   The COPA 1974, s 62(2) lists a number of exceptions to the operation of a loudspeaker:
(a)   for police, fire brigade or ambulance purposes, by the Environment Agency, a water undertaker or sewerage undertaker in the exercise of any of its functions, or by a local authority within its area;

(b) for communicating with persons on a vessel for the purpose of directing the movement of that or any other vessel;

(c) if the loudspeaker forms part of a public telephone system;

(d) if the loudspeaker:
  (i) is in or fixed to a vehicle; and
  (ii) is operated solely for the entertainment of, or for communicating with, the driver or a passenger of the vehicle, or, where the loud-speaker forms part of the horn or similar warning instrument of the vehicle, solely for giving warning to any other traffic; and
  (iii) is so operated as not to give reasonable cause for annoyance to persons in the vicinity;

(e) otherwise than on a highway, by persons employed in connection with a transport undertaking used by the public in cases where the loudspeaker is operated solely for making announcements to passengers or prospective passengers or to other persons so employed;

(f) by a travelling showman on land which is being used for the purposes of a pleasure fair;

(g) in the case of emergency.

13.58 A further exception exists for a loudspeaker between 12pm and 7pm if the loudspeaker:

(a) is fixed to a vehicle which is being used for the conveyance of a perishable commodity for human consumption (eg hot dogs and ice cream); and

(b) is operated solely for informing members of the public (otherwise than by means of words) that the commodity is on sale from the vehicle; and

(c) is so operated as not to give reasonable cause for annoyance to persons in the vicinity. Thus brief messages or music can be used, but not loud and continuous repetition of the same.

13.59 The NSNA 1993, s 8, enables local authorities who adopt Sch 2 to the Act to consent to the operation of loudspeakers for non-advertising purposes outside the hours laid down in s 62. The then DETR suggested that this would enable charitable and other entertainment events to use loudspeakers after 9pm with the approval of the local authority. Applications will have to be made in writing and a reasonable fee may be charged by the local authority. Conditions may be imposed on the consent.

NOISE FROM CONSTRUCTION SITES

Noise control

13.60 Construction work that is reasonably conducted is not a private nuisance. The local authority should consider the interests of the notice recipient in this regard.[1] It may be a statutory nuisance.

1   COPA 1974, s 60(4)(c).

13.61 Noise from construction sites is regulated by the COPA 1974, ss 60 and 61 which apply to the following works:
(a) the erection, construction, alteration, repair or maintenance of buildings, structures or roads;
(b) breaking up, opening or boring under any road or adjacent land in connection with the construction, inspection, maintenance or removal of works;
(c) demolition or dredging work;
(d) any work of engineering construction.[1]

1   COPA 1974, s 60(1).

13.62 Where it appears to a local authority that relevant works are being, or are going to be, carried out on any premises, the local authority may serve a notice imposing requirements as to the way in which the works are to be carried out, and may, if it thinks fit, publish notice of the requirements as to the way in which the works are to be appropriate.[1]

1   COPA 1974, s 60(2). See *Botross v Hammersmith and Fulham London Borough Council* (1994) 27 HLR 179.

13.63 By the COPA 1974, s 60(3) the notice may:
(a) specify the plant or machinery which is or is not to be used;
(b) specify the hours during which the works may be carried out;
(c) specify the level of noise which may be emitted from the premises in question from any specified point on those premises, or which may be so emitted during specified hours; and
(d) provide for any change of circumstances.

13.64 In serving a notice the local authority is required by the COPA 1974, s 60(4) to have regard to the following factors:
(a) the relevant provisions of any code of practice, see Control of Noise (Codes of Practice for Construction and Open Sites) (England) Order 2002[1] approving the guidance contained in BS5228: Noise Control on Construction and Open Sites on the appropriate methods for minimising noise;
(b) the need for ensuring that the best practicable means are employed to minimise noise;[2]
(c) before specifying any particular methods or plant or machinery, to the desirability in the interests of any recipients of the notice in question of specifying other methods or plant or machinery which would be substantially as effective in minimising noise and more acceptable to them;
(d) the need to protect any persons in the locality in which the premises in question are situated from the effects of noise.

1   SI 2002/461.
2   Advice on limiting construction noise is contained in the HSE pamphlet *Noise in Construction* (1995).

13.65   The notice is to be served on the person who appears to the local authority to be carrying out, or going to carry out the works, and on such other persons as appear to the local authority to be responsible for, or to have control over, the carrying out of the works as the local authority thinks fit.[1] The notice must specify the time within which the notice is to be complied with, and may require the execution of such works, and the taking of such other steps as may be necessary for the purposes of the notice as may be specified therein.[2]

1   COPA 1974, s 60(5).
2   COPA 1974, s 60(6).

Appeal

13.66   A person served with a notice under the COPA 1974, s 60 has a right of appeal to a magistrates' court within 21 days from the service of the notice. The grounds of appeal are set out in the Control of Noise (Appeals) Regulations 1975,[1] reg 5 and are similar to those already discussed in relation to appeals against noise level notices.

1   SI 1975/2116.

Offence

13.67   It is an offence for a person who has been served with a notice under this section without reasonable excuse to contravene any requirement of the notice.[1]

1   COPA 1974, s 60(8).

Prior consent for work on construction sites

13.68   Allied with the provisions of the COPA 1974, s 60, there is separate provision in s 61 for a licensing system for work on construction sites. A person who intends to carry out works to which s 60 applies may apply to the local authority for a consent under s 61(1). The application shall contain particulars of:
(a)   the works, and the method by which they are to be carried out; and
(b)   the steps proposed to be taken to minimise noise resulting from the works.

1   COPA 1974, s 61(3).

13.69   If the local authority considers that the application contains sufficient information and that, if the works are carried out in accordance with the application, it would not serve a notice under the COPA 1974, s 60, then it may give its consent to the application.[1] A local authority may attach conditions to a consent.[2] There is a right of appeal against refusal or deemed refusal to a consent or against the attachment of a condition to a consent.[3] The grounds of appeal are set out in the Control of Noise (Appeals) Regulations 1975,[4] reg 6 and are similar to those already discussed. Where there is a prosecution for breach of a s 60(8) notice, then it is a defence to prove that the alleged contravention amounted to the carrying out of works in accordance with a s 61 consent. A consent under the section is not a ground of defence to a prosecution for statutory nuisance under the EPA 1990, s 82.

1   COPA 1974, s 61(4).
2   COPA 1974, s 61(5).
3   COPA 1974, s 61(6), (7).
4   SI 1975/2116.

NOISE FROM PLANT OR MACHINERY

13.70   The COPA 1974, s 68 gives the Secretary of State powers to make regulations:

- for limiting noise levels caused by any plant or machinery; and
- for limiting the level of noise which may be caused by any plant or machinery when used for work on construction sites or which may be caused outside a factory, within the meaning of the Factories Act 1961, by the use of plant or machinery in the factory.

No such regulations have been made.

13.71   The impact of European law can be seen in the Construction Plant and Equipment (Harmonisation of Noise Emission Standards) Regulations 1985[1] made under the European Communities Act 1972. These Regulations came into force on 26 March 1986, and the second, more stringent, standards became effective in September 1989. Compliance with the noise limits is to be assured by a certification procedure run for the Government by consultancies accredited under the National Measurement Accreditation Services. Construction plants must conform to EC noise standards and are subject to periodic examination to ensure conformity.

1   SI 1985/1968.

13.72   The most recent set of regulations in this series are the Noise Emission in the Environment by Equipment for use Outdoors Regulations 2001[1] (as amended) which establish a method of certification whereby the sale or use of certain items is prohibited unless it has been certificated to ensure conformity with noise standards. The equipment in question has a wide definition, covering everything from dumper-trucks and compressors and tower cranes to lawn-mowers and hedge-trimmers.

1   SI 2001/1701.

13.73   Regulation 7 establishes a general duty prohibiting the marketing or use of any equipment listed within Schs 1, 2 and 4. Equipment must conform to the following:

(a)   permissible sound power level;[1]
(b)   conformity assessment procedure completed;[2]
(c)   the equipment must bear the certification marking and the indication of the guaranteed sound power level;[3]
(d)   the equipment must be accompanied by an EC declaration of conformity.[4]

It should be noted that not all items of equipment must conform by the same date. The Regulations provide for phasing in of standards over time from January 2002 until January 2006.

1   SI 2001/1701, reg 8.
2   SI 2001/1701, reg 10.
3   SI 2001/1701, reg 11.
4   SI 2001/1701, Sch 5.

13.74   Contravention of these Regulations is a criminal offence[1] subject to the penalties listed in reg 19, namely a term of imprisonment not exceeding three months or a fine not exceeding level 5 on the summary scale. There is a defence of due diligence under reg 20 for those who can prove that all reasonable steps were taken and that due diligence was exercised in their pursuit of avoiding commission of an offence.

1   SI 2001/1701, reg 18.

AIRCRAFT NOISE

Noise in flight

13.75   Actions for private nuisance and trespass are excluded by statute from being means of pursuing remedies in respect of the noise caused by the flight of an aeroplane over land.[1] Noise caused by aeroplanes other than model aircraft is not a statutory nuisance.[2] Instead the approach to controlling aeroplane flight noise in English law has primarily been to refuse noise certificates to the more noisy types of aeroplane. Noise certificates are issued by the Civil Aviation Authority under the Air Navigation (Noise Certification) Order 1990.[3] In the absence of a noise certificate, an aeroplane subject to the Order is, with certain exceptions, prohibited from taking off or landing in the UK. Reference should be made to the Order itself for the types of aeroplanes covered by it.

1   Civil Aviation Act 1982, s 76.
2   EPA 1990, s 79(6).
3   SI 1990/1514.

13.76   The noise standards with which each of the types of aeroplanes must comply are set out in the British Civil Airworthiness Requirements, Section N (5th edition, 1990), available from the Civil Aviation Authority. The standards are taken from Annex 16, Chicago Convention on International Civil Aviation 1944. The development in the UK law of noise limits on the basis of Annex 16 is required by EC Directives 80/51/EEC, (1980) OJ L 18, p 26; 83/206/EEC, (1983) OJ L 117, p 15; and 92/14/EEC, (1992) OJ L 76, p 21.

13.77   No noise certificate will be issued to an aeroplane that does not satisfy the standards for the kind of aeroplane concerned. In addition, use of the earlier and noisier subsonic jets that meet these standards is being phased out. Chapters 2 and 3 of Annex 16 set two levels of standards for subsonic jets, with the earlier jets being subject to the less strict standards of Chapter 2. Under the Aeroplane Noise Regulations 1999[1] a number of permitted operations by Chapter 2 jets were reduced over the period 1995 to 2002, with operators of those jets undertaking gradually to reduce their use. No operations have been permitted since 2002. The phasing out of Chapter 2 aeroplanes applied to jets with a weight of 34,000 tonnes or capable of seating 19 or more passengers; it did not apply to smaller private jets. The 1990 Order only applies to civil aeroplanes. There are no noise certification requirements in law in respect of military aeroplane noise. However the Ministry of Defence has a Noise Panel that reviews aeroplane noise. It also operates voluntary compensation arrangements for damage or injury caused by military aeroplane noise.

1   SI 1999/1452.

Noise at aerodromes

13.78   There are also statutory controls over aeroplane noise at aerodromes. The Air Navigation Order 2000,[1] art 108 authorises the Secretary of State to prescribe conditions restricting noise and vibrations caused by both civil and military aeroplanes while at aerodromes in the UK. The current conditions are prescribed in the Air Navigation (General) Regulations 1993,[2] reg 13. No action in nuisance may be brought arising out of such noise and vibrations, provided they are within the prescribed conditions.[3]

1   SI 2000/1562.
2   SI 1993/1622.
3   Civil Aviation Act 1982, s 77(2).

13.79   The taking-off or landing of aeroplanes at designated airports may be regulated by the Secretary of State by notice issued under the Civil Aviation Act 1982, s 78(1).[1] Heathrow, Gatwick and Stansted are the three aerodromes that have been designated for the purposes of s 78(1). Notices have been issued that (a) govern the routes, noise limits and procedures to be followed on take-off and landing and (b) set up restrictions on night flights. The notice on limits on night flights at Heathrow has twice been successfully challenged on judicial review, first because it had been determined on the wrong basis and subsequently because of lack of consultation: *R v Secretary of State for Transport, ex p Richmond-upon-Thames London Borough Council.*[2] It was later upheld by the High Court. The Secretary of State is authorised to impose sanctions if the requirements of a notice are not met.[3]

1   See the Civil Aviation (Designation of Aerodromes) Order 1981, SI 1981/651.
2   [1994] 1 WLR 74, [1995] Env LR 390.
3   Civil Aviation Act 1982, s 78(2), (3).

13.80   The noise nuisance caused to occupiers of land near Heathrow Airport prior to 1993 was challenged successfully under the European Convention on Human Rights in *Hatton v United Kingdom*.[1] In 1993 the Secretary of State for Transport introduced a quota system for night time flights from Heathrow. Although intended to reduce noise, the former system of controlling the number of night time take-offs and landings was actually replaced with the (quota) system giving *noisier* aircraft a higher 'quota count' than quieter aircraft. The local residents brought nuisance proceedings which did not succeed in the English courts, but the European Court of Human Rights upheld the complaint. It found that the Government failed in its positive obligation to protect the right to respect private and family life under Article 8 of the Convention when it neglected to conduct independent research into the implications of night flights for the sleep patterns of both those living near the airport and for the economic interest concerned. There had also been a violation of Article 13 of the Convention.

1   (2001) 34 EHRR 1. For an earlier unsuccessful challenge, see *Powell and Rayner v United Kingdom* (1990) 12 EHRR 355.

13.81   The Local Government Ombudsman has been resorted to successfully by local residents complaining of the failure of a local authority to act against excessive airport noise.[1]

1   See, eg, Complaint Nos 95/B/4579 and 96/B1049 Plymouth City Council [2001] JPL 1446.

13.82   Another way of limiting the take-off and landing noise for local inhabitants is through the use by air traffic control of its powers to determine, for example, the route followed by aeroplanes using an aerodrome: Rules of the Air Regulations 1996.[1] Schemes for Heathrow and Gatwick have been applied on this basis, but there are no such schemes operating at present. Heathrow Airport Ltd operates a non-statutory noise insulation scheme.

1   SI 1996/1393.

TRAFFIC NOISE

Control of traffic on roads

13.83   The Road Traffic Regulation Act 1984 ('RTRA 1984'), s 1 gives the power to regulate traffic on trunk roads to the Secretary of State and on other roads to a county council or London borough. Section 2 of the Act provides that a traffic regulation order may provide for the prohibition, restriction or other regulation of vehicular traffic on a road, either generally or specifically. The House of Lords has held that the traffic regulation powers of local authorities may be exercised after environmental considerations have been taken into account. It was held, further, that the power may be used to regulate where particular vehicles may go at any particular times, and to require the modification of such vehicles if they are to be allowed into particular places, provided restrictions do not amount to across-the-board prohibitions or restrictions on vehicles' use: *London Boroughs Transport Committee v Freight Transport Association Ltd.*[1]

1   [1991] 1 WLR 828, HL.

13.84   The RTRA 1984, s 2(4) empowers local authorities to make regulatory provision specifying through routes for heavy commercial vehicles or prohibiting or restricting heavy commercial vehicle use in specified areas or on specified roads, subject to any exemptions contained in the order.

13.85   This power is to be exercised to improve the amenities of localities. It therefore has a straight environmental significance. A heavy commercial vehicle is defined as a goods vehicle having an operating weight exceeding 7.5 tonnes.[1] The procedure for making a regulatory order is contained in RTRA 1984, Sch 9, Pt 3 and, among other matters, requires consultation with the relevant Chief Officers of Police. The Secretary of State has a residual power to direct authorities either to make or prohibit the making of a regulatory order.

1   RTRA 1984, s 138(1).

Vehicle noise

13.86   The statutory basis for this control is the Road Traffic Act 1988 and the Road Vehicles (Construction and Use) Regulations 1986.[1] Section 42 of the 1988 Act makes it an offence to contravene the regulations although there are few prosecutions. Common law liability for nuisance is preserved by the Road Traffic (Consequential Provisions) Act 1988, s 7.

1   SI 1986/1078.

PLANNING CONTROL OF NOISE

13.87   Readers should be aware that the controls on noise that may be imposed when granting planning permission are contained in *Planning and Noise*, PPG 24. Detailed consideration of the planning system lies outside the scope of this book.

1   (1994) HMSO.

CHAPTER 14

Freshwater pollution and remediation of waters

INTRODUCTION

14.01 In any water pollution case there are normally three key elements. The first is the *ownership of the rights* which it is sought to protect. Second, the *cause of the damage* needs to be ascertained and the nature of that damage; for example where a riverbed is polluted it may take the environment some time to recover whilst pollution of the water itself may not be so problematic. Finally, the *legal consequences* of the incident need to be analysed. In such an analysis the statutory regime tends not to be so relevant. Thus in this chapter, while the statutory regime is briefly outlined, no detail is provided; this outline is set out at the end of the chapter.

14.02 There are two types of water pollution incident: (1) pollution of waters (groundwaters, a watercourse or lake); and (2) contamination of drinking water. Each of these will be discussed below, looking at the three key elements outlined above. Marine pollution is dealt with in Chapter 15.

POLLUTION OF WATERS

Ownership of rights

14.03 Where a watercourse or lake is polluted there may be three classes of potential claimant:
(a)   the owners or occupiers of the bed and banks of the watercourse;
(b)   those with fishing rights; and
(c)   anyone else who makes use of the water in it.

The nature of those rights, and the benefits accruing to them, need to be defined. In this section the term 'watercourse' includes lakes or ponds.

14.04 The usual start here is a Land Registry search of the particular stretch affected. This is necessary for both claimants and defendants. Certainly the search should reveal the freehold owners of the bed and banks of the watercourse. However, some rights may not be found in the register and their absence does not mean they do not exist.

Owner or occupier

14.05 The normal rule is that the person who owns or occupies the bank on one side of the river, also owns or occupies its bed up to the middle. If that person has both banks, then he or she has the whole of the bed. The rights such owners or occupiers have are known as 'riparian' rights.[1] A similar rule applies in respect of lakes.

1   *Chasemore v Richards* (1859) 7 HL Cas 349.

Those with fishing rights

14.06 Fishing rights are more complex. The real question is whether the rights a person claims are legally enforceable. Quite often a fisherman will have a mere licence from the occupier of the river to fish in the waters. This will not give a right of recovery for pollution.[1] Other fishermen may either have a lease of the fishery or be freehold owners of rights of fishery which the courts will protect.[2] The exact rights need to be ascertained before any claim is launched by the fisherman.

1   *Hunter v Canary Wharf Ltd* [1997] AC 655, HL – although the position may be different under human rights legislation.
2   *Bidder v Croydon Local Board of Health* (1862) 6 LT 778.

Those who make use of the water

14.07 Finally, a person may have a right to abstract water from the river. If the pollution makes it unsuitable for use then he should be able to bring an action to recover any losses suffered.[1] The legal basis of this is, however, uncertain;[2] but with human rights aspects taken into account it is now more likely that a court would allow recovery in this situation.

1   *Paine & Co v St Neots Gas and Coke Co* [1939] 3 All ER 812 at 816, CA.
2   *Ormerod v Todmorden Joint Stock Mill Co Ltd* (1883) 11 QBD 155, CA.

Nuisance

14.08 The pollution action is brought in private nuisance whether it is for an interference with riparian rights[1] or fishing rights.[2] Liability for the nuisance will rest on the person who caused it or who has taken over an existing nuisance and allowed it to continue.[3] There may also be an action in trespass where solid matter has come to rest on the bed or banks,[4] but usually an action in nuisance will suffice.

1   *John Young & Co v Bankier Distillery Co* [1893] AC 691, HL.
2   *Nicholls v Ely Beet Sugar Factory Ltd* [1936] 1 Ch 343, CA.
3   *Sedleigh-Denfield v O'Callaghan* [1940] 3 All ER 349, HL.
4   *Jones v Llanrwst UDC* [1911] 1 Ch 393.

Negligence

14.09 It may also be useful to bring the action in negligence, for example a spill from a road tanker or where an action in nuisance may be difficult in the light of the claimant's water rights. Over the past thirty years or so there has been an assimilation between the law of nuisance and negligence, particularly where there is an escape from land. The extent to which actions in nuisance and negligence have become assimilated was set out by HHJ Thornton in *Johnson (t/a Johnson Butchers) v BJW Property Developments Ltd.*[1]

1   [2002] EWHC 1131 (TCC) at [47–51], [2002] 3 All ER 574 at [47–51].

14.10 Where matter has flowed from a public sewer it will be important to establish whether it 'escaped' or 'discharged' from the sewer.[1] A sewerage undertaker has no power to discharge matter into watercourses so that any damage caused by the discharge can be the subject of an action in nuisance, without the claimant having to show negligence.[2] As far as an escape is concerned, the rule is that the undertaker will not be liable unless it could be shown that it was negligent.[3] Otherwise, where there is no negligence, in *Marcic v Thames Water Utilities Ltd*[4] the House of Lords held that a sewerage undertaker is only liable for escapes of sewage in accordance with the statutory enforcement scheme under the Water Industry Act 1991 ('WIA 1991'), s 18.

1   *Smeaton v Ilford Corpn* [1954] 1 All ER 923.
2   *British Waterways Board v Severn Trent Water Ltd* [2001] EWCA Civ 276, [2002] Ch 25.
3   *Pride of Derby and Derbyshire Angling Association Ltd v British Celanese Ltd* [1953] 1 All ER 179, CA.
4   [2003] UKHL 66, [2004] 1 All ER 135.

Liability

14.11 Liability for pollution of groundwater was considered by the House of Lords in *Cambridge Water Co v Eastern Counties Leather plc.*[1] There it was held that damage to the groundwater must have been foreseeable at the time when the escape causing the pollution occurred. The House declined to impose liability for 'historic' pollution. Any 'historically' contaminated groundwater will have to be remedied under the contaminated land regime in the Environment Protection Act 1990 ('EPA 1990'), Pt IIA or the Water Resources Act 1991 ('WRA 1991'), ss 161A–161D.

1   [1994] 1 All ER 53.

14.12   The cause of the pollution and its nature and effect will often be available from the Environment Agency. They will investigate any incident and make a report. The report should be open to public inspection under the Environmental Information Regulations 1992.[1] In addition, the Agency may have prosecuted the defendant. If the defendant is convicted, the relevant court should be approached for a certificate of conviction. The facts of the conviction should be pleaded in the particulars of claim.

1   SI 1992/3240.

14.13   Where the polluter has a discharge consent under Pt III of the WRA 1991, its details should be obtained. They should be on the register of consents held by the regional office of the Agency under the WRA 1991, s 190. The contents of the registers must be available for public inspection at all reasonable hours free of charge, and copies can be taken on payment of a reasonable fee.

14.14   The fact that a polluter has a discharge consent and is operating in accordance with it does not absolve the polluter from liability for any pollution damage the polluter has caused.[1]

1   WRA 1991, s 100(b).

Causation

14.15   Causation in a pollution incident need not be ascertained from samples of river water taken at the time, though this is the best evidence. Eyewitness accounts of the state of the river at the time will suffice, though that state will have to be linked to the actions of the defendant.[1]

1   *Trent River Board v Wardle* [1957] Crim LR 196.

14.16   Causation in respect of pollution of water in criminal proceedings was dealt with by Lord Hoffmann in *Empress Car Co (Abertillery) Ltd v National Rivers Authority*[1] where the House of Lords reviewed the law on 'causing' an offence:

- It was considered that, as a first step, the prosecution should identify what it says the defendant *did* to cause the pollution. That something need not have been the immediate cause – maintaining a tank full of polluting matter would be enough for these purposes even if the immediate cause was different.
- Once the prosecution has identified the defendant's act the court must decide whether it *caused* the pollution. It can have done so even if there was another factor involved like vandalism by third parties.
- If the defendant did something which produced a situation in which the polluting matter could escape but a necessary condition of the actual escape which happened was also the act of a third party or a natural

event, the court should consider whether the act or event was a normal *fact of life* or something *extraordinary*. If it was a fact of life, the defendant would still be liable even if he or she could not foresee the particular event. The distinction between ordinary and extraordinary events is one of fact and degree.

1   [1998] Env LR 396.

14.17   Whether this would carry over to civil proceedings remains to be seen, but there seems no logical reason why it should not. Although foreseeability is an essential ingredient in either nuisance or negligence as Lord Hoffmann pointed out, the *particular event* need not be foreseen, just the *likelihood of it*.[1]

1   See e g *Smith v Littlewoods Organisation Ltd* [1987] 1 All ER 710, HL.

14.18   In addition to showing that the defendant caused the pollution, the claimant must also show that the pollutants caused the damage. In *Elliott v Agrevo UK Ltd*[1] the claimant alleged that chemicals from the defendant's factory had entered the groundwaters under his fields and damaged his fruit crops. The court found that chemicals from the factory had passed on to the claimant's land by the flow of groundwater but that they were not at such a degree of concentration to establish on the balance of probabilities that they had damaged the crops.

1   [2001] Env LR D7.

Damages

14.19   Damages in a pollution incident will usually be for the costs of reinstatement of the waters, unless this would be inappropriate, in which case the award will reflect the diminution in the value of the property that results from the pollution. In some cases damages may involve both remediation costs and diminution in value.[1] Where a fishery has been adversely affected, the court may also award a sum for the loss of reputation of the fishery as a result of the incident.[2] Alternatively, if the damage was caused by works done under statutory authority it may be compensated under the relevant statutory provisions.[3]

1   *Blue Circle Industries plc v Ministry of Defence* [1999] Env LR 22, CA.
2   *Marquis of Granby v Bakewell UDC* (1923) 21 LGR 329.
3   *Burgess v Gwynedd River Authority* (1972) 24 P & CR 150.

14.20   A court can also issue an injunction to prevent the continuation of the pollution or to require remediation works. An injunction is considered the proper remedy in a continuing pollution case as the claimant's rights will have been invaded and to award damages only would, in effect, give a defendant a power to buy a right to pollute the claimant's waters against the claimant's wishes.[1]

1   *Shelfer v City of London Electric Lighting Co* [1895] 1 Ch 287, CA.

CONTAMINATION OF DRINKING WATER

14.21   Standards for drinking water are provided under the EC Directive on the Quality of Water Intended for Human Consumption.[1] This Directive has been implemented in England and Wales by the Water Supply (Water Quality) Regulations 2000.[2] These Regulations set out the quality required from drinking water supplied by water undertakers. They are enforced by the Drinking Water Inspectorate and local authorities. Private drinking water supplies are provided for in the Private Water Supplies Regulations 1991.[3]

1   Dir 98/83/EEC.
2   SI 2000/3184 as amended by SI 2001/2885.
3   SI 1991/2790.

14.22   Where a statutory water undertaker supplies water through pipes to any premises and that water is unfit for human consumption, it will be guilty of an offence and liable on summary conviction to a fine not exceeding the statutory maximum or, on indictment, to a fine.[1] The question of whether water is or is not unfit for human consumption will be one of fact. It must be more than unwholesome, but not necessarily injurious or dangerous to health.[2] The supply of unwholesome water may also be a public nuisance.

1   WIA 1991, s 70(1).
2   *Guild v Gateway Foodmarkets Ltd* 1991 SLT 578.

14.23   Where a person has suffered injury or damage through contaminated water, the person will have a right of action against the supplier. If the supplier was a water undertaker there may be an action in breach of statutory duty,[1] but the duty is a general one and so it is not an absolute duty, imposing strict liability.[2] Therefore the action is better brought as one in negligence.

1   *Read v Croydon Corpn* [1938] 4 All ER 631.
2   *Weir v East of Scotland Water Authority* 2001 SLT 1205n, OH.

14.24   In *Read v Croydon Corpn*[1] it was held that a person who supplies to premises water which the person knows will be used for domestic consumption and fails to use care and skill in doing so, will be liable for negligence to anyone injured as a result. A person may also be liable for supplying water that was wholesome when it left his or her pipes but became contaminated in the claimant's pipes as a result of a condition about which the person knew but failed to take any steps to remedy or give a warning.[2] Otherwise, the person will not be liable if the contamination is caused by fittings or a failure of equipment that is the responsibility of another person.[3]

1   [1938] 4 All ER 631.
2   *Barnes v Irwell Valley Water Board* [1938] 2 All ER 650, CA.
3   *Munshaw Colour Service v City of Vancouver* (1961) 29 DLR (2d) 240.

14.25   Suppliers may also be liable under the Consumer Protection Act 1987, Pt I if the water supplied is defective for the purposes of the Act. Where water is supplied under contract there may also be liability under the Sale of Goods Act 1979.

STATUTORY NUISANCE

14.26   Statutory nuisance is mainly dealt with in Chapter 3. However, by the Public Health Act 1936, s 259(1)(a), any pond, pool, ditch, gutter or water-course (but not an estuary[1]) which is so foul or is in such a state as to be prejudicial to health or a nuisance may be treated as a statutory nuisance. The nuisance must be one that is prejudicial to health; e g a pond that was in such a state that it might give rise to flooding could not be dealt with under this section. However, the water does not have to be polluted. A stagnant pond or choked-up ditch that is a breeding ground for mosquitoes or other pests can be a nuisance for these purposes.[2]

1   *R v Falmouth and Truro Port Health Authority, ex p South West Water Services* [2000] Env LR 658, CA.
2   *Renfrew v Woddrop* 1924 SLT 68.

PERSONAL INJURY FROM WATER POLLUTION

14.27   This is mainly dealt with in Chapter 12. However, water pollution cases may involve bacteriological contamination, for example someone affected by bacteria in sewage discharges to water in which he or she was bathing. This will be difficult to attribute to a particular discharger, as there may be a number of sources of the bacteria in question – discharges from ships, domestic discharges, animals etc. In addition, a bacteria can have been picked up by the claimant before immersion in the water – e g from contaminated food.

14.28   Here the particular bacteria involved in the claimant's illness should be identified. This may eliminate animal sources of the illness. Then the claimant should be rigorously questioned as to what the claimant has eaten in the fortnight before to try to eliminate food contamination. If the claim is against a sewage discharger, local hospitals and GPs should be approached to see if there was illness locally that may have led to the bacteria emanating from the sewers within seven days or so of the claimant being affected. The state of currents and tides need to be looked at to see if a discharge from the pipe concerned would reach the waters in which the claimant was immersed. Finally, local weather conditions should be checked to ascertain whether bacteria would survive in the water over the period in question.

REMEDIATION OF WATERS

14.29   Remediation of waters can be carried out by the Environment Agency under the WRA 1991, s 161. This enables the Agency to investigate potential sources of pollution and carry out works to prevent it. Alternatively, if waters are already polluted, it can remove or dispose of the pollutant, remediate the waters and restore the aquatic environment to the state it was before the pollution. It may recover its costs of doing such works from the person who caused or knowingly permitted the potential problem or the pollution.

14.30   However, with the Agency's limited funds it is not able to do much remediation. Therefore, WRA 1991, ss 161A–161D enable the Agency to serve a 'works notice' on a person who is causing or knowingly permitting a situation that may give rise to pollution or who has caused or permitted pollution of controlled waters.[1] The notice may require the person served to do works or operations to prevent the situation or to clean up pollution of waters that has been caused and restore the aquatic environment to the state it was at before the pollution. Details of the regime under ss 161A–161D are provided by the Anti-Pollution Works Regulations 1999.[2] Any appeal to the Secretary of State against the service of a works notice must be made within 21 days from the date of service.[3]

1   WRA 1991, s 161A(1).
2   SI 1999/1006.
3   WRA 1991, s 161C(1).

14.31   Liability for remediation of historic pollution will usually be provided for under the contaminated land regime found in EPA 1990, Pt IIA. That regime is to be used where substances on land are causing, or may cause, significant pollution of controlled waters.[1] This is determined by the relevant authority in accordance with the Secretary of State's Guidance that is set out in DETR Circular 02/2000.[2] If the waters alone are polluted, then the regime under WRA 1991, ss 161A–161D applies.

1   EPA 1990, s 78A(2) as amended by the Water Act 2003, s 86(1), (2)(a).
2   DETR Circular 02/2000, paras B.50 and B.51.

THE STATUTORY REGIME

14.32   Much of the statutory regime now depends on directives issued by the European Community. In 2007 the Framework Water Directive[1] will make considerable changes in the regime, with many of the existing directives being revoked.

1   Dir 2000/60/EEC.

14.33   Currently the main water directives are:
*   The Aquatic Environment Directive of 1976,[1] which deals with some dangerous substances in a series of 'daughter directives';

- The Groundwater Directive;[2]
- The Urban Waste Water Directive,[3] which deals with discharges from sewers and certain industries;

and

- The Freshwater Fisheries Directive;[4]
- The Shellfisheries Directive;[5] and
- The Bathing Waters Directive.[6]

In addition:

- The Nitrate Directive,[7] which is concerned with protecting water from pollution caused by nitrates from agricultural sources.

1   Dir 76/464/EEC.
2   Dir 80/68/EEC.
3   Dir 91/271/EEC.
4   Dir 78/659/EEC.
5   Dir 79/923/EEC.
6   Dir 76/160/EEC.
7   Dir 91/676/EEC.

14.34   In England and Wales the main statutory provision is in the Water Resources Act 1991. Part III of that Act deals with water pollution. It is concerned with the pollution of 'controlled waters' as defined in the Act, namely relevant territorial waters, coastal waters, inland waters and groundwaters.[1]

1   WRA 1991, s 104.

14.35   Controlled waters are classified for quality purposes under WRA 1991, s 82. There are a number of different classifications, based on the use to which the water is put; abstraction for drinking water, for example. There is also a classification system to show the amount of dangerous substances in waters. A wider classification is provided by the Surface Water (River Ecosystem) (Classification) Regulations 1994.[1] Where waters have been classified by the Environment Agency, quality objectives must then be set for them under WRA 1991, s 83. The Secretary of State or the Welsh Assembly must use the powers in WRA 1991, Pt III in such a way that will, as far as is practicable, ensure that the objectives specified are achieved at all times.[2]

1   SI 1994/1057.
2   WRA 1991, s 84(1).

14.36   It is an offence under WRA 1991, s 85(1) to cause or knowingly to permit any poisonous, noxious or polluting matter, or any solid waste matter, to enter any controlled waters. 'Pollute' and its derivatives should be given their ordinary meaning – to make physically impure, foul or filthy: to dirty, stain, taint, befoul[1] – in these cases.[2]

1   OED.
2   *R v Dovermoss Ltd* [1995] Env LR 258, CA.

14.37 It will be a defence to a charge, under WRA 1991, s 85, that the defendant's action was authorised by a competent authority and was done in accordance with that authorisation.[1] The main authorisation here will be a discharge consent given under WRA 1991, Pt III, Ch II. These consents are granted under the provisions of Sch 10 to the Act.[2] Schedule 10 is supplemented by the Control of Pollution (Applications, Appeals and Registers) Regulations 1996.[3] Those processes prescribed for integrated pollution control under the Pollution Prevention and Control Act 1999 will be authorised to discharge to waters in accordance with their IPP authorisation.

1   WRA 1991, s 88(4).
2   WRA 1991, s 88(2).
3   SI 1996/2971.

14.38 If the Environment Agency is of the opinion that a consent-holder is not complying with any of its conditions, or is likely to be in that position, it may serve an enforcement notice on the holder specifying the nature of the problem, the steps necessary to remedy it and a time for compliance.[1]

1   WRA 1991, s 90B(1); added by the EA 1995, Sch 22, para 142.

14.39 Discharges to groundwater are controlled partly under discharge consents, but also under the Groundwaters Regulations 1998.[1] The Regulations are concerned with discharges of List I and List II substances – which are set out in the Schedule to the Regulations. The purpose of the Regulations is to prevent the direct or indirect discharge of these substances to groundwater.

1   SI 1998/2746.

14.40 Specific controls exist in respect of particular causes of pollution or types of pollutant. Regulations made under WRA 1991, s 92 are concerned with the storage of polluting substances. The Control of Pollution (Silage, Slurry and Agricultural Fuel Oil) Regulations 1991[1] impose requirements on the storage of these substances, whilst the Control of Pollution (Oil Storage) (England) Regulations 2001[2] are concerned with anti-pollution requirements in respect of the storage of oil.

1   SI 1991/324 as amended by SI 1997/547.
2   SI 2001/2954.

14.41 Pollution from agricultural pesticides may result from failure to comply with controls imposed under the Food and Environment Protection Act 1985, Pt III. The Control of Pesticides Regulations 1986[1] set out requirements to take reasonable precautions to avoid harm, including pollution of water, when using pesticides. In addition there will a code of practice under s 17 of the 1985 Act.

1   SI 1986/1510 as amended by SI 1997/188.

14.42 Particular protection for fish is found in the Salmon and Freshwater Fisheries Act 1975. Section 4(1) of that Act makes it an offence to cause or knowingly to permit to be released into any waters or the tributaries of waters containing fish, any liquid or solid matter that causes the waters to become poisonous or injurious to fish, spawning grounds, spawn or the food of fish. For these purposes, causing the waters to become harmful to fish completes the offence, even if no fish are actually harmed by the matter that is put into the water.[1]

1   *R v Bradford* (1860) 24 JP 374, CCR.

14.43   In addition to specific statutory controls, requirements made under planning permission may be relevant in a water pollution case. The Environment Agency, water undertakers or a drainage or local authority may have made byelaws that impact on the case.

CHAPTER 15

Marine pollution

REGULATION OF SHIPPING

15.01 Nearly all UK law on shipping and the prevention of pollution from ships derives from international conventions made through the International Maritime Organisation ('IMO'). As far as general standards of ships are concerned, the Safety of Life at Sea ('SOLAS') Convention deals with the construction and equipment of ships and safe navigation. Crew training standards are provided for by the International Convention on Standards of Training, Certification and Watchkeeping for Seafarers 1978. The International Regulations for Preventing Collisions 1972 lay down rules as to how vessels should navigate. The International Convention for the Prevention of Pollution from Ships ('MARPOL') aims to regulate discharges or escapes of substances from shipping.

15.02 Annex I of MARPOL is concerned with oil pollution from ships. Its standards have been implemented in the UK by the Merchant Shipping (Prevention of Oil Pollution) Regulations 1996.[1] Ships to which the Regulations apply must carry a Pollution Prevention Certificate, which will only be issued if the ship complies with the standards set out in Annex I of MARPOL. They must also have an oil record book in which relevant operations must be logged. Offences as to the discharge of oil or an oily mixture from a ship are set out in the Regulations.

1   SI 1996/2154 as amended by SI 1997/1910 and SI 2000/483.

15.03 Annex II of MARPOL lays down Regulations for the control of noxious liquid substances in bulk. It is concerned with the construction of chemical tankers, and, through the International Bulk Chemical Code, the containment of cargoes of chemicals. In the UK, Annex II is effected by the Merchant Shipping (Dangerous or Noxious Liquid Substances in Bulk) Regulations 1996.[1] Ships subject to the Regulations must carry an International

Pollution Prevention Certificate for the Carriage of Noxious Liquid Substances in Bulk. They must also have a cargo record book detailing operations carried out in respect of a particular cargo. Where dangerous goods are carried at sea, Chapter VII of SOLAS applies, which is implemented in the UK by the Merchant Shipping (Dangerous Goods and Marine Pollutants) Regulations 1997.[2]

1   SI 1996/3010 as amended by SI 1998/1153.
2   SI 1997/2367.

15.04   Annex III of MARPOL is concerned with the carriage of dangerous goods in bulk. Annex IV of MARPOL, as revised, regulates the disposal of sewage from ships, but is not yet implemented into UK law. Annex V of MARPOL deals with the disposal of waste from ships. Much waste must be retained on board and disposed of to shore facilities, although some can be discharged into the sea under certain conditions. In the UK, Annex V is implemented by the Merchant Shipping (Prevention of Pollution by Garbage) Regulations 1998.[1] Annex VI of MARPOL will provide for air pollution from ships when it enters into force.

1   SI 1998/1377.

LIABILITY FOR OIL POLLUTION FROM SHIPS

15.05   Liability for oil pollution from ships is governed by two international Conventions, the 1969 Convention on Civil Liability for Oil Pollution Damage ('CLC') and the International Convention on the Establishment of an International Fund for Compensation for Oil Pollution Damage 1971 (the 'Fund Convention'). These Conventions divide liability so that initially it is the ship-owners that are liable. However, if damage goes over a certain amount, then the Fund set up by oil traders comes in to top-up the amounts provided by the owners under the CLC. The Conventions were amended by Protocols in 1992, which came into effect on 30 May 1996. The amended Conventions are implemented into UK law by the Merchant Shipping Act 1995 ('MSA 1995'), Pt VI, Chs III and IV.

15.06   Section 153(1) of the MSA 1995 provides that where, as a result of any occurrence, any oil is discharged or escapes from an oil tanker[1] then (except as otherwise provided) the owner of the ship shall be liable for any damage caused outside the ship in the territory of the UK by contamination resulting from the discharge or escape and the costs of preventive measures to deal with possible contamination in UK territory and for any damage caused by such measures in the UK. Section 153(5) also makes owners liable to compensate for such contamination or measures in the territory of another party to the CLC.

1   MSA 1995, s 153(3), (4).

15.07   Liability for oil pollution from ships other than oil tankers is provided for by the MSA 1995, s 154 in a similar way to s 153. In both sections liability where oil has spilled as a result of a collision between ships and the costs or damage cannot reasonably be apportioned will be joint for the whole of the damage or costs for which the owners would be liable.[1] Liability for certain events is excluded by s 155.

1   MSA 1995, ss 153(6) and 154(3).

15.08 'Damage' for these purposes includes loss.[1] In *Alegrete Shipping Co Inc v International Oil Pollution Compensation Fund 1971*[2] Steel J pointed out that:

> 'The Merchant Shipping Act 1995 draws no distinction between physical and economic loss. I have no difficulty in accepting that the fishermen may be entitled to recover (subject to questions as to the locality of his base and so on). This is because the fishermen's position is such as to give rise to immediate interference with their economic interests. As Lord McCluskey put it in *Landcatch*[3]
>
> > "Nevertheless, it appears to me that the loss of his livelihood is properly described as damage that is caused directly and immediately by contamination resulting from the discharge or escape of oil from the ship. The contamination does not set in train a chain of events that eventually results in his suffering loss or damage. On the contrary, the contamination is both the immediate, direct, and, in such a case, the only cause of his loss." '

Thus a fisherman can recover for lost catches or a hotelier for lost trade. But in either case, the loss of profit must be primary economic loss, not secondary economic loss.

1   MSA 1995, s 170(1).
2   [2003] Env LR 191.
3   [1999] 2 Lloyd's Rep 316.

15.09 As far as pollution from oil tankers is concerned, liability is limited by the MSA 1995, s 157 to the amount at which the Fund takes over. The amount to which the tanker owner is entitled to limit his liability will be determined by the Admiralty Court under s 158.[1] However, this does not apply if the pollution was caused intentionally or recklessly by the owner.[2] Once the court has determined the amount of the limitation fund, claims against it must be made within the time allowed by the court.[3] The court's ruling must be advertised by the owner in such a manner as the court directs.[4]

1   Civil Procedure Rules 1998 ('CPR') 61.2 (1)(iv) and 61.11/PD 61.10.1.
2   MSA 1995, s 157(3).
3   CPR PD 61 para 10.14.
4   CPR 61.11(14).

15.10 Ships, except government ships, that are carrying more than 2,000 tons of oil in bulk must be insured to meet the owners' liability under the CLC. Any such ship must have a certificate showing it is insured and failure to have one is an offence under the MSA 1995, s 163(5).

15.11   The MSA 1995, s 173 provides for oil carriers or importers to contribute to the Fund. The Fund becomes liable to pay compensation or damages to anyone who has suffered pollution damage in UK territory – or in the territory of a party to the Fund Convention – because the damage exceeds the owner's liability as limited by s 157. In addition the Fund may also be liable where an owner's liability is excluded or where an owner or guarantor cannot meet its liability in full.[1] The Fund's liability for an incident cannot exceed that set out in Article 5 of the Fund Convention.

1   MSA 1995, s 175(1), (2).

15.12   The starting point for a claim against the Fund is to obtain its Claims Manual, which can be downloaded from the Fund's website.[1] This sets out the types of claim that can be made and the evidence the Fund Secretariat will require in support of any claim. However, the 2002 Manual points out:

> 'Claimants will ultimately lose their right to compensation under the 1992 Fund Convention unless they bring court action against the 1992 Fund within three years of the date on which the *damage occurred*, or make formal notification to the 1992 Fund of a court action against the shipowner or his insurer within that three-year period (see Articles 6.1 and 7.6 of the 1992 Fund Convention). Although damage may occur some time after an incident takes place, court action must in any case be brought within six years of the date of the *incident*. The same applies to claimants' right to compensation from the shipowner and his insurer under the 1992 Civil Liability Convention. Claimants are recommended to seek legal advice on the formal requirements of court actions, to avoid their claims becoming time-barred.'[2]

1   www.iopcfund.org
2   And see MSA 1995, s 178.

15.13   In practice, issues of liability arising out of a claim against the shipowner or guarantor under the CLC and s 153 of the MSA 1995 determined by the Admiralty Court will bind the Fund in proceedings against it in respect of the same incident.[1] However, the Fund must be notified of the proceedings[2] and will have a right to intervene in them.[3]

1   MSA 1995, s 177(1), (2).
2   CPR PD 61 para 11.1.
3   CPR PD 61 para 11.2.

LIABILITY FOR POLLUTION FROM HAZARDOUS SUBSTANCES

15.14   The International Convention on Liability and Compensation for Damage in connection with the Carriage of Hazardous and Noxious Substances ('HNS') 1996 by sea is not yet in force. When in force it will operate in a similar way to the CLC and Fund conventions, the owners of the cargo carrier being primarily liable but a top-up fund being provided by those who receive HNS cargoes. It will be implemented in the UK by orders made under the MSA 1995, s 182B, the text of the Convention being set out in the MSA 1995, Sch 5A. Until the Convention is in force, liability will be determined in accordance with the common law.

15.15 If during the course of carriage of nuclear matter, as defined in the Nuclear Installations Act 1965 ('NIA 1965'), s 26 (essentially nuclear fuel), an incident occurs in which a person is injured or property is damaged because of the radioactive or toxic, explosive or other hazardous properties of that matter, or ionising radiations from it, the liability for the damage will rest with the operator of the site or other person on whose behalf it was being carried.[1]

1   NIA 1965, ss 7–12 as amended by SI 1990/1918.

LIABILITY FOR OFFSHORE INSTALLATIONS

15.16 The Offshore Pollution Liability Agreement ('OPOL') is a voluntary agreement between oil companies that operate or intend to operate offshore installations and pipelines to guarantee funds to meet certain claims for pollution damage arising out of a spillage or escape of crude oil or natural gas liquids and to pay for the costs of remedial measures taken by public authorities. It also provides a mechanism for settling such claims on the basis of strict liability. The OPOL organisation is based in London.[1] Claims against it must be brought against the relevant operator within one year of the date of the incident causing the loss or damage.[2]

1   www.opol.org.uk
2   OPOL, cl VI.

15.17 Section 23(1) of the Petroleum Act 1998 provides that any breach of duty imposed on any person by regulations made under Pt III of the Act, which is concerned with submarine pipelines, that applies the subsection shall be actionable only in so far as the breach causes personal injury. If OPOL will not accept liability, an action for other loss will have to be commenced in common law.

15.18 The Civil Jurisdiction (Offshore Activities) Order 1987[1] specifies that the law in force in England and Wales shall apply for the determination of questions arising in the English area of the continental shelf out of acts or omissions taking place in a designated area in connection with the exploration for, or exploitation of, natural resources. The High Court has the same jurisdiction for these purposes as it would have if the acts or omissions in question had taken place in England or Wales.

1   SI 1987/2197.

DUMPING OF WASTE AT SEA

15.19 The main convention on this aspect is the Convention on the Prevention of Marine Pollution by Dumping of Wastes and Other Matter 1972, which is known as the 'London Dumping Convention'. It is administered by the International Maritime Organisation from whom the latest text can be obtained.[1] Generally, the dumping of all wastes is prohibited except for those set out in the Annex. The Annex allows the dumping of sewage sludge, however this is prohibited in the North East Atlantic by the OSPAR Convention.[2]

1   www.imo.org
2   The Convention for the Protection of the Marine Environment of the North-East Atlantic (see www.ospar.org).

15.20   In the UK, the dumping of wastes at sea is controlled by licences issued under s 5 of the Food and Environment Protection Act 1995. Exemptions from licensing requirements are provided by the Deposits in the Sea (Exemptions) Order 1985.[1] Registers of information concerning licences are provided under the Food and Environment Protection Act 1985 and in the Deposits in the Sea (Public Registers of Information) Regulations 1996.[2]

1   SI 1985/1699 as amended by SI 1994/1056.
2   SI 1996/1427.

LIABILITY AT COMMON LAW

15.21   Where pollution damage arises from an incident in UK territorial or internal waters, the ordinary UK courts will have jurisdiction as if the incident had occurred on land.[1] The leading case in England is *Southport Corpn v Esso Petroleum Co Ltd*[2] where an oil tanker was stranded in a river estuary and, to prevent further damage, discharged a quantity of oil which polluted the foreshore owned by the Corporation. The courts considered the application of the principles of trespass, public and private nuisance and negligence in this situation. Generally the conclusion to be drawn from this authority is that any such action should be pleaded in negligence. If, as a result of the negligent navigation or management of a ship, pollution occurs causing damage to the claimant, the claimant will be able to obtain compensation from the owner or charterer[3] of the vessel if the negligent act resulting in the pollution was the proximate cause of the loss or damage.[4]

1   *The Waziristan* [1953] 2 Lloyd's Rep 361.
2   [1954] 2 QB 182, CA, affd [1956] AC 218, HL.
3   See *Fenton v City of Dublin Steam Packet Co* (1839) 8 LJQB 28.
4   *Lord Bailiffs and Jurats of Romney Marsh v Trinity House Corpn* (1870) 22 LT 446.

15.22   If damage is caused on the high seas or is suffered within the UK from an incident on the high seas then ordinary UK laws cannot be applied and the case will be governed by 'the general law of the sea'. The maritime law as administered under the Admiralty jurisdiction of the Supreme Court vests a right of action in any person who suffers an injury anywhere in the world, either to his of her person or property, when caused by the maritime fault of the owner of a ship, who is held liable for the acts and omissions of his or her crew.[1] If the vessel is registered in the UK, the action can be brought *in* *personam*; but if it is foreign, the action should be brought *in rem* against the ship itself. Such an action will usually be brought in the District Registry of the High Court and will be an Admiralty claim to which CPR Pt 61 will apply.

1   *The Tolten* [1946] P 135 at 148, CA; *Esso Petroleum* per Devlin LJ at [1956] AC 218 at 227, HL.

LIABILITY FOR POLLUTION IN HARBOURS

15.23   Where pollution is caused due to the negligent operation of a ship in a harbour, the harbour authority may have a right at common law to bring an action in nuisance or negligence against the owner or master of the vessel to recover any expenses incurred in cleaning up the pollutant.[1] In such an action the expenditure by the harbour authority in abating the nuisance will be considered as special damage.[2] A ship may be 'premises' for the purposes of statutory nuisance proceedings.[3]

1   *The Ella* (1914) 30 TLR 566.
2   *The Wagon Mound* (*No 2*) [1966] 2 All ER 709, PC.
3   Environmental Protection Act 1990, s 79(7).

CHAPTER 16

Air pollution

INTRODUCTION

16.01 In 1952 an estimated 4,000 Londoners died from a smog that persisted for five days. The sulphurous smogs of the 1950s have receded but air pollution remains a serious health problem today. The increase in the volume of traffic on the roads, for example, has led to different forms of air pollution caused by nitrogen dioxide and other exhaust emissions. The Department for Environment, Food and Rural Affairs ('DEFRA') publishes an updated general strategies for air quality. Air quality is subject to extensive statutory controls and a number of European Directives dealing with such matters as gases from engines, sulphur in the atmosphere, lead in the air and chlorofluorocarbons. Those controls, however, are not considered in detail in this chapter, which concentrates on the practical aspects of running an air pollution action, and in particular the evidential hurdles faced by potential claimants.

16.02 Air pollution impacts upon individuals at every level, from highly localised nuisances to depletion of the ozone layer and acid rain. It can have a detrimental effect on property through particulate deposition causing depreciation of property value and substantial clean-up costs. Actions based upon air pollution range from the nuisance complaints brought by local residents to restrain odour caused by renderers' operations, to actions brought by companies for compensation for damage to the bodywork of newly imported cars caused by chemicals emanating from chimneys of nearby factories.

16.03 The language is specialised. For example, the phrases 'fall out' and 'air pollution' connote emissions from chimney-stacks, whilst ground-level emissions, eg from the failure to contain offensive odours within buildings, are called 'fugitive emissions'. This chapter provides an introduction to this specialist language.

STATUTORY OUTLINE

16.04   The most important statutory provisions governing air pollution are those contained in the Environmental Protection Act 1990 ('EPA 1990'), Pt I:
- Integrated Pollution Control ('IPC'); and
- Air Pollution Control ('APC').

The concept of IPC means that, in considering abatement measures, regard should not be *confined* to *air*, but should take into account *water* and *land*, and hence 'be integrated'. The EPA 1990 regime was the first to introduce the system of IPC in the UK, covering both IPC as it was called, and APC.

16.05   The regime for Integrated Pollution Prevention and Control ('IPPC') and for APC in England and Wales is provided for by the Pollution Prevention and Control (England and Wales) Regulations 2000[1] ('PPC Regulations'). These Regulations were made under the Pollution Prevention and Control Act 1999 ('PPCA 1999') which has replaced Pt I of the EPA 1990 so as to implement EC Directive 96/61/EC. As with the statutory regime for remediation of land, the cornerstone of the regime is the *Guidance* to the PPC Regulations, obtainable from the DEFRA.

1   SI 2000/1973.

16.06   However, whilst the PPC Regulations[1] came into force on 1 August 2000, *existing* authorisations under the EPA 1990 continue in operation for the time being, and must be replaced by permits under the PCC Regulations by 2007, according to a timescale indicated by Annex IV of the PPC Regulations that sets different deadlines for different industry sectors. Details of the transitional arrangements are contained in the *Guidance*. Part I of the EPA 1990 will be repealed in 2007 when the transitional period ends. Accordingly, where reference to the APC regime is made in this chapter, it continues to be in respect of the EPA 1990, Pt I.

1   SI 2000/1973.

16.07   IPC covers the most complicated processes, which often have the greatest potential for pollution. There are about 5,000 such processes. The Environment Agency Inspectors who oversee these processes are usually scientifically qualified. The permit to operate a process (called an 'authorisation') will usually contain a large number of conditions, many of which will provide for air pollution control.

16.08   The determination of these conditions is broadly a matter of negotiation between the Inspectors and the applicant, but in virtually all cases these negotiations take place against the context of Guidance Notes promulgated by the DEFRA for the industry in question, for example the Guidance for 'Coal, Coke, Coal Product and Petroleum Coke Processes', or Guidance for 'Animal Bi-Product Rendering'.

16.09 These Guidance Notes are particularly important in recommending measures to prevent or minimise pollution, and are incorporated into the statutory scheme pursuant to the EPA 1990, s 7(11).

16.10 So far as material, the EPA 1990, s 7 provides:

'(1) There shall be included in an authorisation ... such specific conditions as the enforcing authority considers appropriate ... for achieving the objectives specified in subsection 2 below ...;

(2) Those objectives are ...

    (a) ensuring that, in carrying on a prescribed process, the best available techniques not entailing excessive cost (BATNEEC) will be used—

        (i) for preventing the release of substances prescribed for any environmental medium into that medium or, where that is not practicable by such means, reducing the release of such substances to a minimum and for rendering harmless any such substances which are so released; and

        (ii) For rendering harmless any other substances which might cause harm if released into any environmental medium ...

(4) ... [T]here is implied in every authorisation a general condition that, in carrying on the process to which the authorisation applies, the person carrying it on must use BATNEEC ...

(10) References to BATNEEC in relation to a process include (in addition to references to any technical means and technology) references to the number, qualifications, training and supervision of persons employed in the process and the design, construction, layout and maintenance of the buildings in which it is carried on.

(11) It shall be the duty of enforcing authorities to have regard to any Guidance issued to them by the Secretary of State for the purposes of the application of subsection (2) ... as to the techniques and environmental options that are appropriate for any description of prescribed process.'

16.11 The EPA 1990, ss 10 and 11 makes provision for variation of an authorisation; s 12 gives power to the enforcing authority to revoke an authorisation; ss 13 and 14 make provision for the service of Enforcement and Prohibition Notices (contravention is an offence); s 15 makes provision for appeals; and s 23 makes it a criminal offence to carry on a prescribed process without, or in breach of a condition of, an authorisation.

16.12 The authorisations, conditions and any enforcement proceedings are required to be put on the Register.[1]

1   See Chapter 8.

16.13   Industrial processes not so complex as to require IPC are dealt with under the EPA 1990, Pt I, Pt B and are subject to control by local authorities. The Environmental Health Department (by means of Environmental Health Officers) will keep an eye on local sources of air pollution, and particularly odour, and will use their powers under the EPA 1990, Pt III (statutory nuisance) where appropriate.[1]

1   See Chapter 3.

16.14   We should also make reference to the Clean Air Act 1993 ('CAA 1993'). The CAA 1993 consolidates the Clean Air Acts of 1956 and 1968. Section 1 prohibits the emission of dark smoke from chimneys; s 2 prohibits the emission of dark smoke from any industrial or trade premises; and s 4 provides that new furnaces must be constructed so that they are, so far as practicable, smokeless. Domestic chimneys are controlled by way of the Smoke Control Areas (Authorised Fuels) Regulations 1991[1] (ss 18–20) whereby a local authority may, by Order, declare the whole or any part of the district of the authority to be a smoke control area and thereby making it an offence to burn other than authorised fuel.

1   SI 1991/1282.

UNDERSTANDING AIR POLLUTION: A PRACTICAL GUIDE

16.15   In many air pollution cases, the primary difficulty faced by the claimant will be identifying the source of the pollution. Often, the key to identifying the source of the pollution will lie with analysis of samples of the pollutant. The chemical composition of the pollutant will often reveal the fingerprint of the polluter, or at least narrow down the possible sources. Analysing the pollutant is therefore the first step in identifying the source of the pollution and the potential defendant. Table 1 below sets out some of the sources of common pollutants.

Table 1: Sources of common pollutants

Source	Potential waste product
Power generation processes (eg coal, oil, gas and nuclear generators)	Carbon monoxide (CO), sulphur dioxide (SO_2), particulate material, radioactive waste
Industrial processes such as mineral, chemical, metal and extractive industries	Heavy metals, polycyclic hydrocarbons, gases and dust

Source	Potential waste product
Incinerators	Waste products depend on the type and size of material incinerated; the temperature of incineration; the residence time; and the amount of excess oxygen
Road traffic	Nitrogen dioxide (NO_2), CO, very fine particles
Industrial processes such as animal by-product rendering or knackers' yards	Highly odorous compounds
Dust	Smuts from chimneys, industrial sites, construction sites

16.16 Airborne pollutants may be divided into two broad categories: gases (eg NO_2); and particulate matter such as dust. Gas is commonly encountered in odour nuisance; dust is the particulate matter most commonly encountered in physical damage claims.

16.17 There are various types of dust (see Table 2 below). The type of dust will reflect the source of the dust, the mechanism of its travel, and effects on members of the public.

Table 2: Types of dust

Pollut-ant	Size (*mm*)	Description	Source	Distance travelled
Dust: Macro deposits	0.5–10	Large individual obtrusive deposits visible to the human eye	Smut from chimneys; commonly caused by incomplete combustion of fuel oil	Up to 300m (short chimneys) or 1000m (tall chimneys)
Dust: Gritty deposits	0.2–1.0	Feels gritty to touch	Unpaved roads/heavy materials handling/ stock-piling	200m if not from elevated source (eg chimney)

Pollut- ant	Size (mm)	Description	Source	Distance travelled
Dust film	0.05–0.01	Most fre- quently occur- ring dust nuisance. Too small to be seen with naked eye	Cement dust from building sites	Maximum deposition within about 10 chimney heights of source
Fume	0.001	Any airborne solid matter smaller than dust (CAA 1993, s 64(1))	Industrial processes	Depends upon height of chimney

16.18   Of the differing forms of dust, the most frequently encountered is a dust film causing soiling ('dinginess'). A dust deposit can cause a clean surface to become soiled in this way within a few hours. The degree of nuisance caused will depend upon the following factors:

(a)   the rate of obscuration of the surface by dust particles;

(b)   the optical properties of the surface exposed to the dust film;

(c)   the optical properties of the dust film;

(d)   the nature of the illumination of the surface;

(e)   the frequency of dust deposition incidents; and

(f)   the size of the area affected.

16.19   The collection of dust is a critical forensic matter in air pollution cases. It is important both for *quality* (transmission to a laboratory for scientific analysis); and for *quantity*. Determination of quantity (within a given time) may itself evidence nuisance. However, it is also very important as a drop-off in concentrations over distance is good evidence that incriminates a point source. Window ledges as collectors of dust (though important to residents) have obvious disadvantages, including the loss of settled dust as a result of weather (eg wind and rain).

16.20   Following the first Clean Air Acts, a British Standard deposit gauge was developed in the 1960s as the technique for collecting dust for measure- ment. However, the modern method of measurement is a Frisbee Dust Deposit Gauge. A Frisbee Gauge is an aerodynamically efficient collector of airborne dust which comprises an inverted spun aluminium Frisbee mounted on a 1.7m high stand, with a foam insert to prevent blow-off of collected particles, and a sampling bottle doped with a biocide agent. This gauge was developed in the 1980s in an attempt to overcome some of the deficiencies of the earlier models, and it is generally accepted that the Frisbee gauge is about 30% more efficient at collecting dust than its predecessors. The Frisbee gauge is now the device of choice in these cases, most particularly where gauges are being set in a line at varying distances from a suspected source so as to test the rate of drop-off of dust over distance from a suspected source.

THE MECHANISM OF POLLUTION

16.21   In seeking to establish a link between an alleged polluter and the person or property injured, the practitioner will often need meteorological evidence. In relatively straightforward cases where there is no dispute as to the source of the pollution (for example, where the claimant suffers an intolerable odour from an adjacent pig farm), meteorological evidence can be dispensed with. However, where for example it is alleged that nuisance dust has been deposited on the claimant's land from one of a number of possible nearby factories, meteorological evidence will be necessary to establish the source and how the dust came to be deposited on the claimant's land (sometimes called a *plausible mechanism of transportation*). In establishing a plausible mechanism, an important feature will be 'distance of travel', which varies according to the type of dust.

Distance of travel

16.22   Following is a brief summary of a large (and not altogether consistent) literature on the limits of distance of travel in relation to particle size/weight/ chimney height. It will be necessary for the expert to express the view not only that wind conditions favour transportation from the source to the claimant, but also that the claimant's land is within the plausible distance of travel of the type of pollutant in question:
(a)   *Macro deposits* – The most common form of macro deposits are caused by incomplete combustion of oil in chimneys ('acid smuts'). The distance of travel of the acid smuts is dependent on the height of the chimney. With chimneys up to 50m they will travel up to 300m. If the height of the chimney is 70m or more the distance may exceed 1000m.
(b)   *Gritty deposits* – These do not travel far except where emitted from tall chimneys. Grit problems caused by dirty surfaces or stock-piles are often associated with strong winds. The mechanism of transportation is 'salta-tion' whereby the particles bounce across the surfaces and off each other, assisted by the wind. The limit of the distance of travel is 200m.
(c)   *Films of dust* – These are particles which are small enough to be dispersed on the wind rather than moving in saltating motion. Nuisance conditions from a ground-level source are usually limited to 200m, but depends on chimney height.

Methods of dust deposition

16.23   Pollutants carried in the air may be deposited on land in a number of ways.

(a)   *Dry deposition* (ie particle fall-out) – This is one mechanism whereby pollutants may be carried from a chimney stack. Where wind is multi-directional, the concentration of deposits is likely to be uniform in all directions around the stack.

(b)   *Wet deposition* – Wet deposition is a very effective means of deposition from a chimney-stack. Consideration needs to be given to whether the pollutant is hydrophobic, eg dioxins. Most rain-bearing winds in Britain are Westerlies or South-westerlies which will tend to shed their water vapour on the western side of any mountains. This may lead to concentrated but patchy deposits of a pollutant.

(c)   *Occult deposition* – This type of deposition takes place where cloud is driven against the hillside. In some areas, this accounts for a significant amount of precipitation and may therefore contribute to the transport of pollutants.

DUST NUISANCE

16.24   Dust is deposited as fall-out in homes and gardens, usually as a visible film over furniture, windowsills, washing or any clean surface. The degree of nuisance experienced depends on the rate of deposition discernible at two levels:

(a)   Significant nuisance is experienced when dust cover is sufficient to be visible when contrasted to an adjacent clean surface (such as when a finger is wiped across the surface). This is particularly annoying when it occurs regularly over long periods.

(b)   Severe nuisance is experienced when dust cover is perceptible without a clean reference surface for comparison. This commonly occurs over short periods during very dusty conditions, eg building-site operations.

16.25   There are no UK statutory or recommended levels of dust deposition that are defined as constituting a nuisance.

16.26   The Irish Institute for Industrial Research and Standards indicates that average deposition rates greater than $200mg/m^2/day$ will cause problems. This standard has been adopted as the 'threshold for serious nuisance for non-toxic soil type dust which is deposited in a regular pattern' in the seminal paper on dust impact by Bate and Coppin.[1] These authors suggest that for black coal dust, which has a higher contrast with a background, a deposition rate of $80mg/m^2/day$ is likely to give rise to complaints. The same authors also canvass an approach based on *increase over existing background level*. The comparison with noise nuisance will be evident (eg BS4142). The approach involves a measurement of the background dust levels in the area in question. These will vary according to whether the area is rural, a small town/suburb, a town centre, or a heavy industrial area. Having established the relevant background (without the source operating), the authors suggest taking a multiple of two or three times the existing background as the threshold of unacceptability.

1   Mines and Quarries, March 1991.

16.27 Nuisance complaints are usually concentrated around periods of peak deposition, occurring during particular weather conditions combined with the operations of which complaint is made. Monitoring will have to be sensitive to this, which is not always easy. For example, if a Frisbee gauge is left for a month to collect dust, this will have the effect of averaging out the deposition over the whole of that period.

16.28 The effect of dust nuisance on a community is mainly to create an air of 'dinginess'. There are specific periods of annoyance and a feeling of frustration during particularly bad episodes of dust. These periods result in direct complaints to the local authority Environmental Health Department. It follows that the local authority Complaints Log is crucial evidence, particularly when combined with meteorological data and a proper understanding of the operating parameters of the suspected polluter. If a good and consistent match can be obtained, then this amounts to a powerful case.

ODOUR NUISANCE

16.29 There are no definitive UK standards for assessing odour levels. As one expert put it, there is no measuring instrument which could adequately substitute the human nose when used together with an established testing protocol.[1] There are such things as 'odourmeters', but they are not recognised in any British Standards, and we do not know of any case where the court has placed reliance on the measurements of such a piece of equipment.

1   See paras **16.31–16.32** below.

16.30 It is generally agreed that complaints are likely to occur when odours become *recognisable*, and the longer that they are recognisable, the greater the level of complaint, particularly if unpleasant or obnoxious.

16.31 A typical odour assessment carried out by a party's environmental consultant will record:
- the weather conditions;
- wind directions;
- time; and
- a description of the operating parameters of the suspect plant (eg doors open or closed, abatement equipment operating or not, activity level high or low).

It will then record the maximum distances (Dmax) at which (around the points of a compass) the odour is recognisable (eg rotten eggs) and at which the assessor (or assessors, if the claimant's environmental consultant has involved the Environmental Health Officer and someone representing the plant) consider that complaints could be expected.

16.32 It is evident from the above that, whilst 'independent' experts can do an assessment in a systematic way, it remains a *subjective* approach, based on olfactory sensibility. It follows that great weight will be given to anecdotal evidence in this sort of case. It is vital, therefore, that the local residents keep very detailed 'odour diaries' including a record of:

- date;
- time;
- wind direction;
- general weather conditions;
- description of the smell (often difficult); and
- intensity (mild to severe).

In the absence of such a log, corroborated by a number of different persons, it is unlikely that an action will succeed.

16.33   It will be necessary to have technical evidence as to the means of abatement being used by the defendant. Typically the gradations are:

(a)   *Containment* – That is, trying to keep the buildings as airtight as possible, e g with negative pressure.

(b)   *Bio-filters* – Involving modest capital investment and cheap to operate.

(c)   *Incineration* – The most expensive, and generally the most effective means.

With some processes (e g rendering) the Secretary of State's Guidance recognises explicitly that it is not possible even using BATNEEC to eliminate all odours arising from the rendering plant outside the process boundary. Whilst this will assist the operator in a statutory nuisance action, it is only a factor to be taken into account (and certainly not a conclusive one) in a private law nuisance action.

REMEDIES IN THE MAGISTRATES' COURT

16.34   The statutory nuisance provisions under the EPA 1990, Pt III are considered in general terms in Chapter 3 above, but the following paragraphs are particularly relevant to dust and odour nuisance.

16.35   The relevant statutory nuisances are set out in the EPA 1990, s 79:

- s 79(1)(b) covers any smoke emitted from premises so as to be prejudicial to health or a nuisance;
- s 79(1)(c) covers fumes or gases emitted from premises so as to be prejudicial to health or a nuisance;
- s 79(1)(d) covers any dust, steam, smell or other effluvia arising on industrial, trade or business premises and being prejudicial to health or a nuisance.

It should be noted that by s 79(7):

- 'dust' does not include dust emitted from a chimney as an ingredient of smoke;
- 'fumes' means any airborne solid matter smaller than dust; and
- 'gas' includes vapour and moisture precipitated from vapour.

16.36 Whether a complainant brings proceedings in the magistrates' court or in the civil courts will depend upon the nature of the nuisance and on the means of the claimant. Broadly speaking, where the primary remedy sought is the cessation of the nuisance (rather than compensation) and where the dispute is relatively simple, for example between neighbours, the informality of the magistrates' court may be preferred (particularly where the complainant does not qualify for legal aid). In cases of dust or smell nuisance from industrial, trade or business premises, and smoke nuisance from a chimney, the defendant will have a complete defence to statutory nuisance proceedings in the magistrates' court if it can show that it has used 'best practicable means' to abate the nuisance.[1] There is no such defence to a private law action in nuisance. This is a powerful incentive to bring a private claim in the county court, even though the expense is likely to be higher.

1   See EPA 1990, ss 79(7), (8).

EVIDENCE

16.37 The starting point is the collation of good anecdotal evidence. A potential claimant should obtain the following by way of primary evidence:
(a)   Anecdotal evidence of the claimant.
(b)   Anecdotal evidence of others, eg neighbours.
(c)   A notebook/diary/log should be kept by the claimant and by neighbours. It should detail the dates, times, duration and source of any smoke, odour or other airborne pollution and indicate the prevailing weather patterns (eg wind direction and whether raining).
(d)   Where dust or other matter is deposited, samples must be obtained.
(e)   If the pollution complained of is dust, the claimant would be wise to have recourse to some objective measure of the dust level. This can be done by means of a dust gauge. There are two types of British standard dust gauge:
   (i)   Bowl Gauge BS1747 Pt 1 (the Frisbee gauge referred to at para **16.20** above); and
   (ii)   Directional Gauge BS1747 Pt 5.

   The differing designs of these gauges mean that the results, although often of the same general magnitude, are not strictly comparable. Both types of gauge have specific uses in the assessment of dust deposition. Deposit figures are only valid for a small area around a gauge, and do not necessarily give much indication of average pollution in the rest of the town or region. Expert input is required if this evidence is to be given weight.
(f)   In a case which involves smoke from a chimney, photographic and video evidence should be obtained where possible.
(g)   In an odour case, expert input may not be necessary, eg where odour is generated from an adjacent pig farm, or it may be required, as in a case of intermittent smell from industrial processes at some distance from the claimant.

(h)   Complaints history. The local authority (Environmental Health Department) usually keeps its own log or written record of all complaints received (even those made orally by telephone). This will be needed.

(i)   Details of any enforcement action, eg Prohibition or Improvement Notices. These will be on the Register.

(j)   Dealings between the defendant and the local authority. All this correspondence will be discoverable by the defendant within the context of civil proceedings. The court will plainly attach weight to the action (or inaction) of the local authority, because it is perceived to be 'independent' within the proceedings. If, for example, the Environmental Health Officer has stated in writing that it is considered that no nuisance exists, then weight is likely to be attached (see *Murdoch v Glacier Metal Co Ltd*[1]). The difficulty arises where the regulatory authority has taken no proceedings, and refuses to state its position unambiguously. In this situation, the history of dealings between the regulatory authority and the defendant, as demonstrated in correspondence, will enable the court to determine whether any inference should be drawn, and in favour of which party.

1   [1998] Env LR 732, CA.

SELECTED CASES

16.38   Whether or not dust or smell amounts to a nuisance will depend upon the character of the neighbourhood and the background air quality. As we have previously noted,[1] what is a nuisance in Belgravia Square may not be a nuisance in Bermondsey. As Mellor J observed in *Tipping v St Helen's Smelting Co*:[2]

'The law does not regard trifling inconveniences; everything must be looked at from a reasonable point of view, and therefore in an action for nuisance to property by noxious vapours arising on the land of another, the injury to be actionable must be such as visibly to diminish the value of the property and the comfort and enjoyment of it ... In determining that question, time, locality, and all the circumstances should be taken into consideration.'

1   See Chapter 2 at para **2.26**.
2   (1863) 4 B & S 608 at 610.

16.39   In *West v Bristol Tramways Co*,[1] the defendants were a tramway company who paved parts of a road on which their tramway was laid. The wood paving was coated with creosote which gave off fumes and injured plants and shrubs belonging to the claimant, a market gardener. It was open to the defendants to use a different form of wood paving which would not have caused the damage. A jury found for the claimant. The Court of Appeal held that although the defendants did not know that the use of creosoted wood might cause damage and were not guilty of negligence they were liable under the rule in *Rylands v Fletcher*[2] for the damage caused by the fumes.

1   [1908] 2 KB 14.
2   (1868) LR 3 HL 330.

16.40 In *Tutton v A D Walter Ltd*[1] the claimants kept bees near land farmed by the defendant company and on which it grew a crop of oil seed rape. The flowers of rape were particularly attractive to bees. The crop was affected by pests to the extend that it required control by spraying with an insecticide. The insecticide was known to be dangerous to bees and the advice to farmers from both government agencies and the manufacturers warned against spraying during the flowering period because of the risk to bees. The defendant, having given a warning only 24 hours earlier to only two of the five claimants, sprayed the field with insecticide, killing the bees. It was held that the defendant owed a common law duty of care to neighbouring bee-keepers since it knew of their presence in the neighbourhood and had knowledge of the danger to bees of spraying during the flowering period.

1   [1986] QB 61.

CHAPTER 17

Waste on land

INTRODUCTION

17.01 This chapter is concerned with liability for waste that has been disposed of to land or to landfill sites. It also briefly describes the regime for liability for radioactive wastes. Waste dumped at sea is dealt with in Chapter 15, while freshwater pollution is covered in Chapter 14.

LIABILITY FOR WASTE AT COMMON LAW

17.02 A person who deliberately disposes of waste on land that he or she does not own or occupy will be liable to the owner or occupier in trespass.[1] Even if the disposer of the waste originally had a licence from the owner or occupier to deposit the waste on the land, once the licence expires the disposer will commit a continuing trespass if he or she leaves the waste there.[2] The claimant will not need to show any actual damage in these circumstances. However, if the defendant has effectively profited by the use of the claimant's land as a tip, the claimant can recover damages on the 'wayleave' principle.[3]

1   *Kynoch Ltd v Rowlands* [1912] 1 Ch 527, CA.
2   *Konskier v B Goodman Ltd* [1928] 1 KB 421, CA.
3   *Whitwham v Westminster Brymbo Coal and Coke Co* [1896] 2 Ch 538, CA.

17.03 If waste matter escapes from one person's land onto the property of another, the action is more properly in *nuisance* as opposed to *trespass*.[1] In addition, the circumstances of the case may show that the escape occurred owing to the negligence of the occupier. While there has been considerable assimilation of the law of nuisance and negligence in cases of escape,[2] nevertheless the acts of negligence that are to be relied on should still be pleaded. In either case the claimant will have to show that he or she has suffered damage as a result of the defendant's action. There may also be liability under the doctrine in *Rylands v Fletcher*.[3]

1 *Tenant v Goldwin* (1704) 2 Ld Raym 1089.
2 See HHJ Thornton in *Johnson (t/a Johnson Butchers) v BJW Property Developments Ltd* [2002] EWHC 1131 (TCC) at [47–51], [2002] 3 All ER 574 at [47–51].
3 (1868) LR 3 HL 330.

LIABILITY FOR WASTE UNDER STATUTE

17.04 'Waste' is defined in the Framework Waste Directive[1] as 'any substance or object in the categories set out in Annex I which the holder discards or intends or is required to discard'. In Great Britain this definition is set out in the Environmental Protection Act 1990 ('EPA 1990'), s 75(2). 'Controlled waste' as defined in s 75 is waste subject to waste management licensing controls. Further provision in respect of such wastes is made in the Controlled Waste Regulations 1992.[2] There are a number of authorities on what is or what is not 'waste' which is a subject that can become quite complex when considering some production residues. However, the general rule is that once a substance or item has been discarded it becomes 'waste', regardless of the intentions of the person who comes into possession of it.[3]

1 Dir 91/156/EEC, amending Dir 75/442/EEC.
2 SI 1992/588. See also SI 1994/1056, Sch 4, para 9(2) 'Directive waste'.
3 *Palin Granit Oy v Vehmassalon Kansanterveystyon Kuntayhtyman Hallitus* [2002] Env LR 843.

17.05 Some wastes are exempted from the provisions of the Waste Directive. These are gaseous effluents emitted into the atmosphere and, where they are already covered by other legislation, radioactive waste, mining and quarrying wastes, animal carcasses, faecal matter and other natural non-dangerous substances used in farming, waste waters (sewage effluent – but not liquid effluent) and decommissioned explosives.[1] The UK exempts more agricultural wastes than strictly allowed under the Directive[2] but regulations may be made to bring these and other exempt wastes into control by EPA 1990, s 63.

1 Dir 75/442/EEC as amended, Article 2.
2 EPA 1990, s 75(7)(c).

17.06 Any person who deposits[1] or causes or knowingly permits the deposit of controlled waste in or on any land without there being a waste management licence in force for the deposit will commit an offence under the EPA 1990, s 33(1)(a). However, there are a number of exemptions from waste management licensing in the Waste Management Licensing Regulations 1994,[2] which should be checked to see if they apply. If waste is deposited unlawfully the Environment Agency should be informed as they may prosecute. If the Agency will not get involved, the occupier of the land, or indeed anyone else, can bring their own prosecution.

1 *Thames Waste Management Ltd v Surrey County Council* [1997] Env LR 148.
2 SI 1994/1056 as amended, reg17 and Sch 3; and see *London Waste Regulation Authority v Drinkwater Sabey Ltd* [1997] Env LR 137.

17.07 The EPA 1990, s 33(1)(c) provides enhanced penalties for when a person unlawfully deposits, treats or keeps controlled waste in a manner likely to cause pollution of the environment or harm to human health. 'Pollution of the environment' and 'harm' are defined in s 29(2) to (5) of the Act. Generally this enhanced offence applies only where waste or substances from it have escaped from the site where it has been deposited or it is being treated or kept.

17.08 The EPA 1990, s 33(7) provides three defences to a charge under s 33(1). They are:
(a) that the acts concerned took place during an emergency;
(b) that the defendant acted under instructions from the defendant's employer and had no reason to suppose he or she was committing an offence; and
(c) that the defendant took all reasonable precautions and exercised all due diligence to avoid the commission of the offence. This 'due diligence' defence is essentially one where the defendant seeks to prove to the court that he or she acted without negligence.[1]

1 See Chapter 7 at para **7.39**.

17.09 Certain wastes will be classified as 'special' wastes in accordance with reg 2 of the Special Waste Regulations 1996.[1] These are wastes that are hazardous to humans or the environment because of their harmful properties, for example asbestos. Part I of Sch 2 to the Regulations sets out a list of wastes. Those assigned a six-figure code number may be special wastes, but only if they have the hazardous properties set out in Pt II of the Schedule. For some such properties, the threshold of harm provided in Pt III of the Schedule must also be exceeded.[2] Where special waste is deposited on land, a record must be made of the location of each such deposit.[3]

1 SI 1996/972 as amended by SI 1996/2019, SI 1997/251, SI 2000/1973, SI 2001/3148. In Wales see SI 2001/3545.
2 See DoE Circular 6/96, Annex B for a more detailed explanation.
3 SI 1996/972, reg 16(1).

17.10 The EPA 1990, s 63(2) makes it an offence to deposit or cause or knowingly permit the deposit of non-controlled waste that has the characteristics of special waste. However, if the deposit was authorised under other legislation, excluding planning legislation, then no offence will have been committed.[1]

1 EPA 1990, s 63(3).

17.11 The EPA 1990, ss 33(1) and 63(2) create criminal offences in respect of the deposit of controlled and non-controlled wastes. Section 73(6) provides for civil liability in respect of such offences. It states that where any damage is caused by waste which has been deposited in or on land, any person who deposited it, or knowingly caused or knowingly permitted it to be deposited so as to commit one of the offences is liable for the damage. 'Damage' here includes the death of, or injury to, any person which in turn includes any disease and any impairment of physical or mental condition.[1]

1   EPA 1990, s 73(8).

17.12   A defendant will not be liable under this section if he or she can establish one of the defences in the EPA 1990, s 33(7).[1] Nor will the defendant be liable if the damage was due wholly to the fault of the person who suffered it or it was suffered by someone who voluntarily accepted the risk of it being caused.[2] 'Fault' here has the same meaning as in the Law Reform (Contributory Negligence) Act 1945.[3]

1   EPA 1990, s 73(7).
2   EPA 1990, s 73(6).
3   EPA 1990, s 73(8); and see sub-s (9).

THE DUTY OF CARE

17.13   The EPA 1990, s 34 provides for a duty of care for waste.[1] This duty is intended to ensure that those who dispose of waste do so properly. Section 34(1) imposes the duty on anyone who imports, produces, carries, keeps, treats or disposes of controlled waste or who, as a broker, has control of such waste. These groups of people are conveniently referred to as 'holders' of waste. The only exception to the duty is for occupiers of domestic property in respect of their household waste.[2]

1   And see Framework Waste Directive (Dir 75/442/EEC as amended by Dir 91/156/EEC), Article 8.
2   EPA 1990, s 34(2).

17.14   It is the duty of the holder of waste to take all such measures applicable to the holder in that capacity as are reasonable in the circumstances to prevent anyone else committing an offence under the EPA 1990, s 33(1), to prevent the escape of the waste from the holder's control or that of any other person and, when the waste is transferred, to secure that it is only transferred to an authorised person or to a person for 'authorised transport purposes' and that it is accompanied by proper documentation. Failure to comply with this duty is an offence under the EPA 1990, s 34(6).

17.15   A Code of Practice on the duty has been issued under the EPA 1990, s 34(7).[1] It sets out common sense guidance on matters such as the storage of waste prior to collection. The Code is admissible in any relevant proceedings.[2] For the purposes of establishing civil liability in respect of waste, a breach of the Code will not be determinative of negligence. It will, however, be a material consideration for the court in reaching its decision.[3]

1   *Waste Management: The Duty of Care: A Code of Practice* (revised March 1996).
2   EPA 1990, s 34(10).
3   *Powell v Phillips* [1972] 3 All ER 864 at 868, CA.

REMOVAL OF WASTE BY STATUTORY AUTHORITIES

17.16 There are a number of powers available to local authorities to remove waste from public or private land. Section 6 of the Refuse Disposal (Amenity) Act 1978 gives a local authority power to remove waste on land in the open air and recover its costs from the person who placed in there. There are also powers under s 34 of the Public Health Act 1961 to enable the removal of rubbish that is seriously detrimental to the amenity of a neighbourhood. In both cases the occupier of the land should be notified about the intended action. An accumulation or deposit of rubbish can be dealt with as a statutory nuisance.

17.17 By virtue of s 215 of the Town and Country Planning Act 1990, if it appears to a local planning authority that the amenity of part of their area, or an adjoining one, is adversely affected by the condition of land in their area, they may serve a notice on its owner and occupier requiring them to take specified steps to remedy its condition within a certain time (which must be at least 28 days). Appeals against such notices can be made to the magistrates' court under s 217 of the Act. Failure to comply with a notice is an offence under s 216 and the authority may also enter the land and carry out the requirements of the notice itself, recovering its reasonable expenses for doing so from the landowner in accordance with s 219.

17.18 Abandoned vehicles can be removed by local authorities under s 3 of the Refuse Disposal (Amenity) Act 1978. Police and local authorities can also remove vehicles by virtue of ss 99 to 103 of the Road Traffic Regulation Act 1984 and Pt II of the Removal and Disposal of Vehicles Regulations 1986.[1] Abandoned shopping or luggage trolleys can be removed from land in the open air under the EPA 1990, s 99 and Sch 4 by a council that has passed a resolution applying those powers within its area.

1   SI 1986/183.

17.19 Under the EPA 1990, s 59, where 'directive' waste is deposited in or on any land in the area of the Environment Agency or of a waste collection authority in contravention of s 33(1), the Agency or authority may require the removal of the waste and cleaning up of the land. The power is exercised by the service of a 'removal notice' on the occupier of the land, in accordance with s 160 of the Act. The notice may require the removal of the waste within a period that must be not less than 21 days from the date of service of the notice. It may also require the taking of specified steps with a view to eliminating or reducing the consequences of the deposit or both.[1]

1   EPA 1990, s 59(1).

17.20 The person served with the notice has 21 days from the date of service to appeal against it to a magistrates' court.[1] The notice will have no effect pending the appeal.[2] In determining such an appeal the court must quash the notice if it is satisfied that the appellant neither deposited, nor knowingly caused or knowingly permitted the deposit of the waste on the land, or if there is a material defect in the notice.[3] Otherwise it may modify the notice or dismiss the appeal or extend time for compliance. As the notice is triggered by an offence under s 33(1) the appellant would have the defences under s 33(7) and would be able to take advantage of exceptions to the licensing regime. Failure to comply with a notice is an offence. Following a conviction for an offence the Agency or authority can take the steps specified in the notice and recover their expenses from the defendant.[4]

1   EPA 1990, s 59(2).
2   EPA 1990, s 59(4).
3   EPA 1990, s 59(3).
4   EPA 1990, s 59(6).

17.21   In addition to their powers to serve removal notices, relevant authorities may also take remedial action against unlawful deposits under s 59(7) of the EPA 1990. This power can be exercised where immediate steps are necessary (i) to remove or prevent pollution or harm to human health or (ii) to eliminate or reduce the consequences of the deposit or (iii) both. It can also be used where there is no occupier of the land in question or the occupier was not responsible for the deposit. If waste is removed under this provision, the removing authority will be able to recover its costs from the person who deposited the waste. It may also be able to recover its reasonable costs from the occupier of the land unless the occupier can prove that he or she neither made nor caused or knowingly permitted the deposit.[1]

1   EPA 1990, s 59(8).

LIABILITY IN RESPECT OF WASTE MANAGEMENT SITES

17.22   A waste management site will be either (i) a landfill site or (ii) a waste transfer station that is licensed under the EPA 1990, s 35. The licensing regime is set out in ss 35 to 43 of the Act and in the Waste Management Licensing Regulations 1994.[1] Details of licences will be available from the public register maintained by the Environment Agency under s 64 of the EPA 1990; which will also be held by waste collection authorities for sites in their area. The particulars that should be entered on the registers are set out in reg 10 of the 1994 Regulations.

1   SI 1994/1056 as amended.

17.23   Waste management licences will contain conditions as to how the site is to be operated. There will also be a working plan, prepared by the operator, providing more detail about the running of the site. As a condition of the licence, the operator will have to run the site in accordance with the plan. Environment Agency inspectors will usually fill in a report after each inspection, which will show compliance with conditions. Whilst a breach of conditions is an offence under the EPA 1990, s 33(1), not every breach is prosecuted. Nevertheless, site inspection reports provide a useful source of information on how the site is run.

17.24 Guidance as to the waste management regime has been issued by the Department for Environment, Food and Rural Affairs ('DEFRA') in the form of Waste Management Papers ('WMP'). These WMPs are in part the guidance issued under ss 35(8) and 74(5) of the EPA 1990. WMP No 4 *Licensing of Waste Management Facilities* is concerned with how a site should be granted a licence. The most useful WMP for guidance on how a site should be run is WMP 26B *Landfill Design, Construction and Operational Practice.* These are HMSO publications.

17.25 The main complaints that arise from waste management facilities are of:
* noise;
* odour;
* dust;
* litter; and
* related nuisances from birds or insects.

These are standard 'nuisance to amenity' claims, the principles in respect of which are set out in Chapter 2 above. In addition, *leachate* from the facility may contaminate water and can be dealt with as a nuisance as shown in Chapter 14 above. This section looks at some particular aspects of claims against waste facilities and, in particular, the issue of *landfill gas.*

17.26 The most modern case on nuisance from landfill sites is *Blackburn v ARC Ltd*[1] which concerned a claim against a large landfill site in Kent. The problems caused by the site were *noise* from traffic using the site, from machinery used for electricity generation from landfill gas and from the gas flare stack. There were also complaints of *litter* blowing onto the claimant's property and of *smells* from poorly covered waste and landfill gas. The court found that the evidence substantiated the claim in nuisance but not of noise, though there had been a noise nuisance in the past.

1   [1998] Env LR 469.

17.27 The first issue was whether the planning permission for the site and its waste management licence authorised the nuisances. The judge held that they did not. Nor did he consider that because the defendants were carrying out certain operations required by licence conditions, this gave them immunity from action – 'Where parties are required to meet certain conditions in order to carry out an activity the steps taken are not ones required by statute or authorised by statute but ones which are required in order to comply with the statute'.[1] He also rejected an argument that the use of land for waste disposal was a 'reasonable use' of land for the purposes of a defence to an action in nuisance.

1   [1998] Env LR 469 at 526.

17.28 The court refused an injunction in this case. The judge considered that to grant such an order would be both difficult to police and enforce and might lead to further troublesome proceedings. He felt it was preferable to leave matters to the regulatory authority. Thus in similar cases a court may follow this approach, being reluctant to add a further level of control over the planning and waste management licensing regimes under which sites operate.

17.29　*Landfill gas* may pose a particular problem.

'Wherever biodegradable material is deposited in landfill sites, microbial activity will generate landfill gas, which is a mixture of flammable and asphyxiating gases. It therefore follows that all sites should be assessed, monitored and, where necessary, have control systems installed to prevent uncontrolled gas migration.'[1]

The gas can migrate through the ground and if it leaves the site can be dangerous in enclosed spaces or can cause damage to plants.

1　WMP No 27 *Landfill Gas* (2nd edn, 1991, HMSO), para 1.1.

17.30　In the Canadian case of *Gertsen v Municipality of Metropolitan Toronto*[1] landfill gas escaped from a site to adjoining private garages. There was an explosion that injured Mr Gertsen. The court found the landfill operator liable to the claimant under the rule in *Rylands v Fletcher*, nuisance and negligence. Given that the gas escapes from the site, an English court today is more likely to treat the case as one assimilating both nuisance and negligence, so that the duty of the site operator to do what is reasonable in all the circumstances to prevent or minimise the risk of the known or foreseeable damage or injury to another and is liable if he or she does not.

1　(1973) 41 DLR (3d) 646.

RADIOACTIVE WASTES

17.31　Radioactive wastes are controlled under the Radioactive Substances Act 1993 ('RSA 1993'). The Act defines 'radioactive wastes' as waste consisting wholly or partly of a substance or article which, if it were not waste would be radioactive material, or a substance or article that has become contaminated by radioactive material or waste.[1] Under the Act the disposal of radioactive waste is subject to the control of the Environment Agency. It will authorise disposals in accordance with the provisions of ss 13 and 16 of the Act. Accumulations of waste must be authorised under s 14. Records of waste disposal sites and of disposals may be required under s 20.

1　RSA 1993, s 2.

THE BASEL CONVENTION

17.32 The parties to the Basel Convention have agreed a Protocol on Liability and Compensation for Damage Resulting from Transboundary Movements of Hazardous Wastes and their Disposal.[1] The objective of the Protocol, as set out in Article 1, is to:

> 'provide for a comprehensive regime for liability and for adequate and prompt compensation for damage resulting from the transboundary movement of hazardous wastes and other wastes and their disposal including illegal traffic in those wastes'.

The Protocol was not in force at the time of writing this chapter.

1   Basel Convention, Decision V/29, 10 December 1999.

CHAPTER 18

Contaminated land

INTRODUCTION

18.01 The Government seeks to re-use previously developed land, however some of this land will be contaminated. Thus the land should be fit for its proposed use, particularly in respect of the health and safety of those who will live, work or play there. In addition, contaminated land may threaten the environment and wildlife. This may affect sites designated under the Habitats Directive or the Birds Directive and lead to a requirement to stop such adverse effects. To deal with this problem, and to ensure that decontamination is paid for by those responsible for contamination or who benefit from the clean-up, the 'contaminated land regime' was enacted through the Environment Act 1995 ('EA 1995'). It is currently contained in Pt IIA of the Environment Protection Act 1990 ('EPA 1990') and came into force on 1 April 2000.

OBJECTIVES BEHIND THE ENVIRONMENTAL PROTECTION ACT 1990, PT IIA

18.02 In para 7 of DETR[1] Circular 02/2000 the Government sets out three objectives for the regime:
(1) to identify and remove unacceptable risks to human health and the environment;
(2) to seek to bring damaged land back into beneficial use;
(3) to seek to ensure that the cost burdens faced by individuals, companies and society as a whole are proportionate, manageable and economically sustainable.

1   Former Department of the Environment, Transport and the Regions, now reconfigured as Department for the Environment, Food and Rural Affairs ('DEFRA').

18.03 The first objective is to remove *unacceptable risks* to human health and the environment. The aim is not to require remediation where it is not needed.

This rejects the approach of restoring land to a pristine condition. Remediation will only be required where either contaminated land is causing significant harm or there is a significant possibility of such harm being caused. This leads to the 'Suitable for use' approach set out in paras 9–15 of Annex 1 to DETR Circular 02/2000. This consists of three elements:

(1) ensuring the land is suitable for its current use;
(2) ensuring land is made suitable for any new use, as planning permission is given for that use;
(3) limiting requirements for remediation to the work necessary to prevent unacceptable risks to human health or the environment in relation to the current use or future use of the land for which planning permission is being sought.

ENVIRONMENTAL PROTECTION ACT 1990, PT IIA

Overview

18.04 The EPA 1990, Pt IIA is concerned with the remediation of land. It is not intended to remediate polluted water, which is provided for by the Water Resources Act 1991, ss 161A–161D. However, it will operate where contaminated land is affecting or likely to affect controlled waters. The potential overlap between the two regimes is discussed in paras 64–68 of Annex 1 to DETR Circular 02/2000. In addition, sites with a current waste management licence or unlawful deposits of wastes, contamination caused by a breach of an authorisation under Pt I of the EPA 1990 and radioactive substances are excluded. Contaminated land cannot be dealt with under the statutory nuisance provisions of the EPA 1990, Pt III.

18.05 The EPA 1990, Pt IIA outlines the contaminated land regime. It is supplemented by the Contaminated Land (England) Regulations 2000[1] and DETR Circular 02/2000 'Contaminated Land'. In particular, the Circular contains, in Annex 3, the Statutory Guidance on the regime.

1   SI 2000/227, as amended by SI 2001/663. For Wales, the Regulations are in SI 2001/2197 (W.157).

18.06 This Guidance is provided for in various sections of Pt IIA. For example, in the definition of 'contaminated land'[1] a local authority, in determining whether land is contaminated, must:

'act in accordance with guidance issued by the Secretary of State in accordance with section 78YA below with respect to the manner in which that determination is to be made'.

1   EPA 1990, s 78A(2).

The regulators

18.07 The main responsibility under the regime lies with the local authority for the area in which the contaminated land is situated. A 'local authority' for these purposes in England and Wales is a unitary authority or, where there is no such authority, a district council. The Common Council for the City of London is also an authority for these purposes. In Scotland the relevant authority is the council for the area constituted under s 2 of the Local Government (Scotland) Act 1994.[1]

1   EPA 1990, s 78A(9).

18.08   However, whilst these local authorities bear the main burden, the Environment Agency (or in Scotland, the Scottish Environmental Protection Agency ('SEPA')) will be responsible for 'special sites'. Special sites are dealt with in the EPA 1990, s 78C. They consist of land prescribed for these purposes under reg 2 of the Contaminated Land (England) Regulations 2000.[1] These are mainly:

• major acquifers;
• sites with waste acid tars;
• oil refineries;
• nuclear sites and defence establishments; and
• sites on which an IPPC operation is being carried on.

The local authority identifies such sites in its area and designates them as special sites after consultation with the relevant Agency. Once land is so designated, the relevant Agency becomes the 'enforcing authority' in respect of it.[2]

1   SI 2000/227, as amended by SI 2001/663. For Wales, the Regulations are in SI 2001/2197 (W.157).
2   EPA 1990, s 78E(1).

'Contaminated land'

18.09   To be 'contaminated land' for the purposes of the regime, the land in question must appear to the local authority for its area to be in such a condition by reason of substances in, on or under it that either significant harm is being caused, or there is a significant possibility of such harm being caused or, pollution of controlled waters *is* being caused, or pollution of controlled waters is likely to be caused. In determining whether the land is contaminated, the authority must act in accordance with the notes of guidance issued by the Secretary of State. The relevant guidance is found in Chapter A of Annex 3 to DETR Circular 02/2000.[1]

1   EPA 1990, s 78A(2).

18.10   The first step is for the authority to determine that three basic criteria are satisfied:
(1)   that there is a *contaminant* in, on or under the land;
(2)   that there is a *receptor* that can be harmed by the contaminant likely to be present on the land – such as children playing in gardens; and
(3)   that there is a *pathway* by which the contaminant can reach the receptor.

If all three elements are present in respect of the land then there is a *pollutant linkage*:

> 'A "pollutant linkage" means the relationship between a contaminant, a pathway and a receptor, and a "pollutant" means the contaminant in a pollutant linkage. Unless all three elements of a pollutant linkage are identified in respect of a piece of land, that land should not be identified as contaminated land. There may be more than one pollutant linkage on any given piece of land.'[1]

1   DETR Circular 02/2000, Annex 3, para A.17.

18.11   If a *pollutant linkage* can be identified, the second step is for the authority is to satisfy itself that the linkage is causing, or is likely to cause, *significant harm* or pollution of controlled waters.[1] 'Significant harm' must be determined in accordance with Annex 3.[2]

- The EPA 1990, s 78A(4) defines 'harm' as 'harm to the health of living organisms or other ecological systems of which they form a part and, in the case of man, means harm to his property'.
- Table A to Annex 3 sets out what constitutes significant harm to the types of receptor concerned. For human beings it is 'Death, disease, serious injury, genetic mutation, birth defects or the impairment of reproductive functions'. It is determined on the basis of risk assessment.
- Table B to Annex 3 sets out what constitutes a 'significant possibility of significant harm': It is concerned with 'a measure of the probability, or frequency, of the occurrence of circumstances which would lead to significant harm being caused'. Thus it does not set out any new types of harm.

Further guidance is available in 'contaminated land reports' on DEFRA's website.[3]

1   The Water Act 2003 will amend this to require the pollution of controlled waters to be 'significant'.
2   EPA 1990, s 78A(5).
3   See www.defra.gov.uk/environment/landliability/index.htm

REMEDIATION STRATEGIES

18.12   The local authority should set out its approach to contaminated land in its area in a written strategy, which it should formally adopt and publish. The strategy should set out the authority's aims, objectives and priorities and its arrangements and procedures for developing its programme for dealing with such land in its area. Once it is determined that, in accordance with the strategy, the relevant land is contaminated this must be recorded by the authority.[1] This record does not have to be entered in the contaminated land register maintained under the EPA 1990, s 78R, nor is there a right of appeal against it. It will be interesting to see whether the courts will allow the judicial review of such a determination.

1   See DETR Circular 02/2000, para B.52.

Remediation notices

'Remediation'

18.13   'Remediation' is defined in the EPA 1990, s 78A(7) to mean:

'(a)   the doing of anything for the purpose of assessing the condition of–

  (i)   the contaminated land in question;
  (ii)   any controlled waters affected by that land; or
  (iii)   any land adjoining or adjacent to that land;

(b)   the doing of any works, the carrying out of any operations or the taking of any steps in relation to any such land or waters for the purpose–

  (i)   of preventing or minimising, or remedying or mitigating the effects of, any significant harm, or any [significant] pollution of controlled waters, by reason of which the contaminated land is such land; or
  (ii)   of restoring the land or waters to their former state; or

(c)   the making of subsequent inspections from time to time for the purpose of keeping under review the condition of the land or waters'.

Serving a remediation notice

18.14   Remediation is secured by an authority serving a remediation notice on the 'appropriate person' under the EPA 1990, s 78E. The Act says that where an authority is satisfied that land is contaminated it *shall* serve a remediation notice. This imposes a duty on it to serve a notice, not a discretion: *R v Carrick District Council, ex p Shelley*.[1] Paragraph C.28 of the Guidance considers volunteered remediation. However, whilst an authority may accept voluntary remediation, that does not absolve it from its duty to serve a notice. Thus s 78H(5)(b) provides that if the authority is satisfied that appropriate action is being taken without the need for a notice, it may dispense with the service of a notice. However, it must record its decision in a 'remediation declaration' under s 78H(6). Before such a notice is served the authority must consult those on whom the notice is to be served and the owner and occupier of the relevant land,[2] or persons who may be required to grant rights for remediation purposes.[3]

1   [1996] Env LR 273.
2   EPA 1990, s 78H(1).
3   EPA 1990, s 78G(3).

18.15   The standard of remediation is based on the 'suitable for use' approach. Remediation of a particular significant pollutant linkage should be achieved by the use of the best practicable technique either to remove or treat the pollutant, break or remove the pollutant pathway, or protect or remove the receptor.

18.16   At this stage economic factors do not play a part in the selection of a best practicable technique. Nevertheless, the authority, under the EPA 1990, s 78E(4), may only specify actions that it considers reasonable having regard to the costs of that action and the seriousness of the harm or pollution caused by the pollution linkage. The Guidance requires the authority to prepare an estimate of the costs[1] of the action and a statement of the likely benefits that would result. The authority does not have to value the benefits. An enforcing authority should regard a remediation action as being reasonable if the costs/benefits analysis shows that those benefits justify incurring those costs. In addition the authority should consider the practicability, effectiveness and durability of the remediation actions it proposes.[2]

1   DETR Circular 02/2000, paras C.30 and C.34–C.38.
2   DETR Circular 02/2000, Annex 3, Ch C, Pt 6.

18.17   The Contaminated Land Regulations 2000,[1] reg 4(1)(g) requires the authority to specify in the notice:

'the enforcing authority's reasons for its decisions as to the things by way of remediation that the appropriate person is required to do, which shall show how any guidance issued by the Secretary of State under section 78E(5) has been applied'.

The content of a remediation notice is prescribed by the Contaminated Land Regulations 2000, reg 4.

1   SI 2000/227, as amended by SI 2001/663. For Wales, the Regulations are in SI 2001/2197 (W.157).

Appeal against a remediation notice

18.18   The EPA 1990, s 78L(1) provides that a person served with a remediation notice, may, within 21 days beginning with the day on which the notice is served, appeal against it. An appeal against a notice served by a local authority is by way of complaint to the magistrates' court. If the notice was served by the Environment Agency then the appeal is to the Secretary of State. The grounds of such an appeal are set out in reg 7(1) of the Contaminated Land Regulations 2000.[1] The 2000 Regulations also set out the procedure to be adopted in the magistrates' court. In particular, reg 8 enables a justice's clerk or the court to give directions as to the conduct of proceedings. The Regulations also deal with appeals to the Secretary of State and hearings or local inquiries to deal with such appeals.

1   SI 2000/227, as amended by SI 2001/663. For Wales, the Regulations are in SI 2001/2197 (W.157).

Failure to comply with a notice

18.19 It will be an offence under the EPA 1990, s 78M for a person served with a notice to fail, without reasonable excuse, to comply with any of the requirements of that notice. The offence is summary only with the usual fine being up to level 5 on the standard scale and a continuing daily penalty of up to one-tenth of that level thereafter for as long as the non-compliance continues after conviction. However, where the notice is concerned with contaminated land which is industrial, trade or business premises[1] then the maximum fine is £20,000 with the daily penalty one-tenth of that. The amount of the fine can be raised by the Secretary of State. Where the failure to comply with a notice that required joint action was because another party failed to meet its obligations, it will be a defence for the person charged to prove that that failure was the only reason why he or she has not complied with the relevant requirement.[2]

1   As defined in EPA 1990, s 78M(6).
2   EPA 1990, s 78M(2).

Registers

18.20 Each enforcing authority is under a duty to maintain a register by virtue of the EPA 1990, s 78R(1). The contents of the register are prescribed by reg 15 of and Sch 3 to the Contaminated Land (England) Regulations 2000.[1] Registers should be open to public inspection and facilities for obtaining copies of entries, for a reasonable charge, should be provided.[2]

1   SI 2000/227, as amended by SI 2001/663. For Wales, the Regulations are in SI 2001/2197 (W.157).
2   EPA 1990, s 78R(8).

LIABILITY TO PAY FOR REMEDIATION

18.21 The basic premise of the regime is that the *polluter* should pay for the costs of remediation. However, by restricting the scope for action against the polluter, many pollution linkages might go unremediated. Therefore the second line of attack is on the *owner or occupier* of the land in question. This reflects the legal principle that the owner of any land is responsible for its condition; further, where remediation works are carried out it will be the owner, or the occupier, who benefits from the improvement in value of the land. Finally, there may be cases where there is no polluter and no owner or occupier of the land. In these cases the *State*, in the form of the enforcing authority, may need to do works to prevent significant harm. There may also be other situations where the *authority* may have to step in.

The 'appropriate person'

The 'appropriate person' – the polluter (Class A)

18.22

'Subject to the following provisions of this section, any person, or any of the persons, who caused or knowingly permitted the substances, or any of the substances, by reason of which the contaminated land in question is such land to be in, on or under that land is an appropriate person.'[1]

For the purposes of the EPA 1990, the 'polluters' are 'Class A persons'. Thus the question here is, did the person concerned 'cause' or 'knowingly permit' the substances to be in, on or under the land in question? The 'substance' for these purposes will include one present as a result of a chemical or biological reaction with the original substance.[2]

1   EPA 1990, s 78F(2).
2   EPA 1990, s 78F(9).

18.23   The Circular, Annex 2, para 9.9 points out that what is caused in this context is the *presence* of a pollutant in, on or under the land. Thus at first glance someone who opens a pollution pathway – e g a developer excavating the site – would not be a causer for these purposes if the substance in question did not migrate from the site. However, the Government, in para D.48(j), seem to consider that a person causing 'the existence, nature or continuance of a significant pollutant linkage' is an appropriate person under the regime.

18.24   In *Empress Cars (Abertillery) Ltd v National Rivers Authority*[1] the House of Lords reviewed the law on 'causing' an offence.
- It was considered that, as a first step, the prosecution should identify what it says the defendant *did* to cause the pollution. That something need not have been the immediate cause (e g maintaining a tank full of polluting matter would be enough for these purposes even if the immediate cause was different).
- Once the prosecution has identified the defendant's act, the court must decide whether it *caused* the pollution. It can have done so even if there was another factor involved, such as vandalism by third parties.
- If the defendant did something which produced a situation in which the polluting matter could escape, but a necessary condition of the actual escape which happened was also the act of a third party or a natural event, the court should consider whether the act or event was a normal *fact of life* or something *extraordinary*. If it was a fact of life, the defendant would still be liable even if the defendant could not have foreseen the particular event. The distinction between ordinary and extraordinary events is one of fact and degree.

1   [1998] Env LR 396.

18.25 'Knowingly permitted' will require both the knowledge that the substances in question were in, on or under the land and the possession of the power to prevent such a substance being there.[1] The Circular points out:

> 'It is also relevant to consider the stage at which a person who is informed of the presence of a pollutant might be considered to have knowingly permitted that presence, where he had not done so previously. In the Government's view, the test would be met only where the person had the ability to take steps to prevent or remove that presence and had a reasonable opportunity to do so'.[2]

However, an owner or occupier of land would not be caught under the EPA 1990, s 78F(2) on this basis unless he or she had done something more than merely own or occupy the land.[3] There is a clear distinction between those who cause or knowingly permit and those who own or occupy land.

1   See, eg, *Price v Cromack* [1975] 1 WLR 988 and DETR Circular, Annex 2, para 9.10.
2   DETR Circular 02/2000, Annex 2, para 9.12.
3   DETR Circular 02/2000, Annex 2, para 9.13.

The 'appropriate person' – the owner or occupier (Class B)

18.26 The owner or occupier for the time being of the contaminated land in question can also be an 'appropriate person' by virtue of the EPA 1990, s 78F(4). For the purposes of the Act they are 'Class B persons'. An 'owner' is defined in s 78A(9) as:

> 'in relation to any land in England and Wales, ... a person (other than a mortgagee not in possession) who, whether in his own right or as trustee for any other person, is entitled to receive the rack rent of the land, or where the land is not let at a rack rent, would be so entitled if it were so let'.

The term 'occupier' is not defined in the EPA 1990, Pt IIA.

Apportioning liability

Apportioning liability – the polluter (Class A)

18.27 The relevant authority must apportion liability in accordance with the Guidance issued by the Secretary of State under the EPA 1990, s 78F(6) and (7). The Guidance for these purposes is contained in Chapter D of Annex 3 to DETR Circular 02/2000.
- In respect of any significant pollutant linkage, the relevant authority must make reasonable enquiries to find those who caused or knowingly permitted the relevant pollutant to be in, on or under the land.[1] These persons are then designated as Class A persons and together constitute a Class A liability group for that linkage.[2]

- The authority then removes from the group anyone who can benefit from a statutory exemption – eg an insolvency practitioner under the EPA 1990, s 78X(4).[3]
- Those left in the group are then examined to see if they can benefit from the exclusion tests set out in Chapter D. They should be informed of the authority's action, be made aware of the Guidance in Chapter D and be allowed to make representations to the authority about their status.[4] While the authority should take into account the information it has itself gathered, '[t]he burden of providing the authority with any further information needed to establish an exclusion, or to influence an apportionment or attribution should rest on the person seeking such a benefit'. Information supplied to an authority that affects another Class A person should be sent to that person.[5] Where some members of a liability group have agreed on how to deal with the problem, the enforcing authority should normally give effect to that agreement.[6]

1   DETR Circular 02/2000, Annex 3, Ch D, para D.11.
2   DETR Circular 02/2000, Annex 3, Ch D, para D.5(c).
3   DETR Circular 02/2000, Annex 3, Ch D, para D.16.
4   DETR Circular 02/2000, Annex 3, Ch D, para D.33.
5   DETR Circular 02/2000, Annex 3, Ch D, para D.37.
6   DETR Circular 02/2000, Annex 3, Ch D, paras D.38, D.39.

EXCLUDING MEMBERS OF A CLASS A LIABILITY GROUP

18.28   Part 5 of Chapter D sets out the tests by which an authority can exclude those who would otherwise be responsible for paying the costs of remediation. They are 'intended to establish whether, in relation to other members of the liability group, it is fair that the Class A person concerned should bear any part of that responsibility'.[1]

1   DETR Circular 02/2000, Annex 3, Ch D, para D.40.

18.29   There must always be one person in a liability group. Thus the exclusion tests only work where there is more than one person. If a polluter meets the criteria of a test but the polluter is the only person left in the group, the polluter cannot be excluded. This means that some people will not be able to benefit from the exclusion provisions even though they might otherwise qualify. In the Guidance it states:

'If the result of applying a test would be to exclude all the members of a liability group who remain after any exclusions resulting from previous tests, that further test should not be applied, and consequently the related exclusions should not be made'.[1]

The tests in the guidance therefore have to be applied in the sequence in which they are set out.

1   DETR Circular 02/2000, Annex 3, Ch D, para D.41(c).
2   DETR Circular 02/2000, Annex 3, Ch D, para D.41(b).

18.30   There are six tests:

(1)   The first excludes certain activities which only lead to a limited responsibility for the contamination. These include giving financial assistance, insuring or providing legal, technical or other advice in relation to the site.

(2)   The second is where one member of the liability group has made payments to another member of it for the purpose of remediating the pollutant linkage.

(3)   The third is that one member should be excluded if he or she sold the land to another member of the liability group who had information about the pollutant linkage.

(4), (5)   The fourth and fifth are concerned with substances that have either changed since they went into the ground or that escaped from the site due to the actions of another member of the liability group.

(6)   Finally, Test 6 excludes those who are only liable because of the introduction of a pathway or receptor by another member of the group.

APPORTIONING LIABILITY WITHIN A CLASS A LIABILITY GROUP

18.31   In apportioning costs between the members of a Class A liability group who remain after any exclusions have been made, the enforcing authority should follow the general principle that liability should be apportioned to reflect the relative responsibility of each of those members for creating or continuing the risk now being caused by the significant pollutant linkage in question. In making an apportionment the authority should consider whether any of the exclusion tests might partially apply and consider reducing relevant costs as appropriate in the circumstances. It should also evaluate responsibility between someone who introduced the substances to the land and someone who knowingly permitted its continued presence.[1]

1   DETR Circular 02/2000, Annex 3, Ch D, paras 73–78.

COMPANY OFFICERS

18.32   The Guidance[1] deals with apportionment between a company and its officers. Yet little is said about how a company officer becomes liable in the first place. The presumption seems to be that the statute allows a company officer to be automatically liable on the basis that an officer may cause or knowingly permit. Paragraph D.86 describes an officer as 'any director, manager, secretary or other similar officer of the company, or any other person purporting to act in any such capacity'. This language reflects the EPA 1990, s 157(1), yet s 157 only applies to *offences* committed under the Act. It does not apply to causing or knowingly permitting under the EPA 1990, Pt IIA. Further, even if it is argued that the entry of the substance was an offence, the relevant officer should still be able to take advantage of any statutory defence.

1   DETR Circular 02/2000, Annex 3, Ch D, paras D.85 and D.86.

18.33   In *C Evans & Sons Ltd v Spritebrand Ltd*[1] it was said that:

> 'a director of a company is not automatically to be identified with his
> company for the purposes of the law of tort, however small the company
> and however powerful his control over its affairs. Commercial enterprise
> and adventure is not to be discouraged by subjecting a director to such
> onerous potential liabilities. In every case where it is sought to make him
> liable for his company's torts it is necessary to examine with care what
> part he played personally in regard to the act or acts complained of ...'.

Thus if these common law principles are applied in respect of liability of
company officers under the EPA 1990, Pt IIA, the courts are likely to be
reluctant to hold that such officers are 'causers or knowing permitters' for the
purposes of s 78F(2).

1   [1985] 2 All ER 415, CA. See also *Williams v Natural Life Health Foods Ltd* [1997] 1 BCLC
    131, CA.

Apportioning liability – owners and occupiers (Class B)

18.34   Owners and occupiers (Class B persons) can only be made liable for
remediation if no polluter can be found. The EPA 1990, s 78F(4) is specific on
this:

> 'If no person has, after reasonable inquiry, been found who is (a "pol-
> luter") the owner or occupier for the time being of the contaminated land
> in question is an appropriate person'.

Paragraph 9.17 of Annex 2 to Circular DETR 02/2000 gives advice on the
application of s 78F(4):

> 'In general ... a natural person would have to be alive and a legal person
> such as a company must not have been dissolved ...'.

The Guidance[1] provides one exclusion where there is more than one member of
a relevant Class B liability group. The purpose of this test is to exclude from
liability those who do not have an interest in the capital value of the land in
question, or full market rent – and hold no beneficial interest in the land to
which the tenancy relates.

1   DETR Circular 02/2000, Annex 3, Ch D, paras D.87–D.90.

APPORTIONING LIABILITY WITHIN A CLASS B LIABILITY GROUP

18.35   Apportionment of costs between members of a Class B liability group
will first look at whether the contamination is in fact related to a particular area
of land and assign liability to the owner and occupier of that area. Otherwise
the enforcing authority should apportion liability in proportion to the capital
values of the interests in the land in question.

1   DETR Circular 02/2000, Appendix D, paras 92, 94 and 95.

Work done by an enforcing authority

18.36 The powers of an enforcing authority to carry out remediation works are set out in the EPA 1990, s 78N and paras 11.2–11.11 of Annex 2 to DETR Circular 02/2000. Orphan linkages – ie a pollutant linkage for which no polluter or owner or occupier can be found – are dealt with in paras D.103–D109[1] of the Guidance. For any remediation action, which is referable to an orphan linkage for which there is a liability group, the enforcing authority should itself bear the costs of carrying out that action. However, if the action can deal with two or more linkages (a shared action) the costs may be recovered from the liability groups concerned.

1   DETR Circular 02/2000, Annex 3, Ch D.

Financial criteria

18.37 Financial criteria do not enter into the designation of persons as 'appropriate persons' nor into a decision to exclude persons from being appropriate persons. Financial circumstances are taken into account in the separate consideration under the EPA 1990, s 78P(2) on hardship and costs recovery. That section requires an authority in deciding whether to recover the costs, or some of them, for doing remediation work itself to have regard to any hardship the recovery may cause to the person from whom the cost is recoverable; and Guidance on the matter issued by the Secretary of State.[1]

1   See DETR Circular 02/2000, Annex 3, Ch E.

18.38 The term 'hardship' is not defined in the Act and therefore carries its ordinary meaning – hardness of fate or circumstance, severe suffering or privation.[1] Thus when all the steps have been gone through to ascertain a final liability group for a particular linkage and to apportion costs within that group for particular remediation actions, the authority must then conduct a hypothetical exercise to see if – if it was taking action itself – it would recover all its costs as apportioned to each member of the group.[2] If it decides that there is at least one member of the group from whom it would not seek to recover all the relevant costs, then it cannot serve a remediation notice and must do the works itself.[3] Having done the work the authority may then recover its costs from those liable to pay them. It may also re-assess liability to pay on the basis of the circumstances existing after the work has been done.[4]

1   DETR Circular 02/2000, Annex 2, para 10.8.
2   DETR Circular 02/2000, Annex 2, paras 10.1–10.4.
3   DETR Circular 02/2000, Annex 2, para 10.5.
4   DETR Circular 02/2000, Annex 2, para 10.6.

CHAPTER 19

Light pollution

'The natural world, our traditional source of direct insights, is rapidly disappearing. Modern city dwellers cannot even see the stars at night. This humbling reminder of Man's place in the greater scheme of things, which human beings formerly saw once every twenty-four hours, is denied them. It's no wonder that people lose their bearings, that they lose track of who they really are, and what their lives are really about.'

Michael Crichton *Travels* (Pan/Macmillan, 1998)

INTRODUCTION

19.01 The current position of light as a nuisance is uncertain. Parallels can be drawn with noise prior to the introduction of the Noise Abatement Act 1960. Is inappropriate light just a minor inconvenience and are those who complain about it overly-sensitive? A growing consensus suggests otherwise: The writer above refers to the societal cost of light pollution. The British Astronomical Association campaigns to protect the beauty and amenity of the starry night sky. The Council for the Protection of Rural England ('CPRE') is concerned because of the adverse impact of artificial lighting on birds (affecting migration and reproductive cycles) and on insects and fish. Although the long-term effect of light pollution on wildlife is yet to be fully understood or assessed, it is being observed.

19.02 Artificial lighting can destroy the local character of a village or the countryside by urbanising rural areas at night despite the careful attention of planners to sympathetic (day-viewed) design, screening and setting. Poor lighting can adversely affect enjoyment and appreciation of the historic built environment and excess light is a waste of energy, resources and money. Bright light shining into a bedroom from the street or from a neighbour's security light can spoil a night's sleep in just the same way as a noisy dog. It can lead to a sense of loss of privacy and stress.

19.03　Light pollution occurs in the developed world and, apart from the Netherlands, England is brighter at night than any other European country. In May 2003 CPRE released data showing that there had been a 17% increase in the amount of land affected by severe light pollution between 1993 and 2000: the problem is getting worse.

THE STATUTORY REGIME

Town and Country Planning Act 1990

19.04　The town and country planning system is an important mechanism for controlling artificial lighting. It impacts at the design stage in the context of new development. Many up-to-date development plans and supplementary planning guidance contain policies empowering local planning authorities ('LPAs') to control lighting design.

19.05　This will be a key issue in certain developments, such as golf driving ranges and industrial estates which have, in the past, been major sources of light pollution. But where the installation is of a smaller scale, one that is not a building or engineering operation, it may be outside the planning regime altogether. Subject to certain exceptions, for example a conservation area, an occupier can buy a 1000 watt light at any DIY store and affix it to a wall without planning permission and the effect can be devastating. For example, in 2002 the members of the Wessex Astronomical Society lost their dark observing site in the New Forest due to one security light on a nearby cottage.

19.06　Where planning permission must be sought, conditions may be imposed to control *external* lighting: the design, location, orientation and power to be agreed in writing with the LPA. Less frequently do LPAs use their powers to control *internal* lighting which can, in the case of large buildings with plate-glass windows (such as a busy hospital which operates throughout the night) affect neighbours' amenity and the character of an area. The illuminance levels (measured in 'lux') should be specified in the condition with care to identify from where the reading is to be taken.

Town and Country Planning (Control of Advertisements) Regulations 1992[1]

19.07　If an illuminated sign is an advertisement, an LPA can, under these Regulations, control the intensity of lighting or its positioning or direction. An 'advertisement' is any word, letter, model, sign, placard, board, notice, awning, blind, device or representation, whether illuminated or not, employed wholly or partly for the purpose of advertisement, announcement or direction. Therefore, the motive for the display is relevant. The creation of light-beams purely for artistic purposes or for religious expression may not be an advertisement and, as such, outside these controls.

1   SI 1992/666.

19.08   In an unreported judicial review[1] laser displays were under consideration. Great Yarmouth Borough Council refused consent for a 'space-flower' searchlight on the roof of an amusement arcade. The powerful light-beam reflected off a series of mirrors to create shafts of light in the night sky and, in the right conditions, a floral pattern was created on the underside of a cloud-base. The display could be seen for some miles both from the town and rural areas. The point of law which Deputy Judge Michael Rich QC was called upon to decide was whether the display was an advertisement. Given the circumstances of the case, he held that it was an advertisement because it promoted the presence of an amusement arcade.

1   See [1993] JPL 650.

Town and Country Planning (Environmental Impact Assessment) (England and Wales) Regulations 1999[1]

19.09   These Regulations extend the scope of planning control in that, as part of the decision-making process, a developer may be required to provide an environmental statement addressing the issues of the environmental impact of lighting. This would be particularly relevant and important in the case of major development in open countryside.

1   SI 1999/293.

Environmental Protection Act 1990

19.10   The categories of statutory nuisances under s 79 of the Environmental Protection Act 1990 do *not* include nuisance by light. An argument might be advanced that where light emanates from a building, the premises are in a state so as to be prejudicial to health or a nuisance,[1] but this argument has never been tested in the courts as far as we are aware. During the passage of the Bill (at the Committee stage of the House of Lords) a specific proposal to include light emitted from premises was rejected. Since *Pepper v Hart*[2] reference may be made to Hansard to assist a court in elucidating the intention of Parliament. In these circumstances it is unlikely that a court would extend the categories of statutory nuisance to include light emitted from premises.

1   See the example of the paperboy at para **19.32** below.
2   [1993] AC 593, HL.

Pollution Prevention and Control Act 1999

19.11   This Act implements Council Directive 96/61/EC on integrated pollution prevention and control and regulates, through a consenting regime, activities capable of causing pollution.

19.12   The Directive defines pollution as:

'the direct or indirect introduction as a result of human activity of substances, vibrations, heat or noise into the air, water or land which may be harmful to human health or the quality of the environment, or which may result in damage to material property or impair or interfere with activities and other legitimate uses of the environment'.

19.13   The corresponding definition under the Act is wider.[1] Environmental pollution which gives rise to harm includes pollution by noise, heat, vibrations or *any other kind of release of energy* and harm for these purposes includes interference with ecosystems and offence to the sense of human beings. At the House of Lords stage of the Bill, an amendment was tabled to specify that light pollution should be included. The then Environment Minister Michael Meacher said that the Government had no objection to 'light being taken aboard too', but indicated that it was not a high enough priority to justify a specific amendment. Given the wide definition and the explicit ministerial acknowledgement, emanation of strong or powerful light from industrial or commercial premises would be subject to integrated pollution control.

1   See Pollution Prevention and Control Act 1999, s 1.

THE MEASUREMENT OF LIGHT AND THE DESCRIPTION OF LIGHT POLLUTION

19.14   Light pollution takes a number of forms:
(a)   *Sky glow* – The pervasive (usually) orange sky glow over urban areas which obscures all but the brightest objects in the night sky. This is caused by the scattering of artificial light by dust particles and water droplets in the sky.
(b)   *Glare* – The uncomfortable brightness of a light source when viewed against a dark background.
(c)   *Light trespass* – Light which spills from beyond the boundary of a property on which the light is located.

Light pollution is the general term used to describe these three forms of excessive or intrusive artificial light.

19.15   When imposing conditions on a permission pertaining to lighting design, the LPA will usually require that details of design, location, orientation and power is agreed in writing before any permanent external lighting is erected. The nature of this formal procedure lends itself to technical specifications. An External Lighting Statement will detail the lighting provision, for example the height of the pole-mounted luminaries and their proximity to the boundary fence; whether lighting is to be recessed, under-canopy etc. Levels of light will vary depending on the use of the area. For example, lighting for a car park will normally be brighter than at the boundary fence. The design of the luminaire is important and should be such as to restrict the light to a downward vertical plane, and the main beam angle directed towards any potential observer should be below 70 degrees.

19.16   Light can be measured, but a full description of this science is beyond the scope of this book. The most commonly used measure of lighting levels is 'lux'. By way of example, moonlight is 0.5 lux, starlight 0.2 lux and a car park may be lit at between 5 and 20 lux. But the numerical measurement is not an absolute standard and location is highly relevant. Some areas are intrinsically dark (such as a National Park); others will be normally very bright (such as a town centre with high levels of night-time activity).

19.17   The Institution of Lighting Engineers ('ILE') provides Guidance Notes for the Reduction of Light Pollution[1] on their website.[2] The ILE would be a good starting point to look for an expert for light measurement.

1   ILE 2000 revised 05/03.
2   www.ile.org.uk

LIGHT POLLUTION AMOUNTING TO A NUISANCE

19.18   The general law of private nuisance has been set out in Chapter 2. Just as with smell and noise, there are no absolute standards breach of which automatically gives rise to a cause of action for light pollution. Nevertheless, it is quite clear that excessive lighting is capable of amounting to a common law nuisance, although this will be a question of fact in every case.

When does light amount to a private nuisance?

19.19   The question for the civil court will be whether or not the light interferes with the claimant's reasonable enjoyment of property: see *Halsey v Esso Petroleum Co Ltd*.[1] Since the law of nuisance is grounded in the protection of property rights, only the forms of light pollution described as 'glare' and 'light trespass'[2] are likely to be actionable. (Sky glow affects the unowned environment and it is difficult to imagine a factual situation where a claimant would have locus standi.) Direct light upon a property affecting a claimant's ability to see the night sky might be actionable, subject to overcoming the legal hurdle of being seen to use the claimant's land for a particularly sensitive purpose.

1   [1961] 2 All ER 145.
2   See para **19.14** above.

19.20   The delicate balancing act of reasonable user which involves issues of motive, sensibility and even social utility must be undertaken in all cases of light pollution. Unlike the prescribed and technical context of town planning conditions, the law of nuisance depends on many factors which renders the outcome somewhat uncertain.

Evidence

19.21   The claimant must be able to satisfy the court of the following:

(1)   *The existence of the light source.* This can be done by direct evidence of the occurrence by the claimant, who should keep good contemporaneous records, eg dates when it happened, the frequency, time, duration. Photographs would also be helpful. Corroborative evidence provided by neighbours, visitors, police, planning officers etc is very useful.

(2)   *Where the light is coming from.* It has to be from another *property.* Light from a spaceship is not a legal nuisance!

(3)   *The effect the light has on the claimant's use and enjoyment of the claimant's property.* In this the claimant must be reasonable. For example, if the complaint is that the light affects the claimant's ability to sleep, it would not be unreasonable to expect the claimant to draw his or her curtains at night. Nevertheless, the character of the locality will be very relevant. The level of darkness a claimant can expect to enjoy in property on the North Norfolk coast will be greater than if the claimant were living in the West End of London. A valid planning permission for a new housing development may have the effect of changing the character of the area, although as a general rule a planning permission does not automatically validate a nuisance which might occur as a result: see *Wheeler v J J Saunders Ltd.*[1] However, it is for the claimant to prove that the light is unreasonably interfering with the claimant's use and enjoyment of his or her property and this depends on the particular circumstances of the individual case.

(4)   *Evidence of intensity* will be very relevant to support item (3) above and the expert evidence of a qualified lighting engineer will be helpful. The engineer will be able to assist the court to understand the level of interference by reference to comparisons and objective criteria without which the court may have difficulty. The lighting engineer will be able to prepare a report and evaluate the interference by reference to the background light levels and intensity. The engineer may also be able to suggest some practical measures to ameliorate the problem, design modifications, timing, lower wattage, infrared etc. This gives the defendant the opportunity to consider the alternatives. If the lighting installation breaches planning controls or is not in conformity with good practice (as evidenced by reference to current ILE recommendations and technical reports, for example) this would demonstrate unreasonableness.

1   [1996] Ch 19.

SOME EXAMPLES

19.22   The following cases provide some interesting examples of light pollution being challenged as nuisance.

19.23   In the New Zealand case *Racti v Hughes*[1] the defendants installed floodlights and camera surveillance equipment in their garden which backed onto the plaintiff's property. Each time the plaintiffs went into their garden at night the sensor-activated floodlights next door switched on and illuminated their garden as well. The plaintiffs felt unable to use their garden as they had done before the installation of the floodlights. The judge held that if the intensity of light was strong enough seriously to disturb a person of ordinary sensibilities or to interfere with an occupation which is no more than ordinarily susceptible to light, it is a nuisance. On the facts, the court held that the defendants were causing an actionable nuisance.

1   1995 NSW Lexis 10736 (NSW Supreme Court 1995).

19.24 A Scottish example involved the lighting of a tennis court and the effect that the light spill had on a nearby trout stream. In *Stonehaven and District Angling Association v Stonehaven Recreation Ground Trustees and Stonehaven Tennis Club*[1] a tennis club erected a powerful floodlighting system with planning permission and subject to conditions. One of the main sea trout pools used by the Stonehaven & District Angling Association was subjected to strong light from the tennis club which altered the nocturnal environment and consequently the behaviour of the trout, which made fishing impossible whilst the lights were on. The Sheriff held that the Tennis Association had caused a nuisance and made an order forbidding the use of the floodlights during the trout fishing season.

1   (January 1997, unreported) Stonehaven Sheriff's Court.

19.25 This case illustrates two important points:
(1)   The use of technical evidence. Both sides instructed lighting engineers to investigate and report on lighting levels. The Sheriff accepted evidence that the lighting arrangement used by the (second) defendant was more suitable for street lighting and that had special tennis court lighting been installed, light trespass onto the river could have been eliminated or at least substantially reduced.
(2)   The pursuers (claimants) were tenants of fishing rights under the terms of a lease which gave them the right to fish for salmon and sea trout type. Thus a clear property right had been interfered with.

19.26 In the unreported Irish case of *Fleming v Rathdown School Trust*[1] the defendant school had upgraded its hockey pitch and, with the benefit of planning permission, replaced the existing perimeter lighting with eight flood-light luminaires. A condition attached to the permission provided that no directional light should go onto neighbouring properties. However, the light did affect the properties equivalent to a bright moonlit night (measured at 20 lux). The light, however, was not directional but refracted, ie glare.

1   High Court Denham J 1993; see Irish Planning and Environmental Law Journal, Vol 5, No 2.

19.27 Three central issues were identified:
(a)   the significance of the difference between directional and refractional light;

(b)   the legal significance of the utility of the defendants' conduct;

(c)   whether any, and if so what type, of remedies would be appropriate.

19.28   The court held that the planning condition had not been breached. The significance between directional and refractional light was relevant only in terms of the extent of the effect it had on neighbours. That the defendants maintained that an open space was for the public benefit and most household-ers would be pleased about that; and that although excessive light in a residential area at night could be a nuisance, a measurement of 20 lux was not. The plaintiffs were not entitled to an injunction, but an order limiting the duration and timing of the lighting was made and some shielding was to be kept and mesh barriers raised whilst the lights were in use.

19.29   This case shows that where practical measures can be taken to reduce the impact of light and where the defendant's use has some social utility, the courts will avoid 'turning off the lights'. It is noteworthy that the Institute of Lighting Engineers Guidance Note recommended the maximum brightness to be allowed in areas of medium distinct brightness (ie urban areas) should be 10 lux.

19.30   The facts of the *Bank of New Zealand v Greenwood*[1] are different from these cases in that this case concerned natural sunlight. The defendants built a two-storey shopping arcade with an angled verandah which on sunny days caused a dazzling glare to be beamed onto the opposite building, the occupants of which sought an injunction to prevent the reflection of the sunlight from the glass roofing panels into their windows. Even though this was not a continuous problem (it happened mainly between October and March and in the late morning and early afternoon) it was held to constitute a nuisance. However, the judge made an order for damages to cover the costs of venetian blinds and would not grant an injunction which would have necessitated the demolition of the verandah.

1   [1984] 1 NZLR 525.

19.31   Whilst it is not possible to elicit any precise principle from the above cases, it is clear that where the cessation of the nuisance would involve great cost or loss of a useful amenity, the courts will seek some compromise and prefer a course of improving the plaintiff's position by taking some alternative measures (with only who should pay the costs of those measures at issue).

19.32   The above cases involved actions for nuisance, which is the usual mechanism for claims involving lighting. However, the case of *Nicholson v Brooks and Brooks*[1] is unusual in that the minor plaintiff, a newspaper boy, brought an action both in nuisance and negligence. He was cycling along the road very early in the morning when the defendants' security light, which was attached to the side of their bungalow, came on and temporarily blinded the boy causing him to crash into a fence and hurt himself. The expert evidence was that the security light was 50% brighter than a car headlamp. The judge found that the light shining onto the highway was a foreseeable risk of danger and that the state of affairs was such to be a danger to persons using the highway and was, therefore, a public nuisance.

1   Unreported, Telford County Court 1997.

CONCLUSION

19.33   Most of the cases referred to above are unreported in the law reports because nuisance cases turn on their facts and do not often create precedent. Individuals are deterred by cost factors from pursuing their claim in the higher courts. But the cases show that the courts do recognise the problem of light pollution.

19.34   The most effective prevention of light pollution is currently achieved at the development stage under town and country planning. But the enforcement mechanisms are not controlled by an individual complainant, who must rely on the civil courts. Permitted development rights and minor lighting installations leave many forms of lighting outside planning control altogether.

19.35   The Select Committee on Science and Technology[1] acknowledged the loss of amenity caused by light pollution to city dwellers who want to see the stars but are unable to do so because of the orange glow which shrouds the sky. It also cited the effects of light pollution on wildlife and the increasing number of complaints made to local authorities about intrusive lighting from domestic, industrial and commercial premises and sporting facilities.

1   Seventh Report, 6 October 2003 (see the Committee's website at www.parliament.uk/parliamentary_committees/science_and_technology_committee.cfm under 'Reports and Publications').

19.36   The Report recommended the following:
(1)   light should be a category of statutory nuisance;
(2)   new Planning Policy Guidance ('PPG') to give clear guidance to Local Planning Authorities.

19.37   The Committee also recommended that the position should be carefully monitored and if the above measures did not produce a reduction in the current levels of sky glow over the next five to ten years, further legislation should be introduced.

19.38   We hope that the Select Committee's recommendation that light should be a category of statutory nuisance is adopted by Government.

CHAPTER 20

Nuclear installations

INTRODUCTION

20.01 'Nuclear installation' means a nuclear reactor or an installation designed or adapted for the production or use of atomic energy or for a process in which preparations are made to that end and involve, or is capable of causing, the emissions of ionising radiation or for the storage, processing or disposal of nuclear fuel or bulk quantities of other radioactive matter.[1] Such installations must have a nuclear site licence, which is granted by the Health and Safety Executive.[2] Nuclear installations are regulated by the Nuclear Installations Act 1965 ('NIA 1965') which will be explored in detail below. The Ionising Radiations Regulations 1999[3] are also relevant, and are discussed below.

1 NIA 1965, ss 26(1) and 1(1)(b).
2 NIA 1965, s 1(1) as amended by SI 1974/2056.
3 SI 1999/3232.

NUCLEAR INSTALLATIONS ACT 1965

Background

20.02 The NIA 1965 implements into UK law the Convention on Third Party Liability in the Field of Nuclear Energy 1960 ('the Paris Convention'). The purpose of the Convention is to ensure adequate and equitable compensation for persons who suffer damage caused by nuclear incidents, whilst taking the necessary steps to ensure that the development of the production and uses of nuclear energy for peaceful purposes is not hindered.[1] This purpose may be important for a court seeking to interpret the provisions of the NIA 1965. The provisions of the Act set out in this chapter are as they were amended by the Nuclear Installations Act 1965 (Repeals and Modifications) Regulations 1990.[1]

1 Paris Convention, Preamble.
2 SI 1990/1918.

Duties imposed

20.03   The NIA 1965, s 7(1) provides that where a nuclear site licence has been granted in respect of any site, it shall be the duty of the licensee to secure that specified operations related to the site do not cause (a) injury to any person or (b) damage to any property (other than that of the licensee[1]) from the hazardous properties of nuclear matter[2] or ionising radiation from other radioactive material or waste discharged from the site.

1   See s 7(3).
2   See s 26(1).

20.04   The specified operations in the NIA 1965, s 7(2) are concerned with operations on the site, for the transport of nuclear matter and matter that has been on the site or transported to or from it.

20.05   'Injury to any person' includes anything that affects a person's ability to have children or a child born with disabilities.[1] 'Damage to any property' here can include a devaluation of that property because it has been contaminated with radioactive material, if the property has to be decontaminated as a result.[2]

1   Congenital Disabilities (Civil Liability) Act 1976, s 3.
2   *Blue Circle Industries plc v Ministry of Defence* [1999] Env LR 22, CA – cf *Merlin v British Nuclear Fuels plc* [1990] 2 QB 557.

20.06   The NIA 1965, ss 8, 9 and 10 modify the duties in s 7 for the UK Atomic Energy Authority, the Crown and certain foreign operators respectively. Section 11 imposes duties on those who cause nuclear matter to be carried.

Liability and compensation

20.07   The NIA 1965, s 12(1) gives a right to compensation for any injury or damage caused by a breach of the duties imposed in ss 7–10. The question of whether personal injury has been caused by ionising radiation is not any easy one to answer, as can be seen from *Reay v British Nuclear Fuels plc*.[1] The right to claim under the Act is the only remedy available to a claimant unless the claimant can separate any damage caused by a breach of ss 7–10 and that caused by ionising radiation that was not in breach of the duties imposed. However there can be no double recovery in such circumstances.[2] Liability is excluded in certain circumstances under s 13, including damage caused as a result of armed conflict, but is extended to damage resulting from a natural disaster.[3] The Consumer Protection Act 1987 does not apply here.[4]

1   [1994] 5 Med LR 1.
2   NIA 1965, s 12(1)(b) and (3).
3   NIA 1965, s 13(4).
4   Consumer Protection Act 1987, s 6(8).

20.08   Once a claimant has established that he or she has suffered damage or injury as a result of a breach of the NIA 1965, ss 7–10, then the person in breach of the duty is liable for the foreseeable losses caused by the breach providing they are not too remote.[1] In a case of widespread damage, total liability is limited to £10 million in respect of a single event.[2] Licensees of sites should have insurance to deal with compensation claims under the Act.[3]

1   Per Aldous LJ in *Blue Circle Industries plc v Ministry of Defence* [1999] Env LR 22 at 33.
2   NIA 1965, s 16(1).
3   NIA 1965, s 19.

20.09   The NIA 1965, s 15(1) allows a claimant 30 years from the date of the occurrence which gives rise to the claim to bring proceedings. If the occurrence was a continuing one, then the 30-year limit starts to run from the last time it happened. However, a 20-year limit is imposed in respect of injury or damage caused as a result of nuclear matter which was stolen from, or lost, jettisoned or abandoned by, the person under the relevant duty.[1]

1   NIA 1965, s 15(2).

20.10   Claims for compensation for a breach of the duty imposed by ss 7–10 of the NIA 1965 should be brought against the site licensee through the courts in the usual way. However, s 16(3) channels certain claims to the Secretary of State for Trade and Industry for his or her decision.[1] This applies if the total compensation payable is over £10 million, the claim is brought 10 years after the relevant occurrence, or more than 20 years after a theft or abandonment. The Secretary of State can refer such claims to the courts or deal with them himself or herself, but if the Secretary of State deals with them an appeal lies to the courts.[2]

1   See NIA 1965, s 26(1); SI 1970/1537.
2   NIA 1965, s 16(4).

IONISING RADIATIONS REGULATIONS 1999

20.11   The Ionising Radiations Regulations 1999[1] are made under the Health and Safety at Work Act 1974, s 15. If a person suffers injury as a result of a breach of those Regulations, a civil action can be brought for breach of statutory duty.[2]

1   SI 1999/3232.
2   Health and Safety at Work Act 1974, s 47(2).

20.12   The Regulations impose duties on employers not just in respect of their employees and trainees, but also exposure of other persons to ionising radiation. However, the duty in respect of non-employees only extends in respect of exposure to radiation from work undertaken by the employer.[1] Duties imposed on an employer are also imposed on the holder of a nuclear site licence under the NIA 1965 insofar as those duties relate to the licensed site.[2] The Regulations require, among other things:

● prior risk assessment;
● restriction of exposure;

- provision of personal protective equipment;
- appropriate information, instruction and training; and
- classification and monitoring of those likely to be exposed to radiation.

1   SI 1999/3232, reg 4(1).
2   SI 1999/3232, reg 4(3).

CHAPTER 21

Human rights

INTRODUCTION

21.01 The European Convention for the Protection of Human Rights and Fundamental Freedoms, as set out in Sch 1 to the Human Rights Act 1998 ('HRA 1998'), does not provide for substantive environmental protection, although it has been suggested that such protection can and should be read into it.[1] This chapter considers the two main environmental liability related rights: Article 8, 'right to respect for private and family life'; and Article 1 of Protocol 1, 'protection of property'. In addition, it looks at recovery of damages where rights have been breached. As well as Convention rights, the reader should also be aware of the Charter of Fundamental Rights of the European Union[2] which, in Article 37, provides for environmental protection.

1   See the dissenting judgment in *Balmer-Schafroth v Switzerland* (1997) 25 EHRR 598.
2   2000/C 364/01.

EUROPEAN CONVENTION FOR THE PROTECTION OF HUMAN RIGHTS AND FUNDAMENTAL FREEDOMS

The Human Rights Act 1998 and common law

21.02 Although Convention provisions can be relevant in private actions between citizens, the focus of the HRA 1998 is on disputes between citizens and the state, or emanations of the state. Thus the HRA 1998 is intended to regulate 'public authorities'. This term is deliberately not defined in the Act[1] but will include private companies set up using statutory powers, such as water and sewerage undertakers, at least when exercising a public function.[2] To be able to claim the protection of the Convention, the claimant must be a 'victim' of an abuse of his or her rights.[3] This may stop pressure groups from claiming a breach of their rights in the absence of any direct harm.[4] In *LM&R v*

Switzerland[5] persons living near to a railway on which nuclear materials were transported were not 'victims' for human rights purposes. To be victims they would have to show a specific risk or specific damage affecting them, going beyond that suffered by the general population.

1   HRA 1998, s 6(3) and (5).
2   *R (on the application of Beer) (t/a Hammer Trout Farm) v Hampshire Farmers' Markets Ltd* [2003] EWCA Civ 1056, [2004] 1 WLR 233.
3   HRA 1998, s 7(1).
4   *Norris v Ireland* 44 DR 132 (1985).
5   (1996) 2 EHRR CD 130.

21.03   The UK courts have held that the common law should be developed in such a way as to conform with the Convention.[1] Thus, authorities such as *Hunter v Canary Wharf Ltd*[2] may have to be revisited if the law set out in them contravenes the Convention.[3]

1   *Aston Cantlow and Wilmcote with Billesley Parochial District Council v Wallbank* EWCA Civ 713 at [53], [2002] Ch 51 at [53].
2   [1997] AC 655, HL.
3   *McKenna v British Aluminium Ltd* [2002] Env LR 721.

Article 8 of the Convention

21.04   Article 8.1 provides that:

'Everyone has the right to respect for his private and family life, his home and his correspondence.'

However, Article 8.2 adds the proviso that:

'There shall be no interference by a public authority with the exercise of this right except such as in accordance with the law and is necessary in a democratic society in the interests of national security, public safety or the economic well-being of the country, for the prevention of disorder or crime, for the protection of health or morals, or for the protection of the rights and freedoms of others.'

The term 'home' here has a broad construction.[1]

'Article 8 may apply in environmental cases whether the pollution is directly caused by the State or whether State responsibility arises from the failure properly to regulate private industry. Whether the case is analysed in terms of a positive duty on the State to take reasonable and appropriate measures to secure the applicants' rights under paragraph 1 of Article 8 or in terms of an interference by a public authority to be justified in accordance with paragraph 2, the applicable principles are broadly similar.'[2]

1   *Buckley v United Kingdom* (1996) 23 EHRR 101.
2   *Hatton v United Kingdom* (2003) 37 EHRR 611 at para 98.

21.05   The European Court of Human Rights has held that a balance has to be struck between the rights set out in Article 8.1 and the exceptions provided for in Article 8.2. In *Lopez Ostra v Spain*[1] the Court ruled that

'regard must be had to the fair balance that has to be struck between the competing interests of the individual and the community as a whole, and in any case the State enjoys a certain margin of appreciation'.

Thus even though a court may find that there has been a breach of Article 8.1, the balancing act required with Article 8.2 may result in the claim failing.

1   (1994) 20 EHRR 277 at para 51.

21.06   Environmental decisions of the courts have borne this principle very much in mind. *Lopez Ostra* succeeded on the basis that the state in that case had not succeeded in striking a fair balance between the interest of the relevant town's economic well-being and the applicant's effective enjoyment of her right to respect for her home and family life. In the initial cases in respect of noise from airports the courts held that the operation of a major international airport pursued a legitimate aim and, given the pursuance by the Government of specific regulatory measure, a fair balance had been struck by it.[1]

1   *Powell and Rayner v United Kingdom* (1990) 12 EHRR 355.

21.07   More recently, the courts have moved away from an approach that simply looks at the balance. If a claimant has suffered harm as a result of a breach of Article 8.1 then, even if there is a legitimate reason under Article 8.2, the public authority concerned may have to compensate the claimant. In *Marcic v Thames Water Utilities Ltd*,[1] Lord Phillips MR, relying on *S v France*[2] considered that that case suggested that:

'Where an authority carries on an undertaking in the interest of the community as a whole it may have to pay compensation to individuals whose rights are infringed by that undertaking in order to achieve a fair balance between the interests of the individual and the community.'

This principle was followed in *Dennis v Ministry of Defence*[3] in which a homeowner near to an RAF training facility was awarded compensation under Article 8, even though the training was in the national interest. Although the House of Lords in *Marcic* overruled the specific decision of the Court of Appeal, this does not mean the principle set out by Lord Phillips is necessarily invalid.

1   [2002] EWCA Civ 65 at [118], [2002] QB 929 at [118].
2   65 DR 250 (1990).
3   [2003] EWHC 793 (QB), [2003] NLJR 634.

21.08   In addition to providing compensation for people whose homes are adversely affected, Article 8.1 may also give a right to information about what causes the effect. In *Guerra v Italy*[1] the court considered that residents affected by a nearby chemical works should have 'essential information that would have entitled them to assess the risks' they were subject to. This principle was affirmed in *McGinley and Egan v United Kingdom*,[2] a case involving nuclear testing on Christmas Island.

1   (1998) 26 EHRR 357.
2   (1998) 27 EHRR 1 but see *LCB v United Kingdom* (1998) 27 EHRR 212.

Article 1 of Protocol 1

21.09   Article 1 of Protocol 1 to the Convention begins by providing that:

'Every natural or legal person is entitled to the peaceful enjoyment of his possessions. No one shall be deprived of his possessions except in the public interest and subject to the conditions provided for by law and by the general principles of international law.'

To that is added a proviso that:

'The preceding provisions shall not, however, impair the right of a State to enforce such laws as it deems necessary to control the use of property in accordance with the general interest or to secure the payment of taxes or other contributions or penalties.'

21.10   The Article comprises three rules. The way they should be construed was set out in *Sporrong and Lönnroth v Sweden*[1] and *James v United Kingdom*:[2]

'The first rule is set out in the first sentence, which is of a general nature and enunciates the principle of the peaceful enjoyment of property. It then deals with two forms of interference with a person's possessions by the state: deprivation of possessions which it subjects to certain conditions, and control of the use of property in accordance with the general interest. In each case a balance must be struck between the rights of the individual and the public interest to determine whether the interference was justified. These rules are not unconnected as, before considering whether the first rule has been complied with, the court must first determine whether the last two rules are applicable. As it was put in *James*, para 37, the second and third rules are concerned with particular instances of interference with the right to peaceful enjoyment of property. They should be construed in the light of the general principle enunciated in the first rule.'[3]

1   (1982) 5 EHRR 35.
2   (1986) 8 EHRR 123.
3   Lord Hope in *Aston Cantlow and Wilmcote with Billesley Parochial District Council v Wallbank* [2003] UKHL 37 at [67], [2003] 3 WLR 283 at [67].

21.11   This Article is more broadly based than Article 8. Effectively it protects the property of individuals and corporations, but an unincorporated association is unlikely to be a 'natural person' for these purposes.[1] 'Possessions' here include not only physical possessions but also licences such as a waste management licence; although this does not mean that a licence-holder is entitled to the continuation of a licence.[2]

1   *Marckx v Belgium* (1979) 2 EHRR 330.
2   *R (on the application of Royden) v Wirral Metropolitan Borough* [2003] LGR 290.

21.12   It is for the defendant to any proceeding under Article 1 to show that the requirement of proportionality is satisfied.[1] However, the proportionality requirement is less stringent here than it is under Article 8 and depends on the severity of the restrictions imposed.[2] This means that states have a wide margin of appreciation and that any controls prescribed or interferences involved must be without any reasonable foundation if a court is to regard them as disproportionate. The fact that better methods exist for achieving the same end does not mean the particular measure is disproportionate.[3]

1   *R (Daly) v Secretary of State for the Home Department* [2001] UKHL 26, [2001] 2 AC 532.
2   *Gillow v United Kingdom* (1985) 7 EHRR 292 at para 154.
3   See *Fisher v English Nature* [2003] EWHC 1599 (Admin) at [46], [2003] 4 All ER 366 at [46].

21.13   The availability of compensation is a material consideration in whether or not a fair balance has been struck.[1] In *James v United Kingdom*[2] it was considered that:

'The taking of property without payment of an amount reasonably related to its value would normally constitute a disproportionate interference which could not be considered justifiable under Article 1.'

However, this does not mean that there could be a claim for devaluation of property as a result of a planning or other decision of the State. Any planning decision would be within the reasonable margin of appreciation that a State has to control.

1   *Holy Monasteries v Greece* (1994) 20 EHRR 1.
2   (1986) 8 EHRR 123 at para 54.

DAMAGES UNDER THE CONVENTION

21.14   Where a court considers that a public authority has acted unlawfully by virtue of the HRA 1998, s 6(1), it may award the claimant damages.[1] In determining whether to award damages, and their amount, the court must take into account the principles applied by the European Court of Human Rights when awarding compensation under Article 41 of the Convention.[2]

1   HRA 1998, s 8(1).
2   HRA 1998, s 8(4).

21.15   The subject of damages under the HRA 1998 was considered by the Law Commission.[1] It concluded that whilst there were areas that might require some further development of the law, generally the law on damages would not require any major changes as a result of implementing the Convention. One area is the award of damages in environmental cases. The European Court awards compensation for 'non-pecuniary' loss – in effect damages for distress and inconvenience.[2] In England and Wales such damages are not awarded in environmental claims. Thus a claim under the HRA 1998 may be advisable if the circumstances allow.

1   *Damages under the Human Rights Act 1998* LC No 266 Cm 4853 (2000).
2   *Lopez Ostra v Spain* (1994) 20 EHRR 277 at para 65.

CLAIMS UNDER THE HUMAN RIGHTS ACT 1998

21.16   A victim of an unlawful act under HRA 1998, s 6(1) may either bring a discrete action under s 7(1) of the Act, or rely on the relevant Convention right or rights concerned in any legal proceedings. A discrete human rights action may be brought in any court; unless it concerns a judicial act, when only the High Court can deal with it.[1] Any such action must be brought before the end of one year beginning with the date the illegality complained of took place or such longer period as the court or tribunal concerned thinks is equitable having regard to all the circumstances.[2] In environmental cases, where the unlawful act often continues for months or even years, the common law rule that the cause of action accrues on each day the breach takes place would probably apply for these purposes. If the action involves asking for a declaration that a provision of primary legislation is incompatible with the Act, the Crown must be notified, and it or an appropriate person, may be joined as a party to the claim.[3] A party seeking to rely on any provision or right under the HRA 1998 must give precise details of the claim in the party's statement of case.[4]

1   Civil Procedure Rules 1998 ('CPR') 7.11.
2   HRA 1998, s 7(5).
3   CPR 19.4A and CPR Pt 19 PD 6.
4   CPR Pt 16 PD 16 para 15.

21.17   Although the rules are much the same for adding a human rights claim into a judicial review or other action, it is important to note that the time-limit comes down to the time allowed to bring the review or other proceedings.[1] A person will only have 'sufficient interest' for the purposes of his or her standing to apply for a judicial review if the person is a 'victim' in accordance with Convention rules.[2] The details of the human rights aspect of the claim must be properly set out in the claim form.[3]

1   HRA 1998, s 7(5).
2   HRA 1998, s 7(7).
3   CPR Pt 54 PD 54 para 5.3.

Index